AMERICAN IMMIGRANT LEADERS, 1800–1910

AMERICAN IMMIGRANT LEADERS 1800–1910

MARGINALITY AND IDENTITY

Victor R. Greene

THE JOHNS HOPKINS UNIVERSITY PRESS   BALTIMORE AND LONDON

The Johns Hopkins University Press
701 West 40th Street
Baltimore, Maryland 21211
The Johns Hopkins Press Ltd., London

The paper used in this publication meets the minimum requirements
of American National Standard for Information Sciences—
Permanence of Paper for Printed Library Materials, ANSI
Z39.48-1984.

LIBRARY OF CONGRESS CATALOGING-IN-PUBLICATION DATA

Greene, Victor R.
  American immigrant leaders, 1800–1910.

  Bibliography: p.
  Includes index.
  1. Minorities—United States—History—19th century.
2. Ethnology—United States. 3. Ethnicity—United
States—History—19th century. 4. Elite (Social sciences)
—United States—History—19th century. I. Title.
E184.A1G86 1987   973'.04   86-20942
ISBN 0-8018-3355-8 (alk. paper)

To the memory of Bernie Witkowski,
the true polka king

Contents

Preface

A work such as this one which attempts to generalize about the six largest white immigrant groups in the American past has set for itself a formidable objective, the reader may agree, but one that I believe is necessary at this time. Occasionally in the past other historians have offered overarching hypotheses that have tried to encompass our complex pluralistic society. But those efforts came with much less information than is currently available to scholars. Several recent developments, such as the late ethnic revival, the popularity of social and grass-roots history and its methods of research, and the general attraction of minorities and the lower class, have made viewing and understanding the outsiders, the non-English speakers, and the non-Protestants in the United States take on new life over the past three decades. This turning away from the movers and the shakers and concentration on ordinary people brought with it an emphasis on the *gemeinschaft* rather than the *gesellschaft,* on the particular community, the neighborhood, and, of course, the ethnic group. This narrowing of focus by many social historians has caused concern among critics, who lament the inhibition of grander generalizations. I have attempted to avoid this limitation of immigrant study by viewing the major groups in U.S. society and trying to learn how their early immigrants accommodated their Old and New World identities.

I approached the task of discerning a common theme among the diverse groups with considerable respect. Using the necessary tools of historical analysis required the use of several languages and the close familiarity any single scholar must have with the plurality of groups. Accomplishing this multigroup study necessitated my seeking the expertise and advice of others. I was fortunate to obtain the help of good translators and generous colleagues whom I cite here and in the text.

I chose to examine the subject of leadership because I felt that, oddly enough, we know less about that strata of society than we should. This claim of the neglect of elites by academics may appear strange given the long tradition of political and military history in the scholarly literature, but certainly students of immigration history and historians generally have hardly begun to integrate foreign-born leaders into America's past. Few if any American history textbooks refer to Francis Hoffmann, Rev. Vincent Barzynski, or Luigi Fugazi. My major contention in this work is that a careful and judicious illumination of the lives of some immigrant group pioneers can reveal important attitudes and sentiments of their followers and show how one could be both ethnic and American. This last enigma has special contemporary significance as Americans celebrate the centennials of the Statue of Liberty and Ellis Island in 1986 and 1992 and ponder the meaning of American national identity.

By emphasizing the founders of these communities, I do not wish to be filiopietist or elitist—one cannot say that in every case leaders dictate to followers. Nor do I wish to exaggerate the power of the rank and file. I have simply explained how particular individuals had the unusual ability to both reflect and influence the feelings of their constituents.

I include these six major white immigrant groups under one generalization explaining their place in American society, but I am not suggesting that group differences are insignificant. Unquestionably, each immigrant community did indeed possess a distinctive heritage that it drew upon and cultivated in the New World. Still, again, certain individuals in all the six groups did rationalize their group's existence in the American context in a similar way; they believed that the adopted society protected its ethnic diversity from total and rapid assimilation.

The number of leaders I have chosen is not large—a handful of prominent figures among the leading Irish, Germans, Scandinavians, Poles, Jews and Italians. The subjects cited are not uniformly the most powerful of group members, nor are they representative of all leaders of their group; many had powerful opponents within their community. Nevertheless all, as pioneer spokesmen, had a sizable following and took a position that resolved some of the inherent conflict between their native and adopted homelands.

Finally, I am aware of the absence of females among those whom I have selected. I would agree with many of my contemporary colleagues that much of historical study in the past either ignored women or placed them in stereotypical roles. Yet, conscious of that deficiency in prior scholarship, I still could not include any women because I could not identify any female pioneers who played the kind of internal role of my selected males in any sustained manner. Women were indeed an oppressed group chiefly because society and immigrant communities denied them wide influence; no female appeared to hold the same commanding position of the clerics, newspaper editors, or group politicians whom I have listed here.

My pursuit of information on the variety of immigrant communities must have placed colleagues in an awkward position. I requested help from experts on a group or community about which they had devoted much of their professional careers, yet I sought their guidance on a topic which I felt they had neglected. Still, they were exceptionally generous with their advice and criticism. The framework of the Immigration History Society allowed me to easily identify and contact the most knowledgeable scholars in the field. By naming them below, I do not mean they endorsed my conclusions. I simply wish to acknowledge the suggestions they made which helped me identify my subjects and sharpen my analysis.

My major intellectual debt is to Professor John Higham of The Johns Hopkins University who, at a memorable seminar on ethnic leadership at his institution in 1976, first alerted me to the complexities of the topic. Furthermore, his reading of my first chapter was especially helpful. My other aides guided me skillfully through the other particular groups: Professor Jay Dolan for the Irish; Kathleen Conzen, Walter Kamphoefner, and Frederick Luebke for the Germans; John Christianson for the Norwegians; Arnold Barton for the Swedes; Moses Rischin and Jonathan Sarna for the Jews; Rudolph Vecoli, Luciano Iorizzo, and especially George Pozzetta for the Italians; and John Bukowczyk and other members of the Polish American Historical Association for the Poles. Each of them read, heard, or heard about sections of the manuscript, and while in some cases they may have disagreed strongly with my conclusions, they all offered comments that substantially improved the work.

I was fortunate to obtain some financial assistance that enabled me to use a wider array of sources and to gain a broader perspective than would have been otherwise possible. Two hospitable hosts in the Federal Republic of Germany, Professors Dirk Hoerder of Bremen and Wolfgang Helbich of Bochum, provided me with a suitable non-American academic environment in which to carry on my research while I was a senior Fulbright scholar in their country in 1980 and 1981. While there I was also the beneficiary of the findings and guidance of Professors Günter Moltmann and Reinhard Doerries of Hamburg.

I express my gratitude fully to the suppliers of all of the photographs, but here I must cite three donors who gave me rich collateral information that enhanced considerably my understanding of their illustrated images. They are Professor Luciano Iorizzo of the State University College of New York, Oswego, Mrs. Nancy Baldi Berlin of Chadd's Ford, Pennsylvania and Mr. Kenneth Rosett of White Plains, New York.

Professor Melvin Holli graciously allowed me to publish an initial version of my study in his and Peter d'A. Jones' *Ethnic Frontier* (Grand Rapids, Mich.: Eerdmans, 1977). Professor Richard Juliani was exceptionally generous in allowing me to use some of his own research on the Italian community in Philadelphia. Ms. Dina Abramovich of the YIVO Institute in New York and Rev. Donald Bilinski of The Polish Museum of America in Chicago both went far beyond the usual servicing of an apprehensive and anxious historian. Mr. Henry Tom and Ms. Ellen Noel of The Johns Hopkins University Press provided the manuscript with the final polish it needed.

I leave finally to two others my deepest gratitude for their encouragement and inspiration. My wife, Laura, has lived with this manuscript for nearly a decade and has helped me with her own literary skill and intelligence. The man to whom this work is dedicated would have been surprised to see his name in these pages. But he, too, belongs here; he knew his audience as well as these immigrant leaders knew theirs.

Victor Greene
Milwaukee, Wisconsin
July 1986

AMERICAN IMMIGRANT LEADERS, 1800–1910

1

Introduction

From time to time throughout history, in the United States as well as in other nations, certain social issues have arisen to provoke lively public debate. Such verbal exchanges have moved people to take action, some in violence and disorder, others in the passing of what was hoped to be remedial legislation. The recent rediscovery of ethnic feeling among people in both the United States and the world at large has once again occasioned a flurry of public and scholarly concern. The debate includes a perennial dilemma that has dogged the modern state—how to accommodate the local, regional, and sub-cultural ties of its people within the larger national loyalty. All central authorities have wondered how to handle the fragmentational and centrifugal tendencies that resist political consolidation and threaten the dominance of the nation-state.

This characteristic tension of modern social and political development has resurfaced as traditional group ties have reasserted themselves throughout the world. The problem of provincialism has beset not only the newly established countries of the Third World, which are struggling to be viable, modern nations, but also the older, more advanced states of the West.

Certainly all societies are interested in their social composition, in particular, the place of their ubiquitous subgroups. Can a pluralistic nation really accommodate active constituent ethnic groups persisting in their traditional ties and not bring about its own breakup and destruction?

This matter of ethnic attachments, and whether and how much to tolerate them, has had a lively history in the Western world. The period from the French Revolution to World War I, the so-called Age of Nationalism, saw many attempts to establish, reestablish, and consolidate many new states. All this state building took place during a massive shift and mixing of peoples inside and outside Europe, worldwide migrations that further complicated the formation of new states. The demographic changes produced many minorities within countries, complicating the problem for rulers seeking a securely loyal population. The United States in particular took the brunt of these vast population transfers and was vitally concerned with the effects, that is, the origins, nature, and consequences, of this epic shift for the sake of its own survival. This movement of the masses to the New World caused certain periods of frenzied nativism in the United States—the 1790s, the 1850s, the 1890s, and especially the 1920s. Considering this huge immigration ominous, many intellectuals and social observers demanded an investigation of the foreigners' impact on American life. This academic concern produced a number of studies on the issue. And following World War II, because of the decline of colonialism, the emergence of nonwhite peoples, the American civil rights movement, and the growing disenchantment with economic and political centralization, the issue of whether to allow ethnic segregation or to encourage or enforce assimilation has provoked discussion and concern.

An important question in this controversy is just how, and how much, the various incoming groups interacted with the Anglo-American majority. The typical twentieth-century sociological investigation, from early in the second decade until the fifties, concluded that most of the foreign-born in the United States were totally assimilated within a generation or two. There the process terminated. According to this so-called straight-line theory, the "melting pot" did its work effectively, homogenizing our highly diverse society. With minor variations, this was the dominant view of leading sociologists, such as Robert Park, William I. Thomas, Florian Znaniecki, Louis Wirth, and Lloyd Warner.[1] The few, pioneering American historians who, like Marcus Hansen, had an interest in immigration in those years generally agreed with that description of a uniform, although certainly uncomfortable, social transformation among foreign-born citizens. In 1951 Oscar Handlin, who was educated in the 1930s, openly acknowledged his debt to Thomas and Znaniecki—he pointed out in *The Uprooted* that he considered his field to be "immigration history," a cultural phenomenon that virtually ended with the first generation. Little group community persisted beyond the children of newcomers, only a feeling of nostalgia, a later generation's yearning to recall the lives of its ancestors.[2]

With the 1960s, though, and with an apparent resurgence of ethnic feeling worldwide, some social scientists questioned the conventional notion of a virtually complete assimilation in the United States. The 1963 work of social scientists Nathan Glazer and Daniel Patrick Moynihan, who studied New York City's population, and the

1964 work of sociologist Milton Gordon, who noted enduring structural diversity, discerned a certain persistence in group feeling among whites of European ancestry.[3] Gordon's work in particular introduced the highly original hypothesis that, although different ethnic peoples maintained different social worlds, they could still become more alike behaviorally and culturally. He was suggesting, then, that assimilation might have been only partial, occurring across, but not obliterating, ethnic "boundaries." A short time later a group of anthropologists led by Frederik Barth supported that differential thesis with empirical research in their aptly titled study, *Ethnic Groups and Boundaries*. Drawing chiefly upon field work in Scandinavia and Africa, Barth and his associates rejected the older idea that ethnic group preservation required separation and physical isolation. Rather, Barth, like Gordon, believed that cultural change, even some assimilation, can take place across ethnic boundaries without breaking those boundaries down. Cultural differences, then, are not tied exclusively to ethnic differences; groups can share cultural values and still remain apart.[4]

The Gordon-Barth theory of assimilation *with* boundary maintenance has considerable significance for the American ethnic historian, because if it is valid, one must now wonder how and with what rationale those ethnic boundaries were constructed in the first place. How were those lines of group demarcation originally built? Because the United States is a relatively young society, having received millions of people from abroad in its short history, numerous organized ethnic communities have been erected, from the English and German structures in the seventeenth century to those of nonwhites in the twentieth. A closer look at the birth of these ethnic societies will help explain, from their very inception, how and how well they were able to coexist with the majority. My work deals with that issue, seeking to learn why these enclaves were organized initially: as a hostile reaction to the hegemony of the Anglo-American majority, and thereby to segregate the group permanently; as temporary sanctuaries for suitable cultural continuity but with assimilation as the goal; or some combination of the two. Knowing the philosophical underpinnings of ethnic associations, that is, of organized ethnic institutions, will help us to understand the nature of those boundaries and the attitudes of the groups toward their host society. Did group members conceive of their community as having protective barriers, or were those walls really swinging doors ready to open and to encourage egress and return?

* * *

One obvious way to study the purpose of those group organizations is to examine their builders. This volume, then, concentrates on those individuals, the early ethnic leaders. Certainly these prominent pioneers were (and many still are) well-known personalities. As leading priests, editors, politicians, colonizers, and businessmen, many already have a sizable biographical literature, which in some cases consists of highly worshipful profiles. Thus, this examination does not "discover" these persons of influence; most are familiar to members of their groups. Still, these people merit review because, even though they are easily identified by group members and by professional historians, their lives are often overlooked in recent findings about assimilation. These leaders have long existed as heroes for the most part, men of ability and accomplishment. But they should also be viewed as types, as agents of their groups' adjustment in America. It is their function as leaders facilitating their followers' ethnic identity, a role really neglected by scholars, that this work scrutinizes.

To their credit, nonhistorical social scientists have already begun to identify a particular social type as crucial in facilitating intercultural contact. They have referred to that role as "ethnic mediator" or "broker." But while anthropologists and sociologists have advanced that particular kind of intermediary, they have confined their attention to primitive societies, not yet applying their theories to the American ethnic scene.

American historians, on the other hand, have lagged far behind their social science colleagues in examining the place of ethnic mediators and their motives. Despite the widespread popularity of American social history, few professional scholars of that genre incorporate the role of ethnic leaders into their accounts. This is in part due to the anti-elitist bias of many students of the masses. Much of their motivation for investigating society has been to view it "from the bottom up." For them the dynamic for change comes from below. Many historians have stressed the need to improve the way history is written, particularly to employ new kinds of sources and new methods. Students concerned with the masses have valued the huge statistical record and oral history for what these types of evidence may reveal about the less articulate classes. But overemphasizing these kinds of records can belittle the significance of particular, prominent personalities who, all must agree, merit special attention.

Quantitative historians of the early 1970s, for example, tended to see ethnic subcultures as essentially unstratified, lacking varied and discrete social and economic levels. They viewed immigrant life as totally proletarian, virtually leaderless, or subject entirely to the external, powerful forces of secular change. Many other even more recent social historians continue to hold that position, a situation indicated by two of the latest assessments of American social and immigration history, which felt compelled to comment on the emergence and influence of an immigrant middle class.[5]

The rise of the literature on the immigrant family also ignores the influence of particular individuals. The studies view the family as responding directly, successfully or not, to the impact of migration, industrialization, technology, or modern values, but not to communal leaders—rabbi, editor, businessman, or priest.[6] A premise of this work is that a *stratified* and *structured* immigrant community did exist early in the New World, and whether its dynamics came from upper or lower echelons, historians must recognize the impact of specific individuals and not just view them as a category of the middle class.

On those occasions in recent scholarship when immigrant historians, themselves normally members of the group, have discussed particular figures of the early immigrant elite, they usually have done so in single biographies, frequently in traditional life histories. These works are valuable on many counts, for illuminating community institutions, for showing the heterogeneity of the group, and for exposing its inner tensions and controversies. Still, they remain incomplete because they minimize or avoid analyzing the kind of relationship that existed between leaders and followers. Prominent figures are not treated in any depth as intermediaries or as ethnic brokers astride the majority and minority worlds.[7] It is this lack of seeing the leaders comparatively, as group interpreters across ethnic boundaries, that my study attempts to correct.

Over the past hundred years a number of leading social philosophers have called attention to the role of the elite in society and have offered valuable clues to the place of ethnic leaders. Two political observers in particular, Gaetano Mosca, who worked in the late nineteenth century, and his student Vilfredo Pareto, who worked around 1930, were probably the first to discern the problem of the elite in a democracy and to generalize about it.[8] One of Mosca's concerns was to resolve the apparent dilemma of whether good leaders are even compatible with a democratic society. In a system in which the people are sovereign, chosen representatives cannot exert too much authority, because they might use their power to create an undemocratic state. Mosca, though, was satisfied that power, talent, and representation can coexist because democracy is fluid and dynamic, always producing new leaders whom the people in turn select for office. The result is a continual, beneficial turnover, or a "circulation of elites," to use the phrase made popular by Pareto.[9] Leaders, then, are representative.

C. Wright Mills, who studied the ethnic elite in the era immediately following World War II, did not share Mosca's optimistic faith in middle-class democratic leadership. Mills was responsible for reviving Mosca's interpretation, but he accepted it only in part, confining the idea of elite turnover to an early phase in history. In the twentieth century, that is, in the advanced corporate age, Mills pointed out that the ruling community appeared to be immune to democratic pressures. A trio of government officials, military leaders, and businessmen ran the nation in their own, not in the people's, interest.[10] Still, it appears likely that Mills would have agreed with Mosca on the more representative character of the ethnic elite, especially in the nineteenth century, during the formation of the immigrant community.

Besides showing the possible compatibility of power and popular representation among a nation's officeholders, Mosca also offered some insight into the variety of people in command. He referred to the existence and importance of second-rank leaders. Whether or not Mosca was correct in representing these subordinate individuals as a reservoir of talent able to move up and replace their superiors, at least he identified a stratified quality of social leadership. Such a picture is helpful in visualizing an ethnic, as distinguished from a national, level of power.

Besides the work of Mosca and the efforts of Mills to revive interest in Mosca's ideas, other, external influences helped to direct modern social research toward leaders of subcultural groups below the first rank. The post–World War II era produced many new Third World countries, and anthropologists in particular became concerned with the process of nation building among these emerging societies. Since in many instances most of these newly apparent political bodies consisted of a plurality of tribal groups, these scholars have sharpened and extended Mosca's treatment of lower-level leaders by studying how they function and perform in their nations. They point out that the second-rank elite serve as critical and necessary links, really as social "brokers," between the villagers and the new central government.

Recent anthropological identification and description of this particular social type adds to an understanding of the condition and function of U.S. ethnic leadership, although one must be careful to note differences as well. That research suggests that in Africa, Asia, and Latin America this intermediary functions amid more traditional subgroups, tribal peoples who are indigenous to their region and not "immigrants" in the sense of incoming white minorities in the United States.

According to these scholars social brokers arise within these infant states as a way for the state to exert political control over its disparate local peoples. The natives in the villages are, of course, intensely provincial in residence and culture, so any attempts at governing them from a distant capital encounters some resistance. The way to communicate effectively with them is to have some human intermediary act as a mediator and interpreter.

A universal characteristic of that role is the existence of dual, opposing pressures coming from the patrons above and the constituents below. The consequence of this difficult condition, according to all scholars, is instability. As the leading anthropologist on peasant society wrote in a seminal essay on the subject, the intermediary's function is sensitive and taxing. These "brokers stand guard over crucial junctures . . . which connect the local system to the larger whole." They occupy their sensitive positions and are "exposed, since Janus-like they face two directions at once . . . they must cope with the conflicts raised in the collision of community and national interests."[11]

Later scholars have further refined the role of these figures, differentiating at least two types—the cultural mediator, for example, the one who has influence only downward among his own kind, and the political intermediary, the figure who exerts effective power in both directions. It is this latter figure, also known as the "patron" who has "clients," whom anthropologists have studied more carefully.[12]

An ironic twist to the growing concern over mediation has emerged recently. While the newly established states are seeking to build a complex and tight-knit economic and social system like that in the more advanced nations and thus to weaken the function of personal mediation, some recent American sociologists have urged that our society return to a type of brokerage similar to that in the underdeveloped lands. They feel that the United States ought to encourage and empower local leaders and institutions as mediators in order to remedy the growing alienation of the citizenry. The return of social brokerage can help restore the confidence of the public, which is hostile to the enlarged political power of the state.[13]

Other anthropological investigation of the mediators in tribal lands dwells upon their being in a difficult psychological state. Living on the boundaries of their group, caught up in discrete and often conflicting social tensions, tribal leaders bear a heavy and unhappy burden, according to Eric Wolf, who adds that the discomfort is

unrelievable. The very "collision of interests" between the gemeinschaft and gesellschaft is the nature of their position. As Wolf
put it, these leaders stand astride two groups whose contending
interests they cannot settle totally because "by doing so [they] would
abolish their own usefulness to others."[14] Some other writers dis-
agree as to whether the broker arbitrates between culturally similar
or dissimilar peoples, but most do accept the contention that it is in
the leaders' own self-interest as leaders to promote, or at least to
maintain, a level of group tension.[15]

This recent anthropological interpretation of the inherent uncomfortable function and character of the group intermediary in
modern, emerging states is entirely in keeping with the longstanding
and conventional sociological view of the extremely difficult position
of American ethnic leaders. As this thesis has it, placed like the tribal
leaders of the emerging people also at the fringes or boundaries of the
ethnic community, these group interpreters also perform their communicating and mediating duties under very trying personal conditions. Their role in this regard is highly unstable, because many
attained their place at least partially from the support of outsiders
among the majority, so they could and did move easily from that
periphery out of the group entirely; that is, they assimilated.

For example, the leading student of U.S. immigrant assimilation
before World War II, Robert E. Park, a well-known sociologist at the
University of Chicago, made some very influential comments on the
adjustment process of the foreign-born. While he did not focus specifically on ethnic leaders, he clearly suggested that group elites held
a tenuous place in American life, and a painful one. This implied
interpretation was carried forward and made more explicit later by
his colleagues.

Park showed clearly that the mortality rate of the ethnic elite was
assured because of the certainty of the entire assimilation process.
Courageously defending the desire of immigrants to establish and
maintain their ethnic associations amid the intolerant hysteria of the
1920s, Park urged Americans to respect the immigrants' natural
desire to preserve past traditions and memories. What everyone
sought—the integration of the foreign-born—was as "inevitable" as
it was desirable because, under natural conditions, it would be "impossible for the immigrants . . . to remain permanently in separate
groups." His prescription to have the assimilation process work best
was simply to leave the newcomers on their own and let their foreign
cultures disappear naturally: "If we give [them] a favorable milieu, if
we tolerate their strangeness during the period of adjustment, if we
give them freedom to make their own connections between old and

new experiences, [and] if we help them to find points of contact, then we hasten their assimilation."[16] He urged, in fact, the nurturing and protecting of the organizations the foreigners constructed, the churches, newspapers, and other self-help societies, because they provided members with the necessary sense of social responsibility and stable personality. These voluntary associations enabled most immigrants to fit easily into the life of the majority without suffering demoralization.[17] There was no question, however, that the alien would be totally transformed.

In a later, even more influential, essay, Park presented the difficult psychological state of group leaders. He revised his earlier suggestion that institutions made for well-balanced immigrant assimilation. Rather, in his famous 1928 article entitled "Human Migration and the Marginal Man," he concluded that no foreigner in the United States, leader or follower, could make the necessary cultural adjustment in a totally satisfactory manner. He posited a universal law that the movement of people apparently leads to marginality whether or not they are members of an ethnic association. Migration itself does have some benefit in that it frees the individual from the past, and in that sense Park admired the migrant as a pioneer. But moving holds problems. In reaching a new society, the immigrant suffers from a conflict of cultures. He is therefore a "marginal man." Using as examples two Jewish writers whom he knew, Park concluded that the newcomer is bound to encounter a "divided self," with "spiritual distress," "inner turmoil," and "intense self-consciousness."[18]

Other writers developed the marginal man theme further, referring specifically to the mental anguish that ethnic leaders encountered at group boundaries. Louis Wirth, for example, one of Park's fellow sociologists at the University of Chicago, was very much aware of the circumstance of oppressed Jews in European ghettoes. He referred grimly in his major work to the immigrant community as an isolated enclave where intermediaries, those who choose to have close contact with the alien community outside, suffer. They cannot remain long on the fringes:

> the price to be paid for [the] freedom and relaxation of being accepted outside as a leader is the loss of intimate contact with the other group. Here and there an individual bridges the gulf and does fraternize with the stranger, but he does so at the risk of excommunication from his own group, without the assurance of a welcome reception on the other.

He must at last choose between one or the other in a dramatic moment. Wirth continued, "He oscillates between the two until a decisive incident either throws him headlong into the activities of the outer world[,] where he forgets his personality and metamorphoses into a new being[,] or else a rebuff sends him bounding into the old familiar and primary group, where life, though puny in scale, is rich and deep and warm." Nevertheless, despite the pressures of the two hostile communities, the overall legacy of these individuals on the fringe is beneficial, for the unhappy hybrids do help in "fusing" the two camps.[19] But the cost of this integration is high—in personal terms, the psychological discomfort of leaders.

Later, sociologists and one social psychologist of the 1930s and 1940s continued to emphasize the rather difficult transition that both group members and especially their leaders endured trying to synthesize their Old and New World cultures. While the outcome generally doomed their ancestral heritage, the ethnic elite encountered a particular pathology. E. V. Stonequist, another of Park's colleagues, continued to develop the "marginal man" concept, going beyond the American to a worldwide setting. There, he believed, *all* traditional European or Western culture was breaking down and thus weakening the ways of life of isolated peoples. But he focused on cultural assimilation in the United States because it was so distinctively pluralistic and because his evidence was closer at hand.[20] He did not accept Park's sweeping conclusion that all immigrants suffered; some foreigners did adjust better than others, particularly the ordinary minority members who were shielded from outside pressure. But intermediaries and leaders of the discordant alien groups undoubtedly did experience personal discomfort, mental stress, disorganization, and even suicide on occasion. Stonequist felt that their sense of accomplishment came largely from the external majority, and if they were able to hold their positions for any length of time, they made excellent interpreters, that is, leaders. Yet in any event, these prominent ethnic figures led unhappy lives, trying to bridge an immense cultural gap between modernity and tradition.[21]

In the best summary of the entire assimilation process another sociologist, William Carlson Smith, restated the notion of a painful marginality for all newcomers, but he more clearly distinguished between that which the leaders and that which their followers encountered. In fact, the trauma *makes* the leader. He agreed with Park that everyone suffers in a clash of loyalties, but he believed that potential leaders do so sooner because of their greater sophistication, their more intimate understanding of their own group, and their being denied majority acceptance earlier. As Smith put it, the outcome is rejection. This refusal of a leader by a group impugns his personal status, violates his ego, makes him race conscious. As a sophisticated and educated person, he resents being an outcast. In time, being unable to penetrate the social order of the upper race, he returns to his own masses, who likewise are victimized by the situation creating the marginal man. He articulates their grievances and, as their experiences and aspirations become increasingly similar to his, they respond to his leadership.[22]

During World War II a leading Jewish social psychologist also looked at ethnic leaders and reached similar conclusions. He described the personal attitudes of Jews in particular toward themselves and toward their group. Himself a victim of severe anti-Semitic prejudice in central Europe, Kurt Lewin sought to learn the response of that minority elite, its emergence, its place, and particularly its self-conception. He probably was familiar with many intermediary figures, both heroic and otherwise, and he referred to this group as leaders of the periphery. As he saw it, potential leaders emerged from prominent figures who had enjoyed economic or professional success. But since all Jews suffered from an enervating sense of self-hatred, he believed, these leaders of the periphery were lukewarm to their followers and even renounced them. These intermediaries, Lewin held, derived their status and power not from the support of their own group members but rather from the esteem of outsiders, of the majority. The elite, then, much preferred external to internal approval, because they in fact wished to leave their people when they could. Although Lewin did refer elsewhere to leaders who arose from deep within the community as being tied more to it, and although he also stated that the earlier leaders were probably more loyal, clearly most of his examples, whom he felt to be the majority of ethnic leaders, were of this peripheral type. The psychological state of these individuals, Lewin concluded, was similar to the sociologists' view of the marginal man; these were people who possessed a "negative balance," clearly a pathological condition.[23] Despite recent anthropological research on "brokers" in Third World countries, Lewin's conclusions on ethnic leadership have not been superseded.

* * *

By all accounts, then, from the earliest Park-Stonequist sociological assessment to later psychological and anthropological interpretations, ethnic leaders who function as interpreters occupy positions that are definitely uncomfortable, even agonizing. Between two distinctively different and at least partially antagonistic cultures, they had to betray one side or the other. The victims were their own people, according to more recent judgments. They suffered continually, torn by opposing ties and sometimes suspected by these polarized groups as well.

Before examining the general subject of ethnic brokerage in America, I want to present an evaluative review of the considerable social science interest in the topic. Such an assessment shows that this earlier investigation of ethnic leadership was seriously deficient in a number of ways. The problem in part has been that, until recently, historical scholars usually left the question of ethnic differences to other disciplines. Hence, generalizations did not have the benefit of a careful historical methodology. For example, of all the sociologists cited, none systematically reviewed the life, thought, and experience of individuals who were influential figures in their group. The subjects cited by these academicians were not intermediaries or social brokers who had arisen from within their communities, so none of the conclusions was the result of empirical research. The individuals were people who really did not qualify as "leaders," although they did express sensitively their feelings of marginality. The subjects were generally writers and ethnic intellectuals, *not* social figures of wide influence, representative of their group. They certainly were not internal leaders. Mary Antin, Ludwig Lewisohn, M. E. Ravage, and Louis Adamic all expressed their marginal sentiments creatively in human terms, and they articulated sensitively the adjustment problems they themselves encountered.[24] But whether these particular men and women were indeed fully or even partially representative, in their total experience, of the ordinary rank and file, the workers and the families, or the group leaders who made up the communities, is still open to question. We really must look elsewhere for the ethnic community elite.

A changed understanding of the assimilation process—that it may not have been a "melting pot"—also calls for a renewed examination of ethnic leaders. It is increasingly clear to recent historical investigators that the assumption of Park and his colleagues—that assimilation, whether painful or not, was total and was largely completed by the maturation of the second generation—is not accurate, or at least needs refinement. Present interpretation suggests that ethnic consciousness and identification did not terminate early but continued, although in altered form, and was transformed.[25] Foreigners and their children did not abandon their ethnic communities totally, but some retained and passed on their group feeling to later generations, the second, third, and beyond.[26] There were individuals who mobilized and really organized their followers into associations that were in fact *the* very immigrant community for its members, helping them to define themselves as a discrete group in the New World.

Thus, understanding that critical question of how immigrants conceived of themselves in relation to the Anglo-American environment requires close scrutiny of those figures who were largely responsible for the identity-defining organizations—churches, fraternal associations, and various newspapers. On the one hand, these bodies could have been agencies of ethnic persistence, created to segregate their groups' members from the society of the larger majority outside, that is, Anglo-America, and to inhibit assimilation and isolate members from alien influences and values. On the other hand, they may have been agents of change, associations organized to provide badly needed social services or education to enable members to function and participate advantageously in the total American milieu.

If the idea of a certain ethnic persistence through the generations is gaining acceptance—if being a Pole in the United States, for example, is a more durable identity than heretofore believed—it is clear that we must rethink our understanding of immigrant leaders and their philosophy about their groups within American society. This study contends that, rather than suffering from effective pressures of rapid assimilation or harboring deep-seated feelings of group inferiority as implied by much earlier theory, the pioneer elite, at least, the initiators of the ethnic communities in the United States, conceived of their group and community life clearly in terms of American principles. While they might have performed their task of community-building under adverse discriminatory pressures, their understanding of their role and position may not have been as agonizing and as painful as previously believed, for they regarded their edifices as rationalized by this nation's democratic ideals. At any rate, it is imperative that historians review the ideas and the community-building rationale of these early immigrant leaders. Students ought not simply to understand their subjects' psychological condition as individually painful or not; they should view these figures as powerful influences upon and representatives of their foreign-born constituents.

* * *

Learning the objective of all organized immigrant institutions as well as the goals of their organizers is not an easy task; it is beyond any single work. Scholars know, for example, that such bodies, formal and informal, were many in number and highly varied in kind. It is likely that many were created so easily as a part of the plethora of America's voluntary associations that many have escaped the historical record. The very ethnic diversity of the United States alone, the multitude of its communities, makes any complete overview of group associations impossible at this time.

Besides the overwhelming variety of groups and organizations, another problem of method concerns the selection of leaders. No single figure among the many communities was totally representative of the group, nor was he or she a group figure of unrivaled influence. The host of voluntary organizations were established by men and women who had widely differing occupational, religious, and philosophical interests and who came from many European regions and settled in just as many U.S. localities.

A final methodological difficulty is the practical one of evidence. Some individuals whom an investigator might select as ideal and predominant figures left no, or only fragmentary, first-hand records of their motives and goals. The materials of other leaders worth studying are for some other reason inaccessible.

Thus, any particular study of immigrant leaders perforce must be selective as to group and individual. But a deliberate survey of America's white immigrant groups in the nineteenth century does suggest a pattern for approaching the incoming millions that this work discusses. For example, the bulk of the immigrants in the last century are of six major ethnic communities, the Irish, Germans, Scandinavians, Poles, Italians and East European Jews. Therefore, this study concerns itself with individuals from these major categories alone.

The more difficult task is to choose particular leaders from these very large immigrant bodies. But here, too, a certain uniformity emerges. A handful of both representative and powerful figures do appear.

Two recent scholars have described the particular type of leader to be studied as individuals who held a high position among their fellows and so were representative of them, *and* whose power rested on their group members' esteem such that they wielded considerable influence upon them. Social psychologist Paul Lazarsfeld has called these figures "opinion leaders" in his studies of the voting behavior of the electorate. Through personal contact as well as from their speeches and writings, particular individuals are able to attract a substantial following among their people. While they, therefore, "set the fashion" as people of influence, they are also like their followers, representing their constituents' attitudes toward outsiders.[27] They articulate inchoate sentiments of followers without persuading their fellows of new ones.

Another observer, historian John Higham, has more carefully distinguished among ethnic leaders themselves and has described them more precisely in a recent review of academic interest in the subject. Using the categories first employed by Kurt Lewin, he referred to three types of leader: the "projective," who hold their status largely if not totally from outsiders; the "received," who base their authority on some receding tradition; and an "internal" elite, who function as the group's representative and advocate.[28] Obviously it is the internal opinion leaders that my work examines, a type that happily defines and clearly restricts subject selection.

A further qualification of the subject that will narrow the choice is that of time. This work deals with the pioneer elite. As the founding architects of organized group institutions, these men had a particularly telling impact upon the philosophical goals and objectives of the arriving group and, to some extent, of later generations. As Professor Higham suggests, it was this elite that helped to bring into focus the consciousness of the group and to broadcast its identity.[29]

Thus, a close reading of the goals of this handful of leading ethnic pioneers, their reasons for organizing, guiding, and administering the institutional life of their countrymen, will reveal some of the thoughts and objectives *all* group members had in trying to place themselves in the American context. As both a mobilizing force and a reflection of the rank and file, this early immigrant elite mirrored the efforts their followers must have made in trying to resolve that rather complex issue of being both ethnic and American.

It is important to add that it is not my purpose in this study to eulogize the founders of immigrant communities in the United States. The leaders were not selfless in their organizing efforts; much of the motivation for what they did was self-interest, reflecting a desire to aggrandize their own power. But there was also a public objective in their work—to facilitate the adjustment of their people—whether they were themselves aware of it or not. Again, the goal here is to show how internal leaders, and hence to a large extent their followers, answered the question of how simultaneously to be a foreign-born member of an immigrant community *and* an American. They first dealt with this issue not years after they arrived or in later generations but at the very inception of their community in the New World. The immigrant institutions established by the elite were far more than simple adjustment devices to provide needed support services for aliens, to disappear, as Robert Park envisioned, once assimilation was complete. Rather, these bodies began as organizations that leaders felt would strengthen, and be sanctioned by, American principles and values.

The philosophical goals of these organizations were entirely in harmony with ultimate American ends. Ethnic pioneers were quite clear in every case about the compatibility of their communities with mainstream U.S. society. Their institutions were not intended to bar group members from participating in the outside world; those wishing to use group agencies to participate in the larger community could do so. Rather, these institutions functioned as educational devices enabling immigrants to feel secure about the compatibility of their ancestral heritage and the principles of their adopted country. It is for that reason that I wish to refer to these immigrant leaders as "traditional progressives," individuals who were trying to synthesize past and future through new group organization in the United States.

Although the task of these individual intermediaries certainly was not easy, and although tensions in attempting to ease pressures inside and outside the group did arise, the position of these traditional progressives and sometimes of their followers did not inherently indicate the marginal pathology, or "negative balance," that has been suggested. In sum, as internal, pioneering leaders, these ethnic interpreters were able to provide themselves and their followers with an intellectual resolution of the problem of being ethnic in America.

2

The IRISH

As one of the first and largest white groups to come to the United States, Irish immigrants have been studied extensively. Their numbers and group characteristics and the timing and circumstances of their emigration are fairly well known. But despite this familiarity, the nature of their group identity—whether they considered themselves to be Irish, Irish American, or American—remains debatable. Earlier historians have described in some detail the circumstances of emigration and have concluded that the Irish immigrants' conception of themselves came essentially from the widespread discrimination of the Anglo-American majority. Evaluating that assessment and suggesting refinements necessitates a brief review of the life of these newcomers in the early nineteenth century and the role of those who helped shape the Irish-American community.

Certainly, as most writers have pointed out, the overall picture of Irish movement to America is a sad one. Their departure from the Old World and arrival in the New World were filled with misery and unhappiness. The overwhelming majority of Irish immigrants were Roman Catholics spurred by the widespread economic dislocation that afflicted the Emerald Isle in the century after 1815. The high birth rate there at the beginning of the nineteenth century; the free trade movement, which ruined Ireland's agricultural markets; the land consolidation and high rents, which produced a mass of agrarian poor; the recurrent potato famines of 1822, the 1830s, and especially the mid 1840s—all joined to produce a wretched existence for most inhabitants. Even with the huge exodus in the first half of the century, which somewhat reduced the pressure of population, there were still twice as many mouths to feed in 1841, over eight million, as there had been fifty years earlier. Those who could left for England and the United States in ever-increasing numbers, from approximately twenty thousand yearly in the late 1820s to over two million during the next two decades. The outflow reached a high point in the early 1850s and still numbered over a million between the American Civil War and the year 1900. In all, about five million went to the United States in the century before World War I, the largest European contingent except for the Germans.[1]

Almost all the American historians who have written about the group have concluded that it was chiefly the wretched character of these immigrant masses—their economic and social deprivation, and especially the confinement and discrimination they faced in urban ghettoes—which brought about group consciousness. Oscar Handlin, Lawrence McCaffrey, and Thomas Brown in particular have emphasized the depressed nature of the arrivals, their feelings of insecurity, and the rising hostility of native citizens, the so-called Protestant Crusade of the 1830s to 1850s, as salient causes of the immigrants' view of themselves. Encountering numerous social problems, being unskilled and poor, living in infested, vice- and crime-ridden urban ghettoes, and frequently being the object of An-glo-American prejudice, alienated Irish immigrants reacted by establishing their own ethnic institutions. These groupings in the saloon, parish, and neighborhood in general provided them with important centers of group reference. As Handlin stated in his classic study of the Boston Irish: "Unable to participate in the normal associational affairs of the [Boston] community, the Irish felt obliged to erect a society within a society, to act together in their own way. In every contact, therefore, the group, acting apart from other sections of the community, became intensely aware of its peculiar and exclusive identity." Lawrence McCaffrey refined this view in a 1971 article entitled "Pioneers of the American Ghetto." He cited in particular nativist condemnation and the group's consequent psychological pathology, which forced them to accept their critics' definition of themselves.[2]

A third writer, Thomas Brown, noted that the general Irish alienation was the cause not only of ethnic organization but also of the vigorous activities of Irish nationalists. Specifically, it was rejection by the Anglo-American Protestant majority which brought about the feelings of loneliness and inferiority as well as the hatred of England. Thus it was essentially psychological discontent which was the wellspring of ethnic enthusiasm. Group resentment shaped the conscious Irish community of the 1840s and 1850s.[3]

Certainly no one can deny the existence of the nearly inhuman living conditions of the ordinary Irish immigrant in Boston, New York, Philadelphia, and other urban centers in the mid 1800s. In fact, the social and religious hostility suffered by the group in cities was probably more pervasive than even these historians have indicated.

But the hardships and traumatic psychological consequences encountered by this group still do not explain fully the justification for
the formation of Irish American communities and group consciousness. If Irish America was founded on a rationale of bitterness
and pain, why were there not more conspicuous pre–Civil War expressions of dissatisfaction with the immigrants' lot, or more re-
emigration to other lands? Obviously, a review of the motivations for
the formation of specific organizations, in particular for the individuals who started self-help groups, mutual aid societies, charitable
associations, and the host of immigrant services, is necessary. Such
an examination reveals that these constructed institutions were
based also on a thorough understanding and, in fact, an endorsement
of American political, or as they called them at the time, "republican,"
principles. In his study, Professor Brown does refer to the appeal of
such American ideals among Irish figures as a basis for organization,
but these ideals were a more significant and more formative factor
than he suggests.[4]

"Irish American" organization, that is, the initial establishment
of a voluntary association restricted to the Irish, long preceded the
famine of the 1840s and even the arrival of the poor masses in the
nineteenth century. The first organized body in America was the
Charitable Irish Society of Boston, begun in 1737. It had two objectives, one historic and one philanthropic. The historic goal was to
celebrate the birth of that well-known Irish patron saint and hero, St.
Patrick, who had Christianized the island in the fifth century, and the
philanthropic goal was to provide financial help to countrymen in
need. As the preamble put it, with "an affectionate concern for the
countrymen" several "gentlemen . . . of the Irish nation" have
formed the society "for the relief of [the] poor and indigent countrymen."[5] A similar group called the Friendly Sons of St. Patrick
began in New York about 1769 with similar purposes.[6]

On the surface, other than having similar ethnic designations,
these two associations had little connection with the millions of Catholic countrymen who filled the Irish sections of American cities a
century later. As Brown and McCaffrey have pointed out, these eigh-
teenth-century organizers were upper- and middle-class merchants,
not the unskilled workers who made up the bulk of later immigrants.
Further, these pioneers were Protestant, not Catholic, and they ex-
pended most of their funds over the years for social purposes such as
celebrating St. Patrick's Day appropriately, rarely for helping the poor
as their charters announced. Hence, these first bodies were hardly
the institutional base for Irish community organization of the 1800s.

Religious and class differences are important matters to consider when reviewing Irish nationalism in the period around 1800. Until that time the Irish movement for freedom was essentially Protestant, and even when Catholics began to support it in the latter 1700s, they did so warily, suspicious of their religious counterparts. Simultaneously, a definite two-class culture existed in Irish society, the group of wealthy merchants and planters clearly distinguished themselves from the cotters and the poor. This obvious social stratification continued into the next century and was evident in Irish American settlements.[7]

Thus, at the start of Irish immigration to America and for a time afterward, these charitable societies in the two leading Irish American centers remained upper-class retreats for well-to-do, leading Irish Protestants and later in the nineteenth century for the increasingly conspicuous "lace curtain" Catholics. The St. Patrick's Day dinners in particular were grand social occasions that the societies sponsored. They became well-known affairs where the elite paraded their finery.[8]

Society members, then, did try to maintain considerable social distance from the incoming lower-class immigrant and to isolate themselves from the masses. Still, despite their determined segregation, these upper-class meetings remained important events in the making of the Irish Catholic community in America for two reasons. First, as most historians have already indicated, these organizations did advance a sense of Irish consciousness and pride. Soon after these bodies had been formed, as early as the mid 1700s, they dropped their religious restrictions and admitted Catholics.[9] Sources suggest that at a rather early date, possibly by the start of the 1830s, Catholics predominated in the Boston Irish society and shortly thereafter made up part of its leadership.[10] Thus, in the first years of mass immigration, the leading Irish organization was already largely Catholic, although it continued to be upper class in character. These societies did help to promote an ethnic more than a religious identity.

Another reason for the ethnic significance of these elite organizations was what turned out to be their major function, celebrating St. Patrick's Day. By so honoring their patron saint, they complemented their identity as Americans. Doing homage to St. Patrick became an important ritual for all immigrants, partly because it reminded them of the compatibility and basic similarity of being both Irish and American. The rationale for the day was not simply to pay their respects to their patron saint but also to celebrate a national hero, one who gave his people a religious identity separate from that of the English and thereby welded together the Irish and American national struggles. Both peoples had been English colonials who had suffered British tyranny, and both sought freedom and democracy or, as they called it, "republicanism." Year after year the societies held dinners that featured speeches and toasts looking forward to winning for Ireland what America had won in 1776, a separate nation based on the Lockean concepts of liberty, freedom, and democracy.

The underlying but clear implication of these elaborate testimonies was that the Irish immigrant working for Irish freedom could do so *as an American.* Group spokesmen referred to the unity of the two national philosophies early on, as soon as American independence was achieved. While at first these upper-class societies often spoke of Irish American compatibility, others, much closer to ordinary immigrants broadcast the same message throughout the nineteenth century.

Recognition of the similarity of Irish and American goals appeared virtually at the moment American independence was won. At the 1784 gathering of the Boston Charitable Irish Society soon after the Treaty of Paris, President McKay welcomed the defeat of England *as an American,* with the toast, "May *our friends, countrymen in Ireland,* behave like the brave Americans till they recover *their* liberties."[11] McKay was already highlighting the similarity of the two national struggles; those "brave Americans" were the Irish participants in the American effort.[12]

Another early Irish American fraternal association more conspicuously indicated the shared national aims by making loyalty to the American founding ideology a requirement for membership. In its 1801 constitution the New York Hibernian Provident Society, dedicated to helping all impoverished immigrants, barred any countrymen who had fought at any time on the British side. It further required an oath to support the political principles found in the U.S. Constitution and the individual states.[13]

A musical toast composed and presented at the society's annual St. Patrick's Day observance three years later dealt more fully with the flight of countrymen from oppression to find fulfillment as Americans, in particular as Tammany Hall Democrats. The lyrics are strained, but the sentiment heralding the universalism of American ideals is clear:

Hark! "tis Erin's voice I hear, calling to the children dear, who
    in merry roundelay, welcome in this glorious Day
While the genius of her Isle heaved a sigh, then a smile, at
    oppression's heavy hand, that forced them from their native
    land. *(repeat)*
Now from persecution free, they hail this land of liberty.
    (repeat 3 times)

Those patriot sons whom round I see, children of St. Tammany
Whose holy zeal in freedom's cause, has filled the world with
    their applause
Charge your goblets, fill them high, the theme deserves to
    reach the sky,
Let Jefferson and Clinton be the guardian of your liberty.
    (repeat 3 times)[14]

And at another observance about the same time, the society expressed the idea that the republican Irish in the United States ought
to be grateful for sanctuary and should be participating as U.S. citizens, that is, by voting and performing military service, to advance
"the happiness and honor of their adopted country."[15]

On the same day two years later a similar New York group, the
Juvenile Sons of Erin, praised the young nation for keeping clear of
"miserable" European governmental "systems" and for possessing
popular self-government, in other words, for being a model, an "example to an admiring world."[16]

Of course, all this rhetoric of affirmation for the new land is
related to the times, the first years of the nation. It was relatively easy
for Irish spokesmen then, before the nineteenth century and the end
of the Napoleonic wars in Europe, to herald their host society in
attractive terms. In 1790, for example, fewer than fifty thousand
Irish natives lived in America, and many of these were Protestant.
The miserable ghettoes and ensuing anti-Irish, anti-Catholic hysteria of later years were not yet evident. But by the 1820s, with the
appearance of city slums such as the notorious, heavily Irish, Five
Points district on New York's Lower East Side, and with the increase
in poor Catholic settlement, a growing feeling of native suspicion and
condemnation did develop.

In the 1830s the New York Friendly Sons of St. Patrick apparently ignored the more visible evidence of Irish misery in American
cities and the rising hostility of the Protestant crusade. The mid-
March observances of that decade remained the occasion for continuing references to the close Irish and American identities rooted
in freedom. For example, at the 1830 dinner, amid traditional decora-
tions and under pictures of the honored triumvirate of St. Patrick,
Daniel O'Connell (the contemporary hero of Irish autonomy), and
Washington, speakers referred to the "mutual respect and affection"
that would always unite the "land we left and the land we live in."
This sentiment of Irish gratitude to America remained the theme of
St. Patrick's Day through the decade.[17]

The older Boston society expressed continued Irish American

loyalty and support of the new land with somewhat more difficulty because the anti-Catholic feeling was more intense there. The 1832 burning of the Charlestown convent and the popularity among Protestants of the salacious Mariah Monk tales inflamed tensions. Yet, sources say that many Irish Catholics still identified closely with President James Boyd when he spoke at the group's 1837 centennial observance. While admitting that his countrymen did deserve some criticism for certain faults, such as drinking excessively, he reminded listeners once again that the Irish in the United States were also American, adhering to American ideals. They, too, hated monarchy and supported liberty. Furthermore, the new arrivals, like the old, chose to come to U.S. shores. Ireland had been good to them, but America was better. "Let all Irish in America never forget the love due to their parent land . . . but let that to the land of their choice remain paramount [because] it is the pole star and hope of republicans all over the world."[18]

Admittedly, as earlier historians have made clear, all the St. Patrick's Day rhetoric in the years before the massive waves of Irish immigrations came from groups and societies that had little close contact with the early Irish peasant-laborers who were finding their way in steerage across the Atlantic. These expressions of Irish gratitude for American sanctuary, the identical goals of the Irish and Americans, came from an upper-class strata of foreigners. Few unskilled workers attended these functions at which loyalty to the United States was upheld. One might wonder, then, if the ordinary immigrant was even aware of the statements of the commonality of Irish and American principles.

The anonymous immigrants probably did consider at some point the idea of America and their place in that alien world. Students of the Irish Catholic masses have strongly implied that these former peasants depended heavily upon the opinions of others, especially of people further up the social scale. The observation is particularly important, as it tends to differentiate the group from other European emigrants, particularly the Germans and Italians.

According to scholarly observers, very few ordinary Irish Americans were individualists; they listened closely to the counsel of others, especially local leaders. According to one writer well acquainted with Irish American social life, the lower classes "looked to the landlord, the agent, or the priest for advice and assistance . . . [they were] accustomed to taking orders and directions, not giving them . . .[and they] developed a sense of dependency upon others that was a handicap to . . . individual progress."[19] An anthropologist acquainted with Irish peasant life, Conrad Arensburg, supports that observation and goes even further. The cotters had only a limited amount of self-reliance, and in the rural districts it was local leaders, the shop-keeper-publican, who wielded predominant influence as a power broker shaping the attitudes of the masses. Another observer, Robert E. Kennedy, has noted the closeness of priest and peasant in the early nineteenth century, the result of long-term English anti-Catholicism. This social harmony began to break down in the 1830s after the passing of Irish Emancipation and the rise of Daniel O'Connell. From those points, a coolness grew between secular Irish nationalists and clerics. Finally, in a conclusion to a recent anthology on the American Irish, the editor, Owen Dudley Edwards, asserted that "most Irish people" respect those who have leadership abilities. "The exceptional" are significant in society and "are necessary to the ordinary." All these judgments on the group's social characteristics suggest that in the early immigrant years the expressed observations of local leaders were important influences on the ideas of national identity held by the larger rank and file of the Irish American community.[20]

Obviously, to discover what the Irish elite was thinking, the scholar should concentrate on figures like popular neighborhood saloon-keepers, politicians, and priests. These community leaders would be ideal types to examine in order to ascertain the views their followers were subjected to. I have selected five particularly significant pioneer Irish American figures with a considerable group following and a significant impact in the two major ethnic centers, New York and Boston, in the nineteenth century. The choice has some flaws. New York and Boston are hardly representative geographically of the total Irish population in the United States, and a discussion of only these two cities neglects other, large colonies in the nation. But my study does not aim for total group coverage. Unquestionably, each member of the quintet rendered here in detail was an important internal leader, someone whose opinion had weight in the community in which he lived—and especially among the lower classes. The figures are Dr. William MacNeven, Thomas O'Connor, and Archbishop John Hughes of New York, and Patrick Donohoe and Patrick Collins of Boston.

All these men expressed ideas and thoughts that had a wide hearing. They were journalists, writers, or effective public speakers who had easy access to a large audience. Additional evidence of their influence came at their death in the form of popular memorials. Also, all lived in the formative period of Irish American life, and all but one attained prominence in the first half of the century. Most important, each of them was a community leader who continued to broadcast the group's upper-class notion of the fundamental harmony and mutual reinforcement of Irish and American ideals. These figures then welded their group's ethnic past to the goals of the new land.

* * *

Dr. William James MacNeven was the first of the leaders to perform that mediating function. He arrived in New York on a day appropriate to his later messages to fellow immigrants, July 4, 1805. He was a United Irishman, a member of an Irish society, created by liberal Protestants like Wolfe Tone, that sought a republic based on French revolutionary ideals.

Prior to his coming to the United States MacNeven hardly seemed like the internal social leader of ordinary Irish Americans that he was to become. His European years showed him as a typical, upper-class, well-to-do emigre, born of the landed, Irish Catholic aristocracy in 1763. He was raised in Prague by his uncle, a baron and physician. At the age of twenty, he, too, became a doctor in Vienna. He returned to Ireland a short time later a cultured gentleman, an accomplished linguist speaking five languages. Back in his native land he became interested in politics and was attracted to the liberal ideas of the time. He joined the United Irishmen and became an Irish representative in Parliament. But the authorities arrested him in 1798, just as the Irish rebellion broke out. Upon his release in 1802 he tried to enlist French aid for the Irish cause, but he failed; thereupon he decided to go to the United States. He immigrated as a member of a famous trio of Irish radical refugees which included Thomas A. Emmet and William Sampson.[21]

The last thirty-five years of MacNeven's life in America were in part a continuation of his upper-class, liberal activities in Europe. He maintained and furthered his professional life, became a professor of medical science in New York, and pursued his many intellectual interests by joining the New York Literary and Philosophical Society in 1823. Still partially oriented to the Old World, he continued to work for Irish freedom, writing a nationalist history in 1807 and organizing and leading the Friends of Ireland, a society supporting O'Connell's modest demand for Irish autonomy.[22]

MacNeven, however, was a rather atypical "exile." He differed from his nationalist colleagues, Emmet and Sampson, in his particular concern for an Irish American identity and in his sensitivity concerning the lower classes. He often spoke about American nationalism to ordinary immigrants while seeking to improve their material adjustment in the new land. With such an activist social philosophy, he was able to communicate with the most anonymous of countrymen, justifying Irish nationalism to all classes on the basis of

American political ideology. He stressed the virtues of American democracy, which he earnestly felt Irish immigrants could and should work for. As he saw it, the goals of the two peoples were not in conflict; as both Irishmen and Americans, the newcomers could easily work for Irish freedom.

Other evidence of his concern for the cotter class is obvious. As a physician, MacNeven attended the immigrants' most practical, medical needs; he often treated infirm members of the working class for little or no charge.[23] His professional specialization was in fact what later colleagues would call "public health." He undertook in particular the humanitarian but likely depressing task of treating the sick and dying arrivals in the 1830s as they disembarked in New York Harbor. His establishment of the city's first free labor exchange offices—one at his own expense in 1816, another elsewhere in 1827, and a third for women in particular—further indicates his continuing social awareness and his proximity to the incoming immigrants.[24] In addition, he felt obliged to aid newcomers in other ways, by publishing a guidebook for them and by organizing and leading, circa 1820, an Irish emigrant society that aimed at colonizing the foreign settlers in the West.

On two occasions MacNeven expressed, formally and in detail, his ideas about how best to relate his Irish listeners' dual national identities. One was at a meeting of naturalized Irish Americans in 1832, where he dealt with the subject directly. At that time during the electoral campaign, some of his political colleagues had urged MacNeven to use his great popular influence with the immigrant electorate to form a separate Irish political organization. He declined because he thought it was unnecessary. As he put it, we "hold our rights as Americans and use them as Americans without reference to alien origins." We in fact *are* Americans, he added, for we Irish found here "not merely an asylum but a country in the United States." By saying this he concluded deliberately that this fortuitous condition did not mean that the group could not coalesce as Irishmen. He welcomed their social organizations and Irish societies chiefly to give help to the struggling old country. All of this suggests that MacNeven clearly identified the immigrant group's differing but compatible loyalties.[25]

Later, too, at a popular St. Patrick's Day celebration in 1837, he continued to uphold the value of American democracy and sanctuary for his fellows. The message came in a speech honoring the contemporary Irish hero, Daniel O'Connell. O'Connell, he recalled, had won concessions some years earlier from Great Britain when it granted Catholics religious freedom. But O'Connell's victory, MacNeven reminded his audience, was something all Americans had obtained many years earlier. The liberator's task now, the immigrant leader advised, was to continue to follow the American model by winning the other rights he and his audience possessed, freedom to speak and to create the organizations and political instruments that would bring about peaceful change. It was the American Revolution in particular, "the happiest . . . ever achieved," said MacNeven, that was responsible for the liberties he and all New Yorkers, Irish and non-Irish, held.[26]

A huge public response to the death of a person is, of course, not always proof of an individual's general influence and following. Throngs of people often attend the funeral of notorious criminals, and once-commanding social figures may die years later in obscurity. But a large audience at the rites of the departed can indicate the individual's appeal. The passing of a well-known social leader is certain to be a large public event. Such was the scene at the ceremonies at MacNeven's death. The burial was a community affair, suggesting the doctor's wide influence.

The setting for the sad event was appropriate: the day was overcast and rainy. Yet despite the heavy downpour, the size of the procession and the mass of spectators made the funeral one "of the largest that has ever been witnessed in this city," according to a local newspaper.[27] As one writer put it simply, MacNeven was at that time the "recognized leader of the Catholic Irish community in New York."[28]

* * *

One of MacNeven's associates, as well known and as anxious to mesh and yet retain the Irish and American labels, was Thomas O'Connor. Like MacNeven, O'Connor also had been a United Irishman. He arrived in New York in 1801, just four years before the physician's arrival. But O'Connor was more of a politician; he was loyal sachem of Tammany, a minor officeholder, and a close aide to Bishop Hughes until O'Connor's death in 1855.[29] And he differed from MacNeven particularly in that his writings, rather than his social actions, were the source of his popularity. With his friend, O'Connor was an avid supporter of Irish emigrant society, but his wide influence came from his association with, and later from his role as editor of, a leading Irish journal after 1814, the *Shamrock and Hibernian Chronicle*. Oddly, even as a writer he followed MacNeven's humanitarian example, using his newspaper to aid immigrants in finding jobs. After 1816, by setting up the Shamrock Friendly Association and turning his journal into a labor exchange, he directed the increasing number of arrivals to employment opportunities. As he put it, getting work for the newcomers was a responsibility of all resident Irishmen in the United States.[30]

While recognizing a social obligation to help immigrant workers, O'Conner simultaneously gave them his ideas about becoming American. That time, early in the century, was especially conducive to a discussion of American and Irish nationalism because such sentiments were becoming well known in both lands. The War of 1812, for example, provided an ideal opportunity for the Irish American journalist to tie the two identities to a common enemy, England, and a common cause, democracy. Ignoring the English parliamentary tradition, O'Connor drew together the Irish and American political symbols. He informed his incoming countrymen of the liberal foundations of their adopted land in his 1813 work, *An Impartial and Correct History of the War Between the United States and Great Britain.* This history of the American Revolution probably had the desired educational impact on his audience, because it ran to three editions by 1816.[31]

It was the change in direction and goals of the early Irish immigrant newspaper, the *Shamrock and Hibernian Chronicle,* from an organ for transplanted Europeans to one for immigrant Americans, which further showed what one might call O'Connor's role as ethnic interpreter. He wanted his readers to know that, as refugees from the Irish struggle, they were in fact *already* Americans.

To understand that shift in the newspaper's goals requires a brief history. O'Connor's associate, Edward Gillespie, had begun the *Chronicle* in 1810 with the major aim of informing readers about Irish events. Comprehending American laws and customs was another, but clearly a subsidiary, goal for his audience.[32] When O'Connor joined Gillespie as co-editor in 1814, Americanist goals took priority. It was probably O'Connor who shortened the paper's name to the *Shamrock* and revised the paper's major objective, which had been to bring about "a political and social amalgamation of the native and adopted citizens." The editors turned now to immigrant adjustment. As they put it, the Irishman differed from the native only in place of birth; in terms of political purpose, they were alike. Again, it was undoubtedly O'Connor's influence that provided the new emphasis.[33]

A further modification showing Irish and American principles as identical came when O'Connor became sole publisher and editor in 1815. As he stated flatly, an "Irishman by birth" was "an American by adoption." And the paper itself was to devote even more space to American events.[34] A short time later he returned to this theme. As he pointed out, differences between the Irish foreigner and the native-born American were trivial. "In spite of [the comments of critics, the two groups] will be one people, with one interest, one cause, ONE COUNTRY."[35]

O'Connor wrote less on the theme of Americanism in the remaining thirty-five years of his life, but he maintained his belief in similar or harmonious Irish and American philosophies to the end. Like MacNeven, he continually viewed American principles as the model for an emerging Ireland, and he always believed that the Irish in America were truly Americans.

At the 1835 St. Patrick's Day observance of the New York Irish Democrats, the theme of the toasts prepared by O'Connor was "America as she is, Ireland as she ought to be," and a few years later, in an essay written for the *Truth Teller* in response to anti-immigrant sentiment, he said that the Irish were *not* strangers to America. Upon arriving in this land, they did not encounter an unfamiliar political order. Rather, they came to see how the democratic rhetoric and theory with which they were already acquainted were being implemented in the New World.[36]

In the 1830s, with the coming of Catholic Emancipation and the intensification of the Irish struggle for autonomy in Europe, a more militant nationalism developed in Ireland. The result was that O'Connor found it necessary to shift his written theme from the similarity of Irish and American values to the ways in which Irish immigrants should relate to their people's national struggle in Europe. He continued to urge his readers to become American citizens and at the same time work for Irish freedom. These loyalties might conflict, but immigrants must act as law-abiding Americans. Any agitation that led immigrants to engage in military action on their own would be wrong and illegal. As he said, "we must not on any account violate the laws of this country because they protect us and because they are good."[37] Thus even if one had both Irish and American responsibilities, they could be compatible.

* * *

The next era, the 1840s and 1850s, certainly tested the faith of the Irish in the new land. Unlike the period during and immediately after the War of 1812, group members a quarter-century later encountered much more opposition and, therefore, had more difficulty in being enthusiastic about America. The Irish poor swelled American cities, and native American Protestants fought the apparent spread of Catholicism with violence and religious intolerance. The new situation forced Thomas O'Connor to write less and to defend his nationality and faith by greater political activity. The new Irish leader of that time, Bishop John Hughes, recognized the Protestant threat, but rather than combating it head on as an anti-Catholic movement, he based his defense on American principles. This assertive and powerful Catholic cleric fought the superpatriotic Americanism with his own idea of Americanism. By so doing, he, too, like MacNeven and O'Connor, revealed to new immigrants the compatibility, not the clash, of Irish and American identities.

Unlike his New York Irish predecessors, Hughes was a prelate in the Roman Catholic church—a bishop and, later, the city's first archbishop. Hence, he held a high institutional position and was less dependent upon the grass-roots support that NacNeven and O'Connor had commanded. Still, Hughes was also an important, perhaps the most important, internal group leader in the two decades before the Civil War. A recent study characterized him as a man who centralized power, moving it from the parishes into his own hands. In a word, he became a religious "boss."[38]

Even beyond his prestige as prelate, Hughes held a strong personal appeal among communicants. His rich oratorical skills enabled him to captivate audiences with stirring sermons, speeches, and addresses. With the mounting Protestant hostility against Catholics in the late 1840s and 1850s, the outspoken Irish-born church leader emerged as his flock's champion, gaining an even larger following. In short, Hughes was *the* Irish Catholic "spokesman," the "chieftain" around whom immigrants then under outside pressure rallied.[39]

While functioning as the lightning rod for nativist assaults from beyond the Catholic community, he simultaneously struggled with the growing pains of his burgeoning archdiocese. Hughes was primarily, then, a religious administrator; he was not centrally concerned with working out an ethnic identity in America, as O'Connor and MacNeven had been. His major task was to safeguard a beleaguered church and its parishioners. Yet Hughes's speeches and deeds clearly show that he did reflect on the matter of relating Irish and American identities for himself and his audience. He did have an assured understanding of the two bonds and, like the others, he justified a modest Irish American sentiment and, in particular, the Irish Catholic faith, on the nation's basic principles, especially its civil liberties tradition.

Although he was certainly not an Irish nationalist in America and was seldom a trumpet for ethnic sentiment, he did on occasion refer to his own personal group identity and the necessity of retaining it. He had come to the United States from Northern Ireland in 1817 at the age of 19, and had quickly joined the priesthood. Even as a young cleric in Philadelphia, he spoke up for Irish freedom, welcoming Catholic Emancipation in 1829 as a moral triumph for O'Connell. He also took part in and spoke at St. Patrick's Day celebrations, referring specifically to Irish virtue and charity, British oppression, pride in his own birthplace, and general Irish American contributions to the Faith, to homeland relief, and even to the 1848 Insurrection.[40] In addition Hughes was, as diocesan head, instrumental in fostering Irish ethnic parishes and starting or assisting other Irish institutions, such as the Irish Emigrant Society, the Emigrant Savings Bank, and the Ancient Order of Hibernians. He was also responsible for the establishment of a number of Irish religious orders.[41] Finally, ordinary Irish immigrants did apply privately to Hughes, as to MacNeven and O'Connor, for advice on personal matters.[42] One historian concluded that Hughes was the "most Irish" figure then in the Catholic hierarchy.[43]

The archbishop's awareness of being Irish and his occasional promotion of this sentiment did have its limits. He did not advocate the total social segregation of Irish American communities; he opposed the various colonization projects attempting to disperse the urban dwellers to the West; and he particularly condemned ethnic-bloc voting. Like O'Connor, he was critical of the more militant Irish nationalists who appeared in the 1840s; he opposed Irish American military aid for Irish freedom and the newly emerged Young Ireland movement. To Hughes, American Catholicism was congenial to Irish ethnic feelings, but he did not wish to formally recognize ethnic divisions among the faithful.[44]

Hughes did accept and support Irish ethnic feeling rooted in American democratic principles, and he had the opportunity to express those sentiments to his people in his response to nativist criticism of Catholics at mid century. He often referred to American constitutional guarantees, which, he asserted, permitted religious and therefore ethnic differences. For example, at one time around 1850 he reacted to Protestant insistence that immigrants abandon their clannishness. Hughes replied that such a dissociation is "not possible," nor is it "desirable" for anyone "to erase from his memory the early recollections of scenes and associations in the land of his nativity."[45]

The prelate reserved most of his public comment for the subject of religious toleration. He frequently mentioned the compatibility between Catholicism and its contributions to American democracy. For example, during the well-known school fund controversy of the early 1840s, Hughes was adamant in his support of the Catholics' struggle to gain public monies for their schools to guard against the Protestantization of public institutions. He emphasized the American tradition of the separation of church and state and insisted that Catholics had given substantial support to that idea. Apparently Hughes felt that the public school had already been compromised by Protestant influence, and he merely saw support of Catholics by the state as a necessary but regrettable defense. He told listeners that Establishments were no doctrine of his faith and that in fact many of the American civil liberties had their roots in Catholic as well as Protestant England. Thus, since his religious group had helped build America, Catholic immigrants must be loyal. America had been a "refuge" and an "asylum" for the persecuted, "the home of conscience and freedom of the West."[46] Thus, in words reminiscent of O'Connor, Hughes, as an Irish Catholic, was proclaiming his faith in America in 1856, when Know-Nothingism was widespread. There was no question of where the immigrants' home was then—according to Hughes, "we had no country [under British domination] until we arrived on these shores."[47]

This early popular and highly influential Irish Catholic cleric was essentially helping ordinary parishioners accommodate their old and new identities. Hughes's effort was an intellectual task partially forced upon him by the crisis of his time, the Protestant Crusade. But whatever its source, this clarification of what the new land offered illuminated for the arriving immigrant what American democracy was in theory. And as such the Irish newcomers could place their culture, their nationality, and their faith within it.

Some local empirical evidence does exist to show that ordinary Irish parishioners accepted the ideals of their adopted land. The association of American patriotism with ethnic identity was a commonly expressed theme among them in the pre–Civil War period. Representative were the activities of the first major Irish parish in New York, the Transfiguration Church, under the direction of a well-loved pastor—oddly enough, Cuban in background, rather than Irish. But this priest, Father Varela, was a liberal democrat deeply in love with American constitutional principles, and he possessed the fervent support of his Irish congregation. In addition, the early parochial school textbooks used by Catholics sought to instill pride in both Irish ethnic traditions and the new nation's founding ideals.[48]

* * *

A similar ideological association and rationale for Irish and American feeling appeared among important representatives of the early group elite in Boston, the leading Irish American city. Group settlement there had been rather slow. As the nineteenth century began, few would have predicted that Boston would be a focal point for Irish immigrants by the middle of the 1800s. Even as late as 1820, despite an established immigrant route through Canada into New England, only 3500 Catholics lived in Boston, while New York and Philadelphia had then eight or nine times that number.[49] But the city's demographic character became markedly Hibernian after 1840, when the Cunard Line made Boston a terminus for the burgeoning immigrant traffic. In five years the number of Irish Catholics jumped dramatically to about one-third of Boston's population of nearly 120,000, probably the largest proportion of the three leading East Coast ports. By the century's end, Boston retained that position, with twice as many citizens.[50]

Historians are familiar with much of the history of the Boston Irish in this period, their wretched living conditions, their Yankee and Brahmin critics, and the lively intellectual life of their religious leaders. But they know little about the frequent efforts of early internal pioneers to make their ethnic and American identities compatible. Three of the most popular figures of the time were Daniel Callaghan of Waltham, Patrick Donahoe, longtime publisher of the *Pilot,* and Patrick Collins, the group's best-known politician.

Most prominent among the very first Irish Catholic settlers is the shadowy figure of a shipyard mechanic, Daniel Callaghan. Regrettably, not much is known about his life or his mobilization of the group, but fragmentary evidence suggests the model of a typical American ethnic organizer. Having arrived in the area about 1817, by the end of the following decade he had rallied a group of approximately seventy people to begin a Catholic parish outside Boston. While well known for his ardent support of Irish Emancipation, Callaghan also professed his loyalty to America.[51] Unfortunately, available records do not reveal more precisely how he made these two identities compatible.

The more significant role and motives of the much better known Patrick Donahoe, editor and publisher of the leading Catholic newspaper, the *Pilot,* is clearer. Throughout most of the century, he was one of the most influential Irishmen in New England. And though he was reputed to be the wealthiest man in the area before 1870, he was still close to his readers. Most historians have viewed Donahoe generally, although not analytically, as an important influence among Irish Catholics and as a friend and employer of leading group nationalists. The *Pilot's* later editors were intellectuals like Thomas D'Arcy McGee, the Reverends John Roddan and Joseph Finotti, and John Boyle O'Reilly. Donahoe began the paper with the clear philosophical goal of serving the newcomers by offering advice and assistance for their social adjustment. He sought their (and thus his own) advancement particularly in political power. Thus he, too, like MacNeven and O'Connor in New York, was a social leader who worked for immigrant aid and progress within the American context.[52]

Donahoe's interest in mobilizing his audience appeared early in his journalistic career. It was articulated more fully later in newspaper editorials. He had arrived in Boston in 1821 as a boy in the pioneer wave, a few years after Callaghan, and entered newspaper work and politics almost immediately, becoming a Jacksonian Democrat like most of his peers. About 1834 he acquired a failing Jesuit sheet from Archbishop Fenwick but had some difficulty reviving it. Nevertheless, after choosing a name for the paper that was more Irish and less Catholic, he was able to widen its appeal and make it prosper. As he established its direction, Donahoe intended the *Pilot* to be the typical immigrant journal. It was to protect the Irish Catholics in America and improve their lot, thus becoming at once a communications link with the homeland, an adviser on social problems, and an educational device for advancement.[53] With Donahoe's acute salesmanship, the paper achieved great success quickly, by mid century, and became known as the "Irish Bible." Its circulation grew from five hundred in 1837 to over fifty thousand in the 1850s, and it was virtually a national Irish publication at its high point in 1872. Its audience then numbered over one hundred thousand.[54]

The *Pilot* functioned in part like the typical immigrant guide. It offered an informational exchange as well as an employment and missing persons bureau before 1860.[55] In that time Donahoe's publishing house handled other social services, too, like receiving immigrant funds (Donahoe helped establish an important Irish Catholic savings bank in 1865), conducting a travel agency, and selling religious articles to new arrivals.[56] He further showed his social concern for poor arrivals in numerous philanthropies, contributing to orphanages, asylums, and Catholic education in both Ireland and America.[57]

So Donahoe spoke to many in the community in his newspaper. While it is true that he did have others as editors, indicating that his was not the only voice of opinion, one must remember that many of the journalistic positions taken were still Donahoe's. He ran the paper singlehandedly for many years after 1837, as both publisher and editor most of the time before 1850. And even when he was not editor, he continued to write editorials.[58] In short, Donahoe himself, and the *Pilot,* were deeply involved in Irish immigrant adjustment in Boston and elsewhere before the Civil War.

Particular editorials provide an idea of Donahoe's message to his readers. Like Bishop Hughes, his contemporary Irish cleric in New

York, Donahoe was motivated by the hostile Protestant Crusade to rationalize Irish ethnic feeling in America. From the late 1830s to the Civil War, Donahoe pleaded with his readers not to be intimidated by antagonistic Yankees who were demanding that they forget their heritage. Instead, he urged them to retain their self-respect and to move along the road of progress in the way America provided, by becoming citizens and getting involved in political matters.

An early essay in the *Pilot* urged readers to combat nativist demands to Anglicize Irish names by remembering the virtues of group heritage. To those who wished to cast aside their "Patrick," Donahoe said in 1839, now was not "the time for us to be ashamed of . . . our patron saint." Only "mockers and blasphemers hold [the name] in derision." And to others who were considering dropping the "O'," they should only recall the name of "our Great Emancipator, Daniel O'Connell." He concluded, "there was nothing in the history of Ireland which persons need feel ashamed of," so Irish Americans should not "despise the names of [their] noble ancestry" or join "the upstarts in adjuring the honored name of St. Patrick."[59] While a similar editorial twenty years later did not come from Donahoe directly, it did continue his thought about resisting Irish name-changing to meet nativist objections. The paper pointedly reminded its readers of the first name of an American founding father, Patrick Henry. The Irish, then, need not be ashamed of their names; they were as much American as Irish.[60]

In the mid 1840s and early 1850s Irish immigration was reaching undreamed-of levels. Again under a barrage of nativist criticisms, the newcomer carried a feeling of inferiority. Shunned, exploited, and excluded from Anglo-American society, most foreigners suffered from poverty, ignorance, and a sense of low self-worth, according to Donahoe.[61] The prescription for this malaise was obvious—to represent the native land honorably, a condition encouraged by the "palladium" of the American Constitution. In fact, Donahoe reminded his readers, their Irish ancestors had been partially responsible in the Revolution for achieving the freedom that produced the United States, and they continued those principles in their own 1798 insurrection. All the newcomers need do now was to become American citizens by obtaining the franchise and resolving their several problems—gaining needed self-respect in the new land and "humiliating" England, the common enemy. Such political involvement, he concluded, did not mean consistent bloc voting as Irishmen, but rather making intelligent decisions as involved citizens.[62]

Soon Donahoe was insisting that Irish immigrants were *by nature* good Americans. Charges of indigence and ignorance in the incoming Irish waves by the *Boston Evening Transcript* in 1850 stung the Irish journalist. He replied with a spirited defense of his followers, accepting the Yankee's characterization of them as "beggarly" but reminding his critic that the immigrants were also the democratic "Bone and Sinew of America." "They bring a certain opulence with them which the Yankee ought to recognize and be thankful for." They were continual "reinforcements to the principle of our republicanism" with "a strong hatred of monarchy" and a "natural love for this sheltering democracy." If at any time "great wealth should prod [Americans] toward aristocracy, we [the Irish] would undoubtedly counteract it." He berated the Anglo-American journal in his conclusion, "Go to your closet and down upon your knees *Mr. Transcript*, . . . thank Heaven for the stalwart beggary!"[63] This defensive outburst probably led directly to several long articles that immediately followed on the theme of the "Irishman in America." Although written by Rev. John Roddan, Donahoe as editor specifically endorsed them. In essence they stated that the Irish could reach their economic, social, and political fulfillment in America without suffering any sense of conflicting loyalties, at least as long as Ireland remained oppressed.[64]

Throughout, then, Donahoe was acting as a group mediator, offering for ordinary immigrants a way to answer their critics. They could be involved and committed American citizens and simultaneously retain their historic identity.[65]

*   *   *

The situation for Irish immigrants coming to the United States after 1860 was different. Because there had been so many Irish immigrants in America for so many years, newcomers did not have to fight for self-confidence; they no longer had to be told to enter the American political lists. The growing Irish influence in the electorate, especially in the Democratic Party, was obvious. Rather, a new era dawned that revealed a more aggressive phase of Irish nationalism in America, and the issue to be resolved was how Irish Americans, some of whom had been socially mobile, even reaching the middle class, could justify their increased support for homeland freedom as American citizens. Patrick Collins provided that rationale.

Patrick Donahoe lived until the end of the century, but due to his and the *Pilot*'s serious financial reverses in the 1870s and to his surrender of the newspaper to the Boston archdiocese, he also gave up the position of major Irish leader to a South Bostonian named Patrick Collins. Collins reflected the improved postwar status of the group, being a middle-class professional, a lawyer-politician and a

nationalist, unlike Donahoe, who was a businessman-journalist defending and helping poor immigrants. The South Bostonian had to
deal with the new concerns of a more stratified Irish America by
defining its place amid the more militant freedom fighters in Ireland
and America. His conclusion was similar to that of other Irish internal leaders, namely, that America offered a universal ideology that he
and his countrymen could share. Despite the potentially trying tension of working for Irish liberty as a U.S. citizen, Collins often spoke
about the compatibility of his and his followers' dual identities.

Very possibly, the initial impetus for Collins's ethnic justification
in America was the same as that for Bishop Hughes and Patrick
Donahoe: the rampant nativism of the 1840s and 1850s. Soon after
Collins had arrived in Boston as a young boy in 1848, a victim of the
Famine, he was physically injured in a Protestant attack on his parish.[66] Whatever his reasons, the youth committed himself to the
Irish nationalist movement early, in 1864. He joined the Fenians,
who at that time sought Irish freedom by military action. With an
acknowledged charismatic talent for public speaking and rallying
listeners, he broadened Fenian support in New England. In a brief
time he became one of the most popular Irish Americans.[67]

Despite this personal success, Collins decided to leave the broth-
erhood in 1866, when the group was planning its raid into Canada.
His rationale indicates his way of working out the matter of dual
loyalty and the point at which he felt one bond violated the other. He
was willing to arm Ireland for victory, but remembering his American
citizenship, he refused to allow American blood to be shed for the
goal. He considered that kind of military intervention by immigrants
to be a violation of American law.[68] In a later statement of his association with the radicals, he justified his membership not simply as an
Irishman but also as an American of Irish descent. Echoing former
immigrant leaders, he urged political involvement for all group members to bring the blessings of America to the Old Country. The aim of
their efforts "should be to give the Irish in Ireland as good and as free
a government as that which the Irish enjoyed in the United States."
And the Irish should exercise the franchise they had here to make
America even better and freer than it was.[69] America was indeed the
great hope of the world:

> As citizens of this land, we are equal sharers in the blessings of
> free, popular government and as a constituent, *yet distinct* [my
> emphasis] part of the [American] nation, we require no excep-
> tional treatment. All we ask is that the government shall be
> administered according to the spirit of the constitution and the

genius of republicanism with a view to the dissemination of
liberal principles throughout the world.[70]

From 1870 to the end of his life in the early 1900s, Collins forsook
exclusive participation in radical Irish nationalism for a preeminent
career in Democratic party politics. But in turning to American affairs of state, he was not, as one interpreter has suggested, totally
abandoning his Irish identity or the community for personal aggran-
disement, although that may have been a motive.[71] He did subordinate his nationalist work after the 1880s, but he still concerned
himself with, and carefully delimited, the role of Irish Americans in
these later years. He sought to widen, not reject, his constituency in
South Boston, and he was rather successful in doing so. He cam-
paigned seriously for Irish support for Grover Cleveland in 1884,
1888, and 1892, emerging as a leading New England Democratic
politician in the process.[72] In his last formal act as an Irish nationalist, he still insisted he was an American. In 1880 he helped host
a visit of the famous Irish land reform leader, Charles Parnell. He led
the American wing of the land reform organization in 1881, winning
much Irish American support and money. But he did so, he said,
with an awareness of his "loving mother Ireland" and his "wife,
America."[73]

   In his later, more purely American, political efforts, he continued to justify himself as an American with Irish roots. At his
widely known 1884 endorsement of Grover Cleveland at Albany, New
York, he spoke of people like himself, born in Ireland, who ought
indeed to retain "Irish affiliation, ties or affections," but who should
do so as "Americans, true and loyal, citizens of the state and federal
system, sharing in the burdens and blessings of the freest people on
earth."[74]

   As a reward for his services after the 1892 election, President
Cleveland appointed Collins Consul-General in London and, although far from his political base, the new diplomat revealed more of
his thinking on his group's ethnic identity in America, this time
before an Irish audience in 1983. He told his listeners that their
countrymen in the New World were obliged to help and support the
Old Country, but they certainly would not lead it.[75]

   Historians generally agree that Collins had a sizable ethnic following in late-nineteenth-century America. A South Boston politician who rose to national prominence partly on an Irish constituency, he had considerable influence in the community. He, like others,
showed many of his supporters that to be Irish was also to be Ameri-

can. Hard evidence of the considerable group and public esteem he inspired became more abundant at the end of his life, when he was Mayor of Boston. He passed away in 1904 while in office. The public service commemorating him was a memorable Irish American occasion. While funerals are not always sober reflections of a person's influence—they are times for eulogies, not objective assessments— Collins's funeral did suggest that he was an effective link and mediator between the immigrant and native societies. In fact, the affair itself helped to harmonize the Boston Irish with the Yankees. It was an occasion for an outpouring of tributes by Irish, Irish American, and American citizens and, perhaps most significantly, by organized societies.[76] The memorials continued years later. Particularly symbolic was a statue of him, unveiled in 1908.[77]

* * *

All of these early Irish American leaders, then, in the group's two major cities, New York and Boston, understood the universal character of American nationality and the place they and their Irish followers had within it. Whatever motivated them to undertake that definition of Irish and American identities—their having a common monarchical enemy, England, around 1812; their desire for status within American society; or, most often, the nativist criticism given them by a hostile Protestant majority—the leaders declared that their people's national goals and those of their adopted land were the same. Both immigrants and natives sought freedom in a representative, "republican," form of government. Thus, highlighting those similar principles, they found it unnecessary to advocate total abandonment of Irish "affections," particularly Roman Catholicism and other group traits, no matter what the more frantic Yankees demanded. These leaders' view of what an American was, therefore, was clearly ideological and inclusive, not ethnically exclusive.

In addition, it is important to realize that this resolution of ethnic identities was not just the private rationalization of a few prominent individuals. These figures were able to broadcast their message about Irish identity within an American context widely, to a large following. As social leaders with ready access to group members, they reached large numbers in sermons, newspapers, and other public forums and gave their message privately in various individual service activities. To what degree their Irish American audience, of an overwhelmingly working-class character, accepted these leaders' explanations of group identities for their own remains largely a matter of speculation. But these men undoubtedly were to a great extent opinion leaders, men with considerable influence in the group's major settlements. So immigrants must have given the idea of an encompassing Americanism serious attention.

Although he was more concerned with Irish nationalism among immigrants than with ethnic identity per se, a recent historian, Michael Funchion, did refer to the ability of the alien masses to see the compatibility of an American ideology with their own group existence. His comments are of special importance because they originated in the experience of a heavily Irish settlement not examined here, namely the Chicago area. The awareness of Irish identity there, he asserts, was partly based on the immigrants' low economic status and the anti-Irish prejudice of outsiders. But more significantly, their group conception was also based on more positive ideas.[78] Group members did not conceptualize their Americanism as synonymous only with "the Protestant Establishment" but also with themselves and with the Irish values they had had while *still in Europe*. The Irish, he asserts, were intrinsically even more "American . . . than most other immigrants." As one Irish Chicagoan wrote after his arrival, "There are none of the foreigners [here] for their hearts and loves were in America" and were devoted to what the nation stands for "long before they thought of sailing" to the New World.[79] This was a feeling that Boston and New York countrymen could share.

3

The GERMANS

As with the Irish, the general statistics about the groups of Germans who migrated to the United States—in particular, the statistics about their large numbers and highly variegated composition—are fairly well known. These immigrants from central Europe made up the largest non-English-speaking group to come to America, about seven million, chiefly in the nineteenth century. They were very much unlike the Irish in that they were so heterogeneous, differing widely among themselves in many characteristics, such as place of origin, class, religion, ideology, and time of arrival.

These immigrants first left the Old World early in American history and came in periodic waves throughout, from the late 1600s to the present. Because their places of origin were the numerous independent German states, most came with little sense of a unified nationality. "Germany" was a country lately formed in 1871, and was finally united from above by Prussian authorities. The people were fragmented and divided by a host of social, religious, and philosophical differences. Among the German immigrants were pietists, Catholics, Protestants, agnostics, democratic liberals, social revolutionaries, fraternalists, and advocates of other ideological persuasions. Immigrant historians generally categorize this group chronologically. The middling peasants, artisans, and intellectuals came before the 1870s, and the poorer agriculturalists and workers later.[1] Their reasons for coming were as varied as their social identities. And even though Germans initially appeared on these shores in colonial times, most arrived in the nineteenth century after the Napoleonic Wars. German America arose in that latter era, the period upon which this essay will concentrate.

It is important to review the forces that motivated these people to leave central Europe because, as we will see, German immigrant leaders kept referring to the necessity of accomplishing those objectives in America. One can distill the complex of causes of movement to two: economic instability and political and religious oppression in Germany. The standard work on German emigration lists the several disruptive material conditions: the recurrent agricultural crises, particularly high food prices; the disruption brought on by the Napoleonic Wars; national free trade policies; the recurrent famines of 1816–17, the 1830s, 1840s, and 1850s; and the occupational displacement wrought by industrialization.[2] Thus, the early emigrants were lower-middle-class peasants, skilled artisans, and tradesmen who usually left with their families. The more proletarian emigrants departed later in the century from the more easterly areas of their homeland.

The other motive for the migration described by the very first recorders was the desire to find philosophical freedom in the new land. The oldest filiopietistic German and American historians stressed this more idealistic objective, and some modern observers have reemphasized its importance. Both early and recent writers have cited the well-known liberal appeal of America for the religious dissenters and political liberals of the 1830s and 1840s, called Dreisiggers and 48ers, especially after the abortive 1848–1850 insurrections in several German states. The descriptive account of the pioneer traveler Gottfried Duden, in 1829, was especially glowing and, many believe, persuasive. He depicted the open, virgin land of the American West as a place to rejuvenate a New Germany, and he thereby aroused many colonizing groups and agricultural societies to look seriously at the New World as their destination.

Thus, in the 1830s and 1840s, particularly after 1848, more Germans with more decidedly political objectives arrived. Some later writers developed a myth about those who came before and after 1848. The post-48ers, they said, established German settlements on the philosophical basis of democratic liberalism (they were named the Greens), while the previously arriving settlers, the Grays, it was said, sought only material gratification and goals. As one German writer put it erroneously in 1912:

> It was the 1848 Revolution that brought literally hundreds of thousands of immigrants to this country, among whom were men of the highest intellectual and social position . . . German settlers who were democratic in character. [Those who arrived before then] did not sympathize either with their ideals or their political associations.[3]

A more recent American historian has explored that Gray-Green dichotomy in a full history of the liberal 48ers. He asserted that, although a rare German democrat may have come to America before 1848, German America before mid century was essentially highly materialist and disorganized, an "army without officers." The 48ers, being committed to democracy, really filled a leadership vacuum.[4] It is not my wish here to revive the old German-American debate over who better represented or served German Americans, the Grays or the Greens. The point to note is the prominence given to the political motivation of German immigrants, particularly those coming just after 1848.

The current trend among students of German immigration is to broaden their view of that political motivation and regard it as having been influential before 1848 as well as after. Recent observers contend that democratic liberalism, or at least a desire to escape oppressive laws in the old country, motivated people from all over the social scale, peasants and artisans as well as intellectuals. Ordinary German emigrants, early in the century as well as later, had experienced oppression at home. They particularly objected to unjust and onerous taxation, and they went to America to alleviate that mistreatment.

One German historian who, with a team of researchers, has examined conditions of emigration, concluded that most of the pre-1850 movement of Germans to the United States was in fact a massive expression of social protest.[5] While Günter Moltmann's idea of emigration as a safety valve for social discontent is not original as applied to the history of immigration to America, Moltmann is original in that he considers the idea to be a vital and pervasive characteristic of the German exodus. The scholar cited a well-known contemporary observer of migration in a recently uncovered early report. Just before 1820, Friedrich List recorded the bitter hostility of emigrants from certain southwestern German states toward their governments. Their solution was flight to the West. Moltmann and List quoted those departing for America as saying that they would prefer to be slaves in America than citizens of a German state.[6] Additional evidence of a widespread political consciousness and motivation among the lower classes exists in the more intense revolutionary fervor among them *between* periods of high emigration and in the sentiments expressed in German emigrant ballads.[7] Still further proof is the vast and heretofore underestimated support that German Americans gave to the liberal democratic movement in Europe in the 1840s and 1850s. Some German liberals seeking governmental reform feared that America was drawing off too much of their grassroots support; they wanted the masses, their supporters, to remain discontented at home![8]

Another recent historian has scrutinized a large group of designedly nonelitist emigrants. He referred to them as "transplanted Westphalians" who went to Missouri in the 1830s. For them and others he, too, felt that discontent with Old World politics was massive among the German lower classes. An illustration of that sentiment was a song written in 1836 by an immigrant woodturner:

> Hail Columbia, praise to thee
> We laud thee high eternally
> Thou hast shown us the way
> Out of our hard servitude
> To save us if we only dare
> To bid our fatherland farewell.[9]

Other stanzas dealt with the chains of slavery and hunger, princes "who drive us to despair," and courts that "conserve our marrow." They also referred to the authorities as a "brood of rats," and condemned the harsh exploitative class system in general. America, on the other hand, was "free: with no class distinctions, no nobles to despise, no limitations on hunting or fishing [important to German peasants], no restrictive guilds, no heavy taxes or compulsory military service." Another song specifically advised that emigration to America—even as a slave—was far more desirable than living in Hesse.[10]

In an article he wrote in 1842, Friedrich List pointed to the only explanation he could find to explain why so many German farmers were then leaving their familiar surroundings for a strange settlement overseas—to escape the heavy exactions of medieval restrictions. It was because there were no "feudal privilege, no taxes, no serfdom, no debasing laws . . . [no] arbitrary oppression" abroad. In America the German found he only had to fight "nature, and if he conquers it, he is a free citizen, sole possesser of the fruits of his labor." That is why he traveled "thousands of miles" to face "the dangers and discomforts of a long journey by sea and by land and bury himself for years in the wilderness."[11]

Not only did the Greens, then, value American freedom, but so did many of the pre-48ers from the lower economic classes. As a farmer outside St. Louis boasted to his brother in Würtemberg in 1845, "You can be a citizen even if you haven't a penny in your pocket."[12]

By emphasizing that America had more representative and more stable government and fewer social and individual controls, German social leaders in America were not expressing conditions about which ordinary immigrants were ignorant. These prominent figures were describing a way of life that had brought many peasants and artisans to America in the first place.

But the appeal of an open and free new land with loose social restrictions did not mean that incoming Germans wished to transform their ethnic character totally. Some hoped to in some way *bring their home with them*. They came early with dreams to establish a new Germany in the American West. Others who did not want to isolate themselves completely from non-Germans still sought to retain at least part of their tradition, particularly their language. This defense of their tongue was not merely a wish to retain familiar speech patterns, words, and phrases, but rather to hold on to something much greater, their culture. *Deutschtum,* they believed, was clearly superior to the culture of native Americans. As Gustav Koerner put it more bluntly in 1834, "in regard to art the Americans are 'half-barbarian' with taste that is not much better than that of the Indian aborigines," who have "rings through their noses." The new land *needed* the newcomer whose artistic heritage was unrivaled.[13]

The drive to protect the language began almost as soon as the first major influx of immigrants appeared in the 1830s. Leaders, particularly journalists, decided to take concerted action. In 1837, thirty-nine prominent figures met at a national convention in Pittsburgh to discuss ways and means of preserving the native tongue.[14] The matter was to preoccupy many leaders thereafter and was to underlie many of the group's objectives in America. As spokesmen expressed it, language maintenance was not incompatible with being American in outlook or sentiment. A dual identity was possible. It became customary to describe this condition at German American festivals by exclaiming that in order to be loyal to his bride [the United States], an immigrant did not have to forsake his mother— "Germania meine Mutter, Columbia meine Braut."[15]

An extended review of particular group leaders will illuminate further how German immigrants could live with two identities without undue tension. Obviously, the attitude of the Germans, who frequently referred to their cultural superiority over Americans, differed from that of the Irish, who considered native and immigrant values to be more compatible and reinforcing. My choice of examples of the German American elite here is not a random one. All of the figures are important group mediators and social brokers who were close to their followers, the rank and file in major German American settlements. Admittedly, because of the enormous size and dispersion of the group and the vast timespan of their arrival, the individuals covered here cannot be representative of all German America. But as a group these leaders did represent, and had a substantial impact on, a large number of people, so it is worthwhile to study them.

As with the Irish, most German American leaders were articulate figures, writers or journalists skilled at communication and able to express their ideas in print. They were also activists who assisted the everyday adjustment of their fellows. In addition, all could be called pioneers who, contrary to the myth of the 48ers, came to America before the European uprisings. The leaders covered here are Johann Andreas Wagener of Charleston, South Carolina; Charles Reemelin and Bishop John Martin Henni of Cincinnati; Franz A. Hoffmann of Chicago; Dr. Franz Huebschmann of Milwaukee, and Friedrich Munch and Gert Gobel of eastern Missouri. This review also refers briefly to other figures. They, too, may have qualified as social leaders and may have been significantly influential and representative, but they did not leave adequate or accessible evidence of their thinking on ethnic and national ties.

* * *

Charleston, South Carolina, was hardly a major German American center in the decades before the Civil War, but it was the home of Johann Andreas Wagener, who nearly single-handedly constructed a vibrant ethnic community in a leading southern city. The rationale he used for doing so was the same as elsewhere in much larger German American communities in the North. Without a doubt, virtually all the central European immigrants settling in and around Charleston knew of and were influenced by the ideas of this commanding German American. His major goal was to make his followers aware of the importance of their political obligations in the American system and the validity of supporting the culture of the ethnic colony.

It is easy to see the ties Wagener had with Germany, and his commitment as an ethnic leader is obvious. He was chiefly responsible for establishing and nurturing the Charleston German American community. Born in 1815 near Bremerhaven, he arrived in New York at the age of 15 accompanied by his brother. The two youths apparently had intended to spend a year traveling in America. His "visit" became permanent when, with the help of friends, he got a job in New York. In 1833 he relocated to Charleston at a branch office of his Northern employer. The Germans in the port city at that time were a small contingent of about twelve hundred "loosely knit" immigrants, chiefly Lutherans from Lower Saxony. There were few peasants, and their settlement was virtually unorganized and leaderless.[16]

The Germans filed into Charleston rapidly in the early 1830s, and they desperately needed a liaison with other Americans. Wagener saw this need and filled it. Despite his youth, he started a retail store and quickly began providing other services for immigrants, becoming a general ethnic advisor, a real-estate agent for those seeking property, and, most importantly, a notary public to help those needing official interpretation.[17] One particular event, a disastrous fire in the late 1830s, demanded the construction of a better-organized German community in Charleston. Wagener determined that the group needed protection, so he started a volunteer fire company and an immigrant insurance company by 1846. He presided over them for the remainder of the decade.[18] At the same time, he established a German Evangelical body, officiating at the founding of the group's first church in 1840. The religious house was more like a community center because, surprisingly, Wagener accepted Protestants *and* Catholics as members.[19]

As anxious to preserve the German language as other leaders would be, in 1843 Wagener initiated a *Teutonbund* that promoted German literature. He also began and edited a semiweekly newspaper, *The Teuton (Der Teutone)* the following year. By the mid 1850s, when the number of Germans had more than doubled since Wagener's arrival, he had either begun or helped to start a German masonic lodge, a turnverein branch, a group theater, a charity association, a colonizing society, and a rifle club.[20]

Thus, Wagener was chiefly responsible for the building of the Charleston German society. These activities assured the existence of *Deutschtum,* yet Wagener also urged immigrants to be Americans, to honor and make use of their political rights in the new land. He glorified the American idea of self-government in particular. Wagener was, therefore, communicating the connection between and the advantages of his peoples' two identities. As he saw it, the newly formed ethnic organizations would help mold the German into a *cultured* and therefore *"thoughtful,"* American citizen.[21]

In one of the early issues of *Der Teutone,* Wagener urged his readers to use the great power that the U.S. Constitution gave them to improve their lot. In an editorial entitled, "The Power of Free Speech: Greater Than Bread," he reminded his audience that oppression, not income, was their reason for leaving Europe. While in America, they had freedom and equality, but these rights would be meaningless unless they joined with other Germans to use those political advantages. Throughout the piece he stressed that Germans in the United States had better, freer lives than their exploited countrymen in Europe.[22] Wagener apparently found it easy to demonstrate his own dual loyalties, because he celebrated American Independence Day conspicuously by serving as chairman of the German Celebration Committee on July 4, 1848.[23] His final wish was appropriate, for he asked that his grave marker indicate his joint ties as a German and an American.[24]

*　*　*

The most important early German settlements in America were in the Midwest, in the so-called German Triangle of Cincinnati, Milwaukee, and St. Louis. Being the farthest east of the three, the Ohio settlement arose first and quickly became heavily German. While Cincinnati's population grew fivefold between 1820 and 1840 to just under fifty thousand, its central European segment increased even more rapidly, making up between a quarter and a third of all inhabitants by the latter year. The result of such a massive influx, first from southeastern and later from northern Germany, was the emergence of a notable group concentration, the famous Over-the-Rhine quarter, with its beer gardens and numerous group institutions. By mid century the German character of the Queen City was known internationally because about fifty thousand of the city's population of over two hundred thousand came from central Europe.[25]

All sources agree that one man, a popular German American merchant named Martin Baum, was chiefly responsible for guiding the first contingent of group pioneers to the southern Ohio city. But unfortunately, the sources neglected to offer Baum's philosophical views on the nature of the immigrants' ethnic and national identities. He is, then, a compelling but mysterious figure whose goals for importing countrymen, other than mundane entrepreneurial ones, remain unclear. Having such fragmentary evidence, one can only conjecture about his thoughts on being German in America.[26]

Born either in Alsace, France, or in Pennsylvania in the mid 1700s, Baum came to Cincinnati just before the turn of the century and became prosperous quickly by running a lucrative general store. As the river city benefited from expanding traffic and commerce in the opening of the West in the early 1800s, Baum became an important labor recruiter, obtaining many German redemptioners in Eastern ports and directing them to his hometown. He rose to wealth quickly by investing in several commercial projects involving transportation, industry, and finance. He was probably the single most important pioneer German leader in Cincinnati. Sources variously characterize him as the immigrants' revered friend, "warm-hearted" advisor, and "influential counselor," the "mighty founder" of these first Cincinnati Germans.[27] He did assist the institutional organization of the German community by sponsoring and funding a Presbyterian church about 1813 and by patronizing performances of German music before his death in 1831.[28] Thus, one can say Baum did initiate *Deutschtum* in Cincinnati, but again, his deeper feelings about his and his group's identity as Americans remain largely enigmatic.

*   *   *

Two later Cincinnatians had far more definite and explicit reasons for their work in immigrant adjustment: they were Charles Reemelin, a journalist and politician, and the Reverend John Martin Henni, a Roman Catholic priest. Both openly heralded the American democratic system early on, and did so even more in the wake of the rising nativist pressures of the time. Reemelin spent much of his energy preserving the language, while Henni defended the Germans' traditional Catholic faith. Yet despite these differences, both understood that the immigrant could have two identities, one inherited and one acquired.

Reemelin was the more articulate of the two and was more conscious of what he regarded as false Americanist pressures on Germans to abandon their cultural life. Responding to the demands for Anglo-American conformity which arose in the 1840s, Reemelin offered his German- and English-speaking audiences. a lesson on the meaning of being American. Since American culture was still largely European, he felt that people on this side of the Atlantic ought to value the immigrants and their contributions to the new land. Reemelin, then, in the middle years of the century, was suggesting how a foreigner ought to treat his Old World inheritance and remain an American.

As with Wagener and the others to be discussed here, Reemelin was no ivory-towered intellectual, and he was in America long before the 48ers. Early in his life he showed that he could lead and influence his fellow Germans. Soon after his arrival from Europe in 1833 at the age of 18, and while he was working as a clerk in a Cincinnati store, he entered politics. His strong egalitarian bias directed him to join the Jacksonian Democratic party, and he quickly assumed a leadership position as a result of his popularity among his employer's customers.[29]

For his own benefit and for the protection of the group, that is, for a mixture of selfish and humanitarian ends, Reemelin sought to mobilize the weak, fragmented, and largely unorganized German element in the city. Together with a few other prominent pioneers, he called a mass meeting at City Hall in 1834 to establish the first permanent fraternal body, the German (Gesellschaft) Society. Two years later the first German Democratic newspaper, the *Volksblatt*, was founded in his store, and by 1848 he had been elected to three terms in the Ohio legislature. He also served as a representative at the state Constitutional Convention and was later appointed to other educational and financial posts in the state government. He wrote articles for both German- and English-language newspapers on political reform and agriculture and was an avid supporter of the German Pioneer Society when it began in Cincinnati in 1868. He edited and was a frequent contributor to the society's historical journal, *Der Deutsche Pionier.* In those thirty-five years he had become a leading German American in the city, and although he encountered some internal opposition to his policies and views, especially among the group's Roman Catholics, he was still a major influence in the ethnic community at that time.[30]

Throughout his life he expressed his contention that, for America's own political, psychological, and cultural welfare, German and other foreign languages should be not only preserved but even officially recognized by the American government. Countering the charges of superpatriots of the day (like the Know-Nothings) that linguistic pluralism would lead to subversion, Reemelin insisted that preservation of the immigrants' languages would weld America's diverse peoples to democratic ideals. Developing and expanding the point that Wagener was making at about the same time in the South, Reemelin believed that foreigners would learn the American political genius best through the use of their own language. Good American citizenship among immigrants required the maintenance of the ancestral tongue, not its demise.

The argument appeared at various times over the years in Reemelin's activities and writings. At the 1834 rally at City Hall, for example, he and other leaders justified the establishment of immigrant societies by citing the necessity to promote immigrants' involvement in the political system.[31]

Five years later he spoke at a meeting of Democrats in his county and asked for state support of German-language instruction in the public schools and the printing of all important state documents in German. Not to do so, he charged, would prevent his people's performing their necessary civic duties and responsibilities.[32] Some years later he said that the state ought not to force any one language on its people (in this case English) but should publish official papers in *any* language necessary to reach large numbers of the foreign-born.[33]

From the early part of his life Reemelin viewed the United States as superior to other nations *because* of its diversity, and he took the offensive to berate pseudo-American patriots, calling them oppressively Anglo-Saxon. By doing so, he was offering a rationale for immigrants to continue using their traditional tongue. The beauty of American culture and politics, he was to suggest in later years, lay not in its Anglo-Saxon traditions alone but in an American cosmopolitanism.

From the late 1860s to his last work in 1892, Reemelin continued to do battle with bigoted Anglo-Americans largely on the theme of an 1868 talk entitled, "The Humbug of Anglo-Saxonism." That humbug, he said, of insisting that non-Anglo-Americans use only English is futile, mean, inhuman, and in fact uncivilized. "To invade [a man's] family and prejudice his children against him by tabooing his native language is one of the most contemptible practices we know of." To lose a language is to be cut off from the roots of one's ancestors and therefore barbaric. "Liberty of development of languages is the only policy fit for a free people."[34]

All this condemnation of Anglo-American conformity led him to make an unusually advanced definition of Americanism in two other essays, statements that anticipated Horace Kallen's idea of cultural pluralism a half-century later. As there is no American "race," he said, there is no one all-embracing language there. The United States is a complex society of many peoples, without one particular national art style or one indigenous population stock—including the American Indians. Americans are held together by the principles of the Declaration of Independence and the absence of religious, social, and political tyranny.[35] Even those supposedly uniquely American institutions, like the separation of church and state, local self-government, and the principles in the Bill of Rights were not originally "American" but were derived from Charlemagne in France and the Puritans in England.[36]

Not only had America benefited politically from its European roots, but it could also mature culturally from having German immigrants in particular preserve their traditions. In 1871, then, Reemelin was repeating the point he had made earlier about language preservation in the 1830s and 1840s—that maintaining *Deutschtum* would benefit America handsomely because the young nation knew woefully little of the fine literature, art, and scholarship of the likes of Humboldt, Goethe, and Schiller.

Reemelin spoke also to those of his German audience who, out of either arrogance or fear, might totally eschew American outsiders. He stated that their justifiable protection of cultural tradition did not permit complete isolation. Just as he rejected the conformity of Anglo-Americans, Reemelin also rejected ghettoization. The mutual infusion of cultures was necessary. "We must move out of our German shell" he said, and demonstrate what is good and worthwhile in

German character, thereby advancing "American morals and values."[37] This 1871 essay appeared in the widely read journal, *The German Pioneer*, and according to authorities, was particularly representative and significant in the thinking of many German Americans for the next half-century.[38]

* * *

The Cincinnati Germans, like those elsewhere in America, were a fragmented group, consisting of factions of differing social and ideological persuasions. A large element less responsive than most to Reemelin's leadership was the city's many Roman Catholics. Yet while they did not regard Reemelin as their American interpreter, they did have their own internal mediator whose conception of Germans as Americans closely approximated that of his fellow Cincinnatians. That Catholic leader was the Reverend John Martin Henni, a Swiss German cleric who later went to Milwaukee and became this nation's first German Catholic prelate. An extraordinarily popular religious leader, Henni, like Reemelin, also urged his communicants to honor American governing principles while simultaneously keeping their group traditions. Even more than Archbishop Hughes was for the New York Irish, Henni was indeed a *German* Catholic leader.

Henni's early activities showed his great popular support and his strong ethnic consciousness in the Queen City and beyond—in southern Ohio and even throughout the state. He became the symbol of German Catholicism by the time he left for Milwaukee in 1844. He arrived in Cincinnati from Europe in 1829 when 24 at a time when the burgeoning Ohio population was desperately short of Catholic priests, particularly German-speaking ones. Cincinnati's Bishop Fenwick immediately ordered the young Swiss German priest to traverse the state and minister to the many immigrant colonies which were then proliferating. Basing his forays into the hinterland from the city of Canton, Henni became acquainted with and helped to organize thirteen other Ohio parishes. One writer has called him the German "Las Casas" for his widespread missionary work. Another called him the German Catholic "apostle" in America.[39]

It was quite understandable, then, for a new bishop to call Henni back to Cincinnati in 1834 to take charge of the pioneer German Catholic parish that was just forming there. As more German Catholics poured into the burgeoning river town, Henni emerged as "an effective and popular community leader as well as a religious one."[40]

Henni implemented his goals for his urban constituency as well as for many German Catholic farmers in the community in order to ease the adjustment of the German Americans. Underlying his ac-

tivities were three objectives: to ensure parishioners' adherence to
Catholicism amid increasingly hostile Protestant nativism, to make
them more familiar with their own German culture, and to assure
their appreciation of American democracy. The latter two goals were,
of course, the very same held by Wagener and Reemelin. Hence,
Henni was another German American interpreter.

It is difficult to identify which of the three aims took priority in
the mind of the Swiss German cleric. They may have changed at
different times. He certainly promoted German ethnic culture in a
number of ways: by encouraging a bookseller to circulate and sell
German books in 1836, by helping establish a German book society
in 1842, and by supporting the start of a German musical ensemble
in 1838.[41] His religious concerns were frequently bound up with his
ethnic ones. For example, he wished to establish a seminary that
would train German-speaking priests, even though this was opposed
by the American church hierarchy. The Catholic prelates initially
refused his request because of the cost, the potentially divisive nature
of his project (the church was unwilling at that early date to sanction
too much ethnic recognition) and the continued, though inadequate,
availability of European clergy. Henni contended that the emerging
German Catholic community needed its own spiritual advisors and
would not readily accept Old World clerics. The German American
communicants would work best with German American priests. Ultimately, Henni did win the hierarchy's approval of such a seminary in
1843 just prior to his departure for Wisconsin.[42]

Henni combined his religious and ethnic ends as well as his
American goal of civic education by setting up a newspaper, *Der
Wahrheits-Freund im Weltlichen,* in 1837. The paper was the first
German Catholic organ in the country. Beginning with a few hundred subscribers, it quickly became popular, although, oddly, it had
more readers outside Cincinnati than within. It sold thirty-three
hundred copies by the end of the first year and ultimately almost
fourteen thousand later in the century.[43] Its initial, stated goal was to
respond to the critics in the same manner that Archbishop Hughes
was to do personally in New York and that Reemelin was then doing
in Cincinnati. That is, the paper was to remind readers of the cherished principles of American democracy which really protected
Catholics. Henni therefore contended that his faith and his nation
were compatible. This new German American journal, then, was
both a defense of, and an educational document for, German Catholics. Henni's major biographer called it a "school for citizenship"
which translated and conveyed extensive information on legislative
action and the general American legal tradition. For example, it pub-

lished most, if not all, major government documents.[44]

The initial issue, appearing July 20, 1837, was an example of what was to follow in later numbers. There Henni printed a two-page translation of the Declaration of Independence and indicated that the Founding Fathers had produced in Philadelphia a governmental model for the civilized world. He also lamented that the recent celebration of the nation's birthday had had insufficient spirit, and he implied a hope for a more meaningful observance next time.[45]

Clearly, then, this lively German Catholic priest was working for an enlightened German American community, one aware of both its Old World inheritance and its New World advantages. Henni's goals, as we have seen, were those of other German American leaders, although he had the additional religious motive of keeping his people within the Catholic fold.

Henni's elevation to bishop in the mid 1840s suggests his effectiveness with communicants in Cincinnati. His success was such that a rumor even circulated that Henni was being sent to Milwaukee as a prelate not simply for his personal advancement but because he was becoming too powerful. The heavily Irish American hierarchy, it was rumored, wanted to rid itself of a very popular German Catholic priest in the heavily German city.[46]

*　*　*

Undoubtedly the most successful German American internal leader among all the pre-48ers discussed here was Francis Arnold Hoffmann of northern Illinois and southern Wisconsin. He was active in more areas that his contemporaries, as a minister, teacher, politician, banker, journalist, and agriculturalist. And he attained the highest place of power, being elected lieutenant governor of Illinois during the Civil War. Even at the end of his life, in "retirement," he continued to reach and influence more incoming foreigners than Reemelin, Wagener, Henni, and the others.[47] His message to his audience was the same as theirs—to be active in preserving German culture while also being an involved American.

The German population in Illinois and around Chicago in mid century was different than that farther east. Settlement on the shores of Lake Michigan occurred later, starting in the 1840s, with more emphasis on political and economic motives than on religious ones. Immigrants were more often Prussian in origin rather than southern, and these Midwest colonies were even less cohesively organized than the older ones to the east. All during his career Hoffmann was very sensitively aware of non-Germans in the region, probably because his countrymen did not dominate Illinois as they did southern Ohio, southern Wisconsin, and eastern Missouri. German-speaking immigrants, for example, made up at most only a fifth of the early Chicagoans in 1850, and the proportion really declined thereafter.[48]

Hoffmann rocketed to ethnic preeminence, and in the process he realized early the need of his countrymen and himself to deal with Anglo-Americans. From soon after his arrival about mid century until his death almost fifty years later, he was the region's leading German American mediator, recruiting waves of newcomers and easing their adjustment. His major means in reaching and maintaining that position, and the advice that he gave to followers, was to learn English quickly and become active in politics.

Hoffmann first built up his ethnic following. He reached the Windy City probably in 1840 at the age of 18, having left his home in West Prussia. Almost immediately he settled at nearby Dunkley's Grove (now Addison), which was a town of his fellow Westphalian countrymen. They needed a schoolteacher, and Hoffmann applied for the post and was accepted. The young man apparently endeared himself quickly to the townspeople with his winning personality and "rough ingenuousness," and with amiable charm, a lively sense of humor, and a captivating musical ability. The inhabitants of Dunkley's Grove rewarded him with a number of important local positions: he served as their religious leader, postmaster, and town secretary.[49]

While holding this variety of village offices, Hoffmann considered himself, then, in the mid 1840s, as essentially a religious leader, so he felt obliged to obtain formal training. To do this, he went off to Michigan, where he was ordained a Lutheran minister. When he returned home, he counseled Germans in northern Indiana and Illinois colonies, especially Shaumberg, where he settled in 1847.

Although he successfully improved his spiritual position among his parishioners, Hoffmann was always aware that he was in a non-German, Anglo-American world. His various positions in local government and his role as group translator convinced him of his need to improve his English. Early on, he began writing articles in both English- and German-language publications. As with most Germans of that time, he was occasionally active in the more accessible Democratic party. By 1850, partially for health reasons but also for more practical advantage, he moved to Chicago, where he became a lawyer, businessman, politician, and ethnic organizer. A year after his entering the legal profession in 1852 he was elected alderman of a heavily German ward.

By the early 1850s, then, Hoffmann was the leading group spokesman among the Democrats, and he continued to build up his political and ethnic position by writing and sending to Europe an annual trade review of the area. This publication resulted in his becoming consular representative for four German states. More significantly, he became a guide and recruiter for hosts of new immigrants traveling from his native land to the city.

Hoffmann not only directed German arrivals to Chicago but he did much to promote German culture there. Even before he physically moved to the city, he was editing a newspaper there in 1845. In addition, he helped to start a singing group and an important art and science body about 1853. The latter organization led directly to the construction of the city's major German cultural center, Das Deutsche Haus, in 1855. It was Hoffmann who laid the cornerstone, and the structure served as the focal point for the Chicago German community until the famous fire in 1871.[50]

Having become the most prominent German in the state by the early 1850s, Hoffmann reached the pinnacle of his Anglo-American influence in the years up to and during the Civil War. He joined the newly formed Republican Party, which nominated him twice as its candidate for lieutenant governor of Illinois, and he was elected to that office the second time at the start of the war. But he also maintained his powerful ethnic position as immigrant recruiter, for he secured thousands of German settlers for the Illinois Central Railroad lands in the 1860s and 1870s.[51]

Even after his so-called retirement in 1875 to his Jefferson, Wisconsin farm home for health reasons, he continued to be a significant German guide. It was from there, at Riverside, until his death in 1903 that he wrote a long series of instructive and immensely popular articles for Germans under the pen names "Hans and Grete Buschbauer."[52] The essays, later a widely circulated newspaper supplement called "Der Haus und Bauerfreund," were written in simple, familiar peasant language and were directed mainly toward farmers specifically to educate them in the use of advanced farming techniques and practices. Actually, the pieces were engagingly written advisories counseling farm families on personal problems. The column appeared in Milwaukee, Chicago, and Buffalo newspapers with a huge readership of 150,000.[53] As German-American observers put it at the end of his life, Hoffmann was a person of "remarkable personal magnetism" whom German farmers "greatly admired."[54]

On numerous, important occasions throughout his life, Hoffmann dealt personally and openly with the matter of German immigrant identity in America. The philosophy expressed was similar to that of other German American mediators, to retain *Deutschtum* but still be involved citizens. One particularly critical moment came in 1854 during the debate over the Kansas-Nebraska Bill. Hoffmann felt it was especially important that German Americans exercise fully the civic responsibilities given them by the Constitution. He, along with numerous other Germans, was critical of the Democratic party because it was lenient toward the expansion of slavery. He also objected to the bill more specifically because of its anti-immigrant tone. At a German meeting in Chicago Hoffmann exhorted his listeners to utilize their rights enthusiastically. Voting or "citizenship," he said, was "one of the [country's] greatest blessings imaginable," but it carried "with itself certain [additional] responsibilities," as being "vigilant watchdogs of legislation" such as the Kansas-Nebraska bill. His audience, he said, ought to work against the bill because it not only extended slavery into the territories, but it also actually "enslaved" foreigners who were barred from voting there.[55] Thus, here at a crucial moment when immigrant affiliations were shifting from Democrat to Republican, Hoffmann highlighted the use of the suffrage and political action by German Americans.

Yet while fostering such involvement, Hoffmann at the same time believed German Americans had a duty to their heritage. Partial proof of his devotion to cultural maintenance was in the conduct of his own family life, which was decidedly ethnic. He had married a woman of English stock in 1844 when he was a religious leader. But he insisted even over his wife's objections that they would have a German home. He had her learn the language, and together they maintained an ethnic household for the rest of their lives, speaking only in that tongue and observing Old World customs.[56]

Hoffmann's reason for revering *Deutschtum* and assuring its preservation was similar to that given by other German American leaders, that is, its superiority. He explained his rationale in an 1884 essay entitled "Deutsch," written by the "Buschbauers," Hans and Grete, in the "Haus und Bauerfreund" supplement. In this instance he offered his remarks particularly to farm wives who directed the household and had the major task of raising American-born children. His opening sentence was his theme, "Germans we are and Germans we wish to remain in this free land." The American democracy, he said, needed the cultural polish that only Germans could give. The immigrants could make such a contribution and still be American because it is entirely possible to have a cultural identity that is separate from the civic and political one. And as he explained to immigrant mothers, they could convey their traditions to their American-born offspring through German language instruction. Language preservation, then, through the establishment and maintenance of schools and the press, was the key to his objective.[57]

An even more revealing occasion where Hoffmann showed the dual civic and aesthetic functions of German immigrants and the beneficial result of their relationship came at the ceremonial laying of the cornerstone of the Deutsches Haus in Chicago in 1855. The arrangements committee had selected the proper day and the main speaker to illuminate Americanism for the German-speaking audience: it took place on Independence Day, and Hoffmann gave the keynote address. The immigrant leader spoke to a "very large concourse of people," identifying clearly the obligations of his audience to America and Germany. The house before them would be an "asylum" of German culture, Hoffmann told them, a needed haven for Germans and, by implication, for any American in a society where the "destroying spirit of money-making . . . rules so predominantly." Again, Germans offered a needed enrichment in America. But he added, as did Reemelin in Cincinnati, that the existence of this sanctuary would not mean that he or his listeners sought isolation or wished to form "a clan," or "a nation in the nation." They would always be true Americans, too. Even amid the widespread hostility of bigots, all true American citizens would acknowledge the United States to be their home, the place for all lovers of freedom. Yet again, culture and nationality are divisible. It would not be necessary to "expel from our hearts the love of our Fatherland . . . the land of . . . Hermann, . . . Schiller, . . . Goethe, . . . Mendelssohn, . . . [and] Mozart; the land of all that is bright and great in art and literature."

Hoffmann concluded with a graphic description of typical German immigrants. They, too, each wished to be the "true American in America, . . . unified . . . in a duality." On the one hand, they were devoted "to our old German home, . . . [its] spirit . . . art, and happiness," yet on the other, they had a "true love for our new free Fatherland, the country of free elections . . . freedom, equality, and independence."[58]

* * *

Hoffmann, there and elsewhere in his life, explained the existence of the immigrants' dualism, how they could live with it and in fact gain their identity from it. Because he spent the last part of his life in southern Wisconsin, he could be considered an ethnic intermediary in that state as well. But his function there came late in the century. The title of pioneer German leader in Wisconsin goes to another, a contemporary of Hoffmann's early life, the energetic Dr. Franz Huebschmann of Milwaukee. Like the Illinoisian, this prominent physician also conceived of his Americanism in terms of the same cultural and political dichotomy. Huebschmann's career differed from Hoffmann's in that the doctor never attained the latter's commanding position in both the ethnic and American worlds. He never reached Hoffmann's influence because there were more Germans in Milwaukee, so there was greater fragmentation and more virulent factionalism. Huebschmann also had a far more abrasive personality, as shown in his greater commitment to radical ideas. Still, he did hold an important mediating position briefly in the 1840s and early 1850s, and as such could be called a significant German American internal leader.

By 1840 Milwaukee was rapidly developing its nationally known character as one of the most German of all American cities. Wisconsin's fertile soil, its liberal alien laws, its accessibility to Europeans, and its generally avid recruitment of foreigners all attracted hosts of Germans to it then and in the following decades. The small contingent of about two to three hundred of these immigrants had little in common in 1840, and even ten years later the settlers of middling economic background came from a variety of provinces, Mecklenberg, Prussia, Bavaria, and Hesse-Darmstadt.[59] This fragmentation and regional diversity and the general state of disorganization were characteristics that Huebschmann found intolerable when he arrived in 1842.

He had left his homeland as a confirmed liberal, hating the rigid caste system in the Old Country, so he was attracted to Wisconsin's rough social democracy.[60] But the opportunity for class harmony which he saw in the state did not produce the favorable conditions of development for the German community. He, too, wished to see the flowering of *Deutschtum,* but he was particularly concerned about the lack of what he regarded as the prerequisite for cultural growth, a united, politically active community. Culture had to be and could be protected by favorable political conditions and a cohesive immigrant bloc. He was also sensitive to the rampant nativism in the 1840s, even more so than other German leaders.

Like the New York Irish physician, MacNeven, Huebschmann forged his ethnic following in part if not largely from his professional work as a doctor, ministering to the masses. From his practice he soon became "known for his kindness and consideration" among his countrymen.[61] With this reputation as one who brought medical relief to the poor and infirm, he organized a number of German cultural bodies, a singing society in 1847, the city's leading language and literature school in 1861 (a "People's Literary Society"), and Milwaukee's first German newspaper. Huebschmann raised the money for the journal, recruited its editor, and formulated its initial editorial policy.[62]

Huebschmann's primary goal, however, was mobilizing his fellow Germans into a powerful voting bloc, getting as many as possible involved in elections. Early successes at group unification, for which he was probably mostly responsible, took place in 1843 and 1844 at several demonstrations of German solidarity. First, he led a parade of countrymen to celebrate winning a grant of federal aid for the Milwaukee harbor; it was the first unified German occasion. At another assembly, with Irish help, he rallied community support for a liberal suffrage provision for foreigners in the new state constitution.[63] He was also the moving spirit of the German Democratic Association in 1844, a body formed to mobilize his countrymen politically and to implement specific ethnic goals. One goal was to have the post office hire a German-speaking clerk who could read addresses on immigrants' letters and direct them properly.[64]

Huebschmann's election in 1846 to the state constitutional convention allowed him to articulate his support for giving aliens the vote, a proposal Whigs and conservatives then sought to block. Contrary to their charges, he stated before the convention that the foreigners did know and cherish republican institutions. Their loyalty was proven by their participation in the just-completed Mexican War. He also told his fellow delegates that by granting immigrants suffrage, and thereby making them equal to the native-born, they could assure that the foreign-born would be devoted, valuable citizens. The result would be a unified Wisconsin population. The convention responded sympathetically, approving the request for a very liberal residency requirement for voting among white male foreigners over 21.[65]

Huebschmann continued his political leadership into the early 1850s, winning various local and state offices and successfully blocking anti-German temperance legislation. But possibly due to his secular radicalism, he began losing the support of more conservative Germans, especially Catholics, and after 1853 he was away from the community, having accepted an appointment to federal office in northern Wisconsin. Nevertheless, in the formative period of the Milwaukee German community it was Huebschmann who rallied disparate elements and built a number of cultural institutions, all the while working to mobilize his followers and educate them in the principles of American democracy. He led in setting the "cultural as well as political and social mold of the German community."[66]

* * *

In addition to the Cincinnati and Milwaukee areas, the third major settlement of Germans was in eastern Missouri, outside St. Louis.

There, as in the other centers, immigrants moved and clustered to enjoy the liberal political conditions. Yet certain leading figures upheld the idea of maintaining ethnic culture as well. The opportunity to remake Germany on liberal lines in the mid Mississippi River valley cannot be underestimated as a cause for German settlement in the area. An early catalyst for such a project was a book published in 1829 by Gottfried Duden, a German traveler in the region. Duden described the exciting, open, free, and stable democratic society that could be established there, especially with the availability of cheap land. His *Report* came at a highly opportune historical moment, because many Germans sought to leave Europe. They condemned the Old World for its oppressive class conflict and sought an egalitarian community elsewhere. According to Duden, the American wilderness offered the ideal setting.[67]

Several colonizing societies formed and prepared to set up their projects there. The major one in the university community at Giessen eventually produced two early immigrant leaders in Missouri, Friedrich Munch and Gert Gobel. These men understood the virtues of American and German traditions, the enlightened way the New World ran its government, and the aesthetic richness of their peoples' ancestry.

Munch was already a social leader of departing emigrants even before they arrived in Missouri; he was in fact a colonizer with a definite philosophy. Deeply disappointed in Germany's slow progress toward an egalitarian political system, and hating the aristocratic and militaristic control as well as the heavy tax burden on the masses, he formed the Giessen Emigration Society about 1830 to provide the remedy. Its 1833 manifesto announced its goal "to seek a new Fatherland in the free states of North America."[68] So Munch led a contingent of about 350 to the St. Louis area the next year and proceeded, according to one recent historian, to "mold the minds" of the Germans there more than any other individual.[69] Later known as "Papa" Munch among his constituents, a "household word" among German settlers, he was active in many German American organizations and wrote widely during his life on a number of political and literary topics. He had a successful political career as a Republican before, during, and after the Civil War.[70]

As one might expect, throughout his life Munch was a committed democrat, and he loved his adopted land for its egalitarian principles, particularly when compared to his homeland. He glorified Missouri in a poem directed at Europeans:

O, you brothers far on the Rhine
If only you were here with us

If you, too, drank Missouri wine
If you were free, free like us.[71]

Life on the frontier in the Mississippi River valley had beneficial social attributes in addition to its political virtues. The isolated farmsteads, he felt, fostered happier families, an absence of indigence, and particularly the peaceful co-existence of differing religions, something nearly unknown in Europe.[72]

Munch was also a German, and he made a good statement of his faith in his ethnic inheritance at a Milwaukee festival of Turners in 1857. The title of his address described the issue: "Is the Preservation of the German Element Necessary in the United States?" Munch's affirmative response was rooted in the same idea of all the others discussed here—he felt that language preservation was especially advisable for Germans. He used the example of the linguistic difference between the familiar "Du" and the formal "Sie" to show that such distinctions were critical to Germans but often little understood by others. In fact, he concluded, people who differ in language really differ in culture. So for a German to forget his native speech was tragic, an unfortunate deprivation, not just for him personally, but also for Americans. Surrendering the German tongue, he warned in his talk, was doubly harmful—it meant the disappearance of beloved "untranslatable" songs (lieder), which apparently were especially revered by his listeners, and, worse, it meant the loss of the "entire treasure of our ideas." Those immigrants who kept the language would enrich American society and politics. He concluded the thought by lamenting, "we will wither [away] when our mother tongue [Muttersprache] will neither be heard nor understood by us."[73] Elsewhere he reiterated Hoffmann's concern about what to do with American-born children, advocating instructing them in *both* German and English so they could acquire the best attributes of both cultures. For all German Americans, then, a cultural synthesis was possible.[74]

Another popular figure among the German immigrants in Missouri, Gert Gobel, coincidentally came in Munch's colonizing party, or rather with his family in 1834 at the age of 18 years. The youth's father, David, was a professor who had joined the Giessen Emigration Society and had brought his family with him to realize its rustic ideals. As a liberal intellectual immigrant, therefore, David became what was called a "Latin farmer." Having little aptitude for agriculture, he soon moved into St. Louis as a teacher, but his son, Gert, stayed in the hinterland and farmed until mid century, when he decided to enter local politics. He was more successful than his father among the townspeople, and being a "fluent speaker" and "good conversationalist," he became "a recognized leader" of the German element in the counties surrounding the city.[75] These largely immigrant counties elected him to a number of public offices: he was a county surveyor in the early 1850s and a state legislator and later senator in the 1860s. Gobel assumed a state-appointed post in 1870 and spent the rest of his life as a writer, working frequently as a correspondent for a St. Louis German newspaper and completing his autobiography, *Longer Than a Man's Life* in 1877.[76]

This published life history is a summation of his activities, essentially a long, colorful account of a foreigner's confrontation with the American wilderness rather than a discussion of views on ethnic identity. But a few sections are pertinent to my study because they show the same enthusiasm for American democracy held by Munch and his father as well as the typical confidence in *Deutschtum*. For example, he dealt with the question of how Anglo-Americans received the immigrant pioneers. Their reception, he observed, was based largely on the philosophical preconceptions the Germans themselves held of society! A few had come with elitist notions of caste and had abused and derided American freedom as "boorish" and "arrogant," and as a result, those Germans found their own reception hostile. Those who had come with faith in democratic principles made an easier adjustment. Thus, Gobel suggested approvingly to his readers, America welcomed only like-minded, liberal, egalitarian Germans; others were to be unhappy.[77]

Nevertheless, like all the other German leaders covered here, Gobel felt that the immigrants were obliged to do more than just subscribe to democratic principles. In a brief section on "sprachvermichung" (language mixing), he lamented the "deterioration" of the mother tongue in America. While such a cultural decline was a disgrace, he said, he predicted it would not continue as long as educated Germans, writers, and journalists like himself continued to publish. Thus, he felt certain that ultimately the language would be properly preserved. As with the other leaders, he justified such maintenance not simply because it promoted cultural continuity, but because it allowed immigrant participation in American affairs.[78]

*   *   *

From Charleston, South Carolina, to eastern Missouri, then, this group of early German American leaders understood clearly the involved matter of their dual identity. One bond did not conflict with the other; each had its own virtue which was mutually supportive— the American one encouraged political involvement for all, and the

German one provided superior cultural resources, the necessary civilizing influence. The leaders told their immigrant audience that they should realize those practical advantages of American democracy—a system of government for which their European relatives were struggling at home. Retaining the best characteristics from two cultures was neither a transitional nor an unstable condition, for as Reemelin, Henni, and Hoffmann pointed out specifically and the others indirectly, maintaining language did not mean total segregation, it simply made it easier to become involved in the larger society. And children in particular were to be taught *both* languages.

This picture of German American duties was drawn by all these leaders, and they were social mediators in five states. As with the Irish, the important question once again arises as to whether ordinary immigrants, the rank and file, held that same conception of a dual ethnic identity expressed by their elite. German-speaking newcomers came in huge numbers, were highly fragmented, and settled over a long period of time over a wide geographical area. Thus, encompassing generalizations are certainly problematic. But the leaders described here were important men of influence and were themselves representative of a wide constituency. They could not, of course, "speak for" all their countrymen, even in the localities they dominated. But given the fact that many immigrants left Germany and went to America to live in freedom, the leaders were expressing a faith in the New World that followers already held in inchoate form. Furthermore, all these prominent figures were involved in wide-ranging communication and held substantial grass-roots support— as generally elected office holders or, in Henni's case, simply as popular individuals. And their ideas about German American identity were surprisingly similar. Therefore, their message of synthesizing their former and adopted loyalties must have reached a substantial part of German Americans, who learned that they need not suffer from marginality or inner identity conflict. Finally, this resolution of how to be at once German and American came early from prominent persons who helped build immigrant institutions, even before the arrival of the liberal 48ers.[79]

Illustrations

William James MacNeven, the early New York Irish leader.

Archbishop John Hughes of New York.

Das Deutsche Haus, Chicago, a German American cultural center in the mid 1800s. Francis Hoffmann laid the cornerstone in 1855. Note the American flag flying above it.

"Hans Buschbauer," former Lieutenant Governor Francis Hoffmann, seen smoking a peasant pipe in his study at Riverside Farm, Jefferson, Wisconsin, about 1890. He probably wrote many of his articles of advice to farm families from here.

Memorial for Johann Enander (right), headstone in ancient runic design. The bottom inscription reads, "This stone set up by Swedes in America was unveiled May 22, 1921." (Below) Vasa, Hans Mattson's first home parish, a Swedish colony he began in Minnesota.

Rabbi Kasriel H. Sarasohn
(left), probably about 1890,
with traditional yarmulke.
(Below) Cover pages from
two of Alexander Harkavy's
most popular works in
Yiddish. Note the dates, at
the start of the massive
eastern European
immigration.

דער
ענגלישער לעהרער.
א לעהרבוך פיר יעדען זיך אויסצולערנען ענגליש אהן א לעהרער.
מיט ביילאגע:
דיא אונאבהענגיגקיימס ערקלערונג פון דיא פעראייניגטע שטאאטען אין יודיש.
פון
אלכסנדר הארקאווי.
ניו יארק:
פערלאג פון קאצענעלענבאגען און סאפירשטיין.
פרייז 65 סענט.

THE ENGLISH TEACHER.
A MANUAL OF THE ENGLISH LANGUAGE.
WITH APPENDIX :
The Declaration of Independence in Judæo-German translation.

BY
ALEXANDER HARKAVY.

NEW YORK:
Katzenelenbogen & Saphirstein, Publishers.
1891.

וואשינגטאן
ר ערשטער פרעזידענט פון דיא פער-אייניגטע שטאאטען.
מיט ביילאגע:
"יא ,אונאבהענגיגקייטס ערקלערונג", אין ענגליש און יודיש.
פון
אלכסנדר הארקאווי.
ניו יארק:
זיגמנד קאנטראָאוויץ, פערלעגער.
1892.

WASHINGTON,
the first president of the United States.

with supplement:
The Declaration of Independence, in Jewish version.

BY
ALEXANDER HARKAVY.

NEW YORK:
Sigmund Kantrowitz, Publisher.
1892.

„Uncle Sam" odsłania pomniki polskich bohaterów.

Original cartoon from the Washington *Evening Star* showing the new Kościusko and Pułaski statues at the 1910 Polish Congress in Washington, D.C. Caption reads, "Uncle Sam's unveiling of the statues of Polish heroes."

Dr. Franciszek Eustachy Fronczak of Buffalo, with the Polish government's Polonia Restituta medal (1919) most prominent.

America's leading Italian "pappa della colonia," Cavaliere Luigi V. Fugazi of New York.

Philadelphia Italians and others pay their last respects to Charles C. Baldi. The caption read, "Visual proof of the immense outpouring of grief of the city and the community of Philadelphia at the funeral of Commendatore Baldi."

4

The **NORWEGIANS** and the **SWEDES**

Until recently, historians of northern European immigration to America had characterized their subjects as assimilating quickly and easily into the host society. Unlike the Germans, who cherished their traditional language in the early days of their arrival, or the Irish, whose Catholic faith and fervent nationalism set them apart from the Anglo-American majority, the Swedes and the Norwegians, observers have written, retained few political or cultural traditions to retard their integration. Highly literate immigrants in general, these peoples learned English quickly, held little loyalty to the Old Country, and blended in fairly easily with American society. Scholars do make some distinctions between the two major Scandinavian peoples in America; the rate of assimilation for the Swedes, for example, was faster than that for the Norwegians. But certainly in both cases the overwhelming majority in both groups acquired their American identity faster than that of almost any other group of foreigners.[1]

The well-known conditions of departure for early Scandinavian emigrants certainly suggest widespread dissatisfaction with homeland authorities and an eagerness to forget many national and ethnic ties. These pioneers left with strong feelings of dissent from the established state church and with a desire to find inexpensive land upon which to support their families. They clearly hungered for the cheap territory that the vast, open, American West offered them in the mid nineteenth century. That these peoples sought spiritual and material freedom in a new land with little nativist hostility directed against them might indicate that northern Europeans did not much concern themselves with matters of ethnic identity and change. The idea of adjusting their traditional and adopted country loyalties might not have been a conscious exercise by some at all. Others may have gone through the process individually without reflecting on or comparing their Scandinavian and American group identities. The transition or process of becoming American might well have been for them swift and thorough. This study will not attempt to trace precisely the speed and extent of assimilation for the nearly two million northern European immigrants who arrived in the United States between the mid nineteenth and early twentieth centuries.[2] Still, the transformation was, for some, a group issue. Certain immigrant leaders with wide influence among the groups did raise and largely resolve the matter of how a Swede or a Norwegian could simultaneously be American and European, and their thinking on the question reflected that of a good number of followers.

The Swedish immigrants in particular did not experience the kind of spirited nationalism in the nineteenth century that was felt by most other Europeans, say the Irish or the Poles. Nor did they possess the kind of aggressive feelings of cultural superiority characteristic of the Germans. But Swedish American leaders did cherish their forebears—not so much their *distant* predecessors in Europe but rather their *immigrant* forebears who first came to America. As late-nineteenth-century group leaders put it, it was their own seventeenth-century ancestors in colonial times who brought with them qualities that made them and their descendants *both* Swedish and American. These values included a reverence for the separation of church and state and for a number of desirable personal qualities. The prominent nineteenth-century figures who referred to those virtues were the Reverend Tufve Hasselquist, the group's major religious leader; Johann Enander, a popular newspaper editor and leading promoter of a Swedish American identity; and Hans Mattson, the major group promoter in the most Swedish state in the union, Minnesota.

Although they came from the same general region of Europe as the Swedes and were close to them culturally and socially even in America, the Norwegian immigrants encountered an identity adjustment that differed somewhat from that of the Swedes. Being more of a subjugated people—they were under Swedish control until 1905—the Norwegians retained a stronger feeling of group nationalism and group loyalty, and were thereby somewhat less interested in a rapid and complete assimilation in America. The question of being both Norwegian and American, and the problem of defining the meaning of both conditions, concerned all the group leaders deeply; in fact it led to a split that forced them into two rather hostile camps. Again, while some Norwegians may simply have shed their foreignness readily soon after their arrival, a significant number of others confronted the change as an issue in the same manner that their leaders did.

Most of the Norwegian elite agreed on the necessity of preserving their Old Country identity and culture—to that extent few were totally assimilationist. Far more than the Swedes, they honored their European traditions and heritage. But the Norwegian consensus over preservation ended with heated, divisive debates over how best to achieve that goal outside their ancestral land, in American society.

A bitter intragroup exchange erupted in the 1870s over precisely how and by whom people should be instructed about their heritage—by means of parochial schools or the public school system. Norwegian American clerics believed church schools ought to be the place for such group education; lay leaders insisted that educating the immigrants to their identity ought to be the task of the American common school. The winners of this controversy, that is the camp joined by most of the rank and file, were secular spokesmen, individuals like educator Rasmus Anderson and his friend, businessman John Johnson of Wisconsin, as well as the very popular political figure, Knute Nelson of Wisconsin and Minnesota.

It was this trio who advanced the notion of how Norwegians in this country were to learn about themselves as Europeans and as Americans. The vehicle was the public school and its curriculum. They held that the common schools had the job of making Americans, but that job included reminding students of their traditional heritage. American public education, then, in the heavily Norwegian districts was to *include* the instruction of Scandinavian culture and certainly was not to neglect it. Like the Germans, Anderson and his colleagues agreed that all Americans must know about European civilization and its vital role in New World culture. These Norwegians designated early the specific institution to propagate that proposition. With Scandinavian civilization being taught in the public schools, *both* native-born Americans of any background and Norwegian immigrants would be aware of the latter's share in American life.

People in both major northern European groups in America considered the issue of defining themselves, relating their past and present. The controversy among the Norwegians arose and was resolved by the 1880s, before the Swedes considered the question, so we will review the former group first. To fully understand the intense Norwegian debate and its relationship to the group as a whole requires some background concerning their coming, their numbers, their character, and their location in America.

* * *

Nearly a million Norwegian immigrants arrived here over a long period, from early in the nineteenth century to the start of the twentieth. The first boatload to leave as a community did so on July 4, 1825 in a well-known voyage from Stavenger on Norway's west coast. The group's continuous migration, however, did not start until about 1840. It peaked in the 1880s and declined after then until just before World War I. The common motive for the earliest arrivals was religion; most were followers of or sympathetic to the several pietistic awakenings like the Haugian movement, which swept Norway in the earlier period. These dissenters chafed at the austere and authoritarian state Lutheran church.

Later, around the start of the Civil War, the general reason for coming changed; emigrants left more for purely economic and material ends. These later arrivals, who by then included Lutherans, came to obtain the cheap land of the upper Midwest, which the American preemption statutes and the Homestead Act of 1862 made available.

Most of the Norwegian settlements in America, then, sprang up in that region around mid century. Between the 1830s and the 1850s they were located mainly in southern Wisconsin, northern Illinois, eastern Iowa, and southern Minnesota. Late in the 1860s and 1870s they spread to western Minnesota and eastern Dakota. Those areas remain the focal point of most Americans of that ancestry today.[3]

By the third quarter of the century Wisconsin became the leading recipient and first center of Norwegian immigrants. It contained about forty thousand in 1870, just over a third of them all, while Minnesota took second place with about thirty-six thousand. It is no coincidence that these two states were the setting for the "common school" controversy about how these Scandinavians should perpetuate group tradition.[4]

*   *   *

Although many of the Norwegian leaders of both religious and lay camps—the Norwegian Evangelical Lutheran Church figures on one hand and Rasmus Anderson on the other—never commanded the devotion of masses of immigrants in the way that Bishop John Hughes, Patrick Collins, or Johann Wagener did, Anderson's impact on the rank and file was still significant. The men he influenced, his associates Johnson and Nelson, were much more charismatic, and they helped convey Anderson's message to the masses.[5]

Anderson's pugnacious and even rebellious character made him a notable figure early in life. Born the son of an immigrant in 1846 in Koshkonong in southern Wisconsin, he continually questioned authority and enjoyed challenging his superiors. For example, as a youth he led a student strike against the rigid discipline of one of his early schools, Luther College, from which he was expelled.[6]

When he was rather young he decided to enter teaching, and he obtained a position at an academy in his hometown. He almost immediately launched on his life's goal, promoting knowledge of his ethnic group. With friends he established the Norwegian American Education Society (NAES) about 1868. The organization quickly acquired about one hundred members.[7] Its simple purpose was the essence of Anderson's ideas thereafter—to use the public schools to educate Norwegian Americans in their own tradition. Anderson knew that that objective was directly contrary to the work of Norwegian Lutheran religious leaders at that time.

The church in the late 1860s actually had just shifted from the position of the NAES to an advocacy of total parochial school education. When the Norwegian Evangelical Lutheran Synod was formed in 1853, it was desperately short of pastors, just like other immigrant churches in America before and after. To provide the necessary ministers, the synod approached the recently established University of Wisconsin and petitioned it to found a seminary to produce pastors. The request was not unusual for that time, because the emerging public school system in the Midwest was usually under such heavy religious influence. But the university in this instance rejected the proposal. Norwegian church leaders had already worked closely with fellow German Missouri Synod Lutherans, and with the university's refusal, they became even more convinced of the value of their co-religionists' separatist educational philosophy.[8] They arranged with the Germans to handle pastoral training in 1855 and later launched a parochial school system on the German Lutheran model. Claiming the responsibility of providing for the entire educational needs of all Norwegian immigrants, the Norwegian Synod condemned the emerging public school as inadequate to meet their people's requirements. The Reverend A. C. Preus, the group's major religious leader, was especially critical. The common school, he charged, was a miserably weak institution, employing inadequate and inexperienced teachers who were, of course, not Lutheran. They also could not provide the proper student discipline and respect integral to Norwegian American life. Worst of all, public schools were nonreligious; their refusal to offer spiritual guidance was an intolerable condition for educating the immigrants.[9]

This synodical position, expressed in the 1850s and 1860s, obviously irritated and challenged Anderson and his NAES supporters. They criticized in particular the clerics' insistence that Norwegians isolate themselves from American influence. Although they did not express it as such, the NAES considered their people to be Americans. For Norwegians to withdraw and nearly become hermits under church authority was not only intellectually and morally wrong; it was dangerous. Anderson and the NAES agreed with their opponents that the beauties of Norwegian religion and culture were too little known in America by both Norwegians and Americans, and the situation demanded a remedy—education. But instead of suggesting that they retreat into isolated enclaves to forestall contamination from outside, as other groups advocated, Anderson insisted that Norwegians should broadcast their heritage and show in universally accessible institutions how they and all Americans have benefited from their coming. The public schools, then, were not a threat to the group's existence but rather an opportunity to promote it.[10] Anderson obviously had confidence in his own group traditions, but his position was not the same as that of the Germans, whom we have already seen. He felt that his heritage was not superior to American culture, but rather that it offered an important and significant contribution to American values.

As Anderson viewed it, the crucial agents to lead the campaign to enlighten all Americans were the teachers. At a synodical meeting in 1868 he proposed that the church support the training of Norwegian Lutheran instructors who would work in public schools and colleges. These teachers would then go on in those institutions to offer courses in Scandinavian culture. The synod rejected this proposal.

Anderson then decided to launch out on his own and set an example. He obtained an appointment in 1869 at the University of Wisconsin and later described his task in terms that clearly show how he felt about the compatibility of being Norwegian and American.

> The majority of the Norwegians [in America] were either ignorant or indifferent in regard to their inheritance. It was necessary to do a lot of missionary work among them in order to arouse in them enthusiasm for their ancestors and respect for their language and literature. *I wanted them to be good Norwegians and loyal Americans at the same time* and I wanted to impress the Americans with the fact that they were greatly indebted to the north of Europe for their liberties, laws and institutions. Along these lines I conducted my campaign.[11]

Anderson's rationale for teaching Norwegian traditions, then, was similar to that of Bishop Hughes's reference to the Catholic basis of many of the principles of the American Revolution. As the Norwegian American teacher told his wife in 1885, we "have treasures of which no other European can boast" but too few of us realize that.[12]

Although he was not a popular teacher of Scandinavian literature at the university, he did make an impact as a speaker, writer, and especially as a colleague to others in his field.[13] He continued as professor of Scandinavian languages at Madison until 1883, translating many of his group's legends and stories into English. He spent much time showing that Norwegians, not Columbus, discovered America. Most significant is his reputation as the father of Scandinavian studies in America, which he got because of his influence on his colleagues, on his successor at Madison, and on instructors at Minnesota and other universities.[14]

The major historian of Norwegian immigration has offered his assessment of Anderson's place in his generation. The educator did so well in transmitting the cultural treasures of his ancestral land that "he generated a literary contagion among his countrymen. He was a popularizer of boundless energy whose gift as a writer was matched by his skill as a speaker and by a singularly provocative personality."[15]

*   *   *

The irascible academician roused bitter opponents, chiefly clerics, but he also attracted dedicated allies, leading figures who were far more popular with the ordinary group member. One was the businessman John Johnson of Madison, who was likely the leading Norwegian layman of his day.[16] Johnson was very close to Anderson, and while their relationship was not always a harmonious one, he generally helped his friend and followed Anderson's lead. He had aided him in organizing the NAES in 1868 and 1869. In addition, he was partially responsible for Anderson's position at the university, and he offered a five thousand dollar scholarship there to any Norwegian graduate of a public school. Johnson was at least as enthusiastic as Anderson about the superiority of the common school. In fact, he went further than other laymen in claiming that religious education was an unnecessary expense. The public school, he insisted, was the "cornerstone and bulwark of our political and social system," and it made much more effective citizens than the parochial institutions.[17]

With Anderson's energetic publicity and Johnson's material aid, it was clear that by the early 1880s Norwegian immigrants in Wisconsin and Minnesota had generally accepted the public school as their primary educational institution.[18] Actually, the clergy itself had never been unanimous in supporting parochial instruction. They and their parishioners knew that some of their religious schools suffered some of the same deficiencies for which they criticized the public schools. The parochial institutions also were inadequate places for education, being poorly financed, and were even inferior to the tax-supported ones. Some leading pastors openly admitted this.

Even the Reverend Bernt Muus, one of the most outspoken clerics, reluctantly accepted the practice of sending children to secular institutions in some cases. This widespread support of public education by the group's rank and file did not come about simply because of the greater expense of parochial schools or the eagerness of parents to have their children obtain American instruction. Some outwardly welcomed knowledge about being Norwegian and American. A recent historian conclusively assessed Anderson's general influence: "Through the force of . . . his argument, Anderson [by the late 1800s] had pulled his countrymen in his direction."[19]

* * *

Another friend of Anderson's, and probably the best-known Norwegian American of the late nineteenth and early twentieth centuries inside and outside the community, was the leading Minnesota political figure, Knute Nelson.[20] Nelson shared in thought and in deed Anderson's faith in public schooling for his group, and he spoke of it often to constituents. He also contributed to the immigrants' feeling of being American by making his personal commitment to public life. The first Norwegian elected to prominent national office, he reached the position of U.S. Senator *and held it* largely on the basis of strong ethnic support.

That a Norwegian American politician should have commanding position among his group is no surprise. Norwegians in America generally esteemed public life, like the Irish in the East and certainly more than their fellow Scandinavians, the Swedes. This avid interest in office holding has been ascribed to a number of group characteristics, including their long-standing local democratic traditions in Europe (the ones that Anderson publicized), their familiarity with English, their nearly universal ownership of property, their tight-knit farming communities, and their relatively heavy concentration of population in the upper Midwest.[21] Whatever the sources of their strong political interest and sensitivity, certainly an unusually high percentage of Norwegian immigrants were involved in community affairs. In 1881, for example, of the many Scandinavians who filed for public office in Minnesota, well over two-thirds were Norwegian.[22]

Nelson's life, his statements and actions, clearly suggest that he considered his ethnic background important, yet at the same time he demonstrated his feeling for America. Whether the motives for this synthesis of his traditional and adopted identities came from a sincere personal commitment or from his practical wish to be elected by his countrymen is not entirely clear. Still, it is the place Nelson held in the minds of immigrants that is important. During his career, according to a recent observer, Norwegians revered Nelson as "their pioneer politician."[23]

In the educational controversy of the 1860s and 1870s Nelson clearly sided with Andersonian liberals in upholding the public school. And later, his prominent position contributed substantially to the immigrants' confidence in public education.

Nelson was familiar with Anderson early in life; he probably knew him as a youth. After immigrating from Norway to Chicago as a child of six with his widowed mother in 1849, Nelson settled the next year in Anderson's hometown in Wisconsin. While still a youth he served in the Civil War and quickly entered politics as a Republican state legislator, attending closely to his heavily ethnic constituency. In a warm letter to Anderson in 1868, for example, he said he regretted that his legislative proposal encouraging foreign-language instruction in the state's public schools, an idea both men supported, had failed.[24] Nelson was more successful in raising the stature of Norwegian newspapers. In the same year, he proposed and implemented the printing of government documents in foreign languages, and he also worked to gain for the immigrant press the same privileges held by the state's English-language papers.[25]

At the same time that Nelson was trying to have the state formally recognize an immigrant institution, he was also acting as an assimilating agent among his people. In effect, he was instructing his Norwegian constituents about the power they could wield in local American politics, encouraging them to become involved in public issues. By giving such encouragement he was aiding their Americanization. This was the same role that some of the German leaders, such as Henni and Wagener, played earlier. The winning of ethnic rights and status required American political involvement, and Nelson's constituents learned the message.[26]

In his later political career, too, Nelson continued as the Norwegian American intermediary. He followed the westward migration of many Norwegian immigrants into Minnesota, moving there in 1871 to further capitalize on his image as the group's representative. Within three years he was again in the state legislature, representing, as one would expect, a heavily ethnic district in the western part of the state. His ideas as immigrant broker did not change; he continued to promote Anderson's proposal of including Scandinavian instruction in public education. In fact, he sought and ultimately obtained an appointment as a member of the Minnesota Board of Regents in 1882, and as a result he was instrumental in establishing a Scandinavian professorship at the state university the next year. Throughout, he continued to seek Anderson's help and counsel.[27]

The final stage of Nelson's political life was the most successful for him personally because he won a number of high state offices. He was elected to the House of Representatives in the 1880s, and he went on in the next decade to win the Minnesota governorship and a place in the U.S. Senate.

One might expect that as he scaled the political ladder of success his feelings for his Norwegian ethnic identity might have weakened, even disappeared, since he was less dependent on particular group support. He did indeed become less of a Norwegian partisan, but he continued to voice his strong support and faith in the foreign-born who were moving into his state. During the late 1880s and the 1890s, a time of rising nativist criticism, he often advised his congressional colleagues not to despair of the newcomer, at least not the kind who settled in his state, Scandinavian farmers.

In one speech that Nelson gave in the House of Representatives in response to the huge public outcry against the foreign-born, whom many condemned for being responsible for the Haymarket Square riot, he reminded his audience not to blame *all* immigrants, certainly not the rural ones. As he put it, the immigrants in his region were not at all like the urban workers from the East who tended to support radicals. His newcomers were law-abiding farmers who owned property and were a credit to the nation.[28]

To counter the more spirited criticism of foreigners in the next decade, Nelson described to the U.S. Senate the dual identity of those who had come to his state from overseas. In an address reminiscent of that of German leaders a half-century earlier, Nelson used the mother-bride metaphor in which immigrants considered their native land as the former and America as the latter. A different kind of bond exists for each, but both are compatible. The immigrants, he said in 1896,

> came [to Minnesota] poor and empty handed . . . but possessed
> of an intense desire and purpose to become good American
> citizens. . . . As the good wife, though loving her mother, still
> gives her husband the uppermost place in her affections, so do
> the foreign-born sons and daughters of Minnesota, though
> loving the lands of their birth, still place [America] uppermost
> and foremost in their love and affection.[29]

Although, of course, not all Norwegians in Minnesota considered Nelson their leader or representative, it is certain that he held a high place in the esteem of many. Those who wrote to him for help occasionally used the widely known nickname of "Uncle Knute." Another example of Nelson's continuing recognition of his ethnic origins was the realization of a long-planned visit to his native Norway in 1899.[30]

All three of these Norwegian American pioneers, Anderson, Johnson, and Nelson, then, in their actions, writings, and speeches, showed their people that they could be both Norwegian and American and that the duality would benefit both themselves and the larger society around them. No strain need accompany the tug of the past and the present.[31]

* * *

If a conscious Norwegian American identity sprang conspicuously from a controversy over education and from the group's involvement in politics, the forces illuminating the essence of Swedish America were more obscure. Less nationalistic than the Norwegians, most of the Swedes who came to the United States were dissenters from, or people disenchanted with, the Swedish state church. Like the Norwegians, they, too, sought to escape life in the homeland, and they welcomed the economic and political attractions of the New World. But still, some of them did not assimilate immediately upon arrival. They too, built ethnic institutions, though they were admittedly more modest than those of the Norwegians. Their major cohesive force was the church, particularly the Augustana Synod. As expressed by their major pioneer, the Reverend Tufve Hasselquist, the Swedes were bound to their adopted country because it had no national religious establishment, and it therefore protected their rights of nonconformity and dissent.

As with the Norwegians, it was first religious and later economic reasons that motivated the Swedish trek to the United States in the last half of the nineteenth century. With the possible exception of the eastern European Jews, no other group was more eager to leave its homeland. Increasing lay dissatisfaction with the dry formalism and rationalism of the state Lutheran church in the 1830s spawned a number of nonconformist pietistic groups. One group led by Eric Jansen decided to go to America just before mid century. His followers settled in Illinois in 1845 and were soon joined by other sects, even some unhappy Swedish Lutherans. Until the Civil War the numbers of incoming Swedes were small; the center of the group remained in Illinois, the home of about a third of all arrivals to 1870.

As with the Norwegians, a reason for later movement to the United States was the availability of inexpensive land. Besides this, a famine in Sweden in 1867 compelled about one hundred thousand to leave for America between 1868 and 1873. They, too, settled mostly in the upper Midwest, chiefly in Minnesota and the Dakotas in those later years.[32] After the 1870s, the majority of the Swedish immigrants were laborers.

The pioneer period for this group, the formative time of the Swedish American community, was before the 1880s. Ethnic institutional development was slow, and when it did emerge, it was mainly connected to the church.[33] The Augustana Synod in the United States was Lutheran, the same Protestant denomination as in the Old Country, but it was hardly like the church in Sweden.

The most significant personality in this early period was undoubtedly the long-dominant religious figure, the Reverend Tufve Hasselquist. He was like the other Swedish immigrant leaders of the day in that he did not promote many of the group's cultural traditions, although he constructed his church to allow for the maintenance of ethnic identity. Hasselquist was not the first important Swedish cleric in America, but he was undoubtedly the most influential. His stature and impact are best seen in a review of how he came to the Midwest.

It was the founder of Swedish American Lutheranism, the Reverend Lars Paul Esbjorn, who brought Hasselquist to the New World. A pastor in the Swedish state church, Esbjorn had become unhappy with it and, like many after him, had decided to emigrate to America. He did this not only to escape strict church control but also to save the faithful in America. Disturbing accounts had crossed the Atlantic that Swedish immigrant pietists and other Protestants in the New World were winning away many Lutherans. Esbjorn went to Illinois in 1840 and immediately set up a Swedish Lutheran parish. He sought help from the Swedish religious authorities in his drive to hold congregants and to begin other Lutheran churches. Two other clerics equally disenchanted with the state church policies responded to his pleas. They were Hasselquist, who immigrated in 1852 at the age of 36 and took over the Galesburg, Illinois, parish that Esbjorn had started, and the Reverend Erland Carlsson, who went to Chicago.

Although he was credited with "saving" many Swedish Americans from abandoning Lutheranism, Esbjorn still remained unhappy. His discomfort came from two sources in the 1850s—envy over Hasselquist's extraordinary popularity with Swedish Americans and a disagreement with him over doctrine. Hasselquist had certainly won the hearts of his parishioners, gaining their "respect and admiration" with his "winning personality." They particularly liked his unpretentious style of preaching and his simple, puritanical ideals.[34] Hasselquist also antagonized Esbjorn in particular by presenting his more liberal ideas and attitudes in the new environment. He more readily accepted departures from Swedish church practice, advocated closer ties with other Lutherans, and in particular fervently endorsed the American principle of church-state separation.[35]

When Hasselquist was elected head of the newly formed Augustana Synod in 1860, it is understandable that his jealous opponent, Esbjorn, became homesick and retired from the scene. He finally returned to Sweden in 1863. In the meantime, Hasselquist was appointed professor of theology and president of the Augustana Seminary, thereby attaining the pinnacle of his power among Swedish Americans. He was the "most versatile and . . . ablest leader" as well as the "guiding light" of Swedish American Lutheranism.[36]

Hasselquist's commanding influence came not only from his attractive personality and his liberal attitude toward native-born Americans, but also from his contribution to ethnic mobilization. He established the first and for some years largest Swedish American newspaper in America, *Hemlandet* (The Homeland), in 1855.[37] His popularity also came from the fact that he had organized other Swedish Lutheran parishes from New York to Minnesota, and this newspaper enabled him to maintain contact with those congregants far beyond his home church in Galesburg. One must keep in mind that the Swedish press was generally powerful because these Northern Europeans were one of the most highly literate of all immigrant groups.[38]

There is no doubt as to Hasselquist's strongly assimilationist philosophy. He was continually openly critical of his own traditional Swedish Lutheranism, and he did encourage English-language instruction in his seminary curriculum. Unlike his Norwegian counterparts, he was hostile to parochial schooling, and he certainly honored the principles of his adopted land and wanted his people to become American quickly.[39] *Hemlandet* was really more assimilationist than Swedish. As Hasselquist put it, as editor, he wanted readers to be educated fully in American public debates. "He regarded an ignorant . . . population as a menace to any country . . . [and] in a democracy such as the United States . . . it was all the more important that [so many foreign-born] people be informed regarding public affairs."[40]

Although he was a critic of the Swedish state church, Hasselquist still did not want to see his audience integrated immediately into mainstream America. He took several actions to build a Swedish American community. For example, his objectives for establishing *Hemlandet* were not simply to inform readers about American issues but also to keep the audience aware of events in the homeland. In a letter of justification for the publication of the paper written just prior to the paper's first issue, Hasselquist told Pastor Carlsson that he was going to supply what many people were yearning for, an organ that provided news from Sweden. Thus, he implied that such information was as necessary as a knowledge of American events.[41] Also, though he was not as committed to language preservation as were Anderson and the Norwegians, Hasselquist did feel it necessary to offer formal Swedish-language instruction at the seminary. In 1872 he advised potential Swedish seminarians who intended to go to America to make sure that they had a firm knowledge of their own language and history as well as English.[42] Elsewhere he even went so far as to urge that the two languages be given parity at Augustana. He felt that graduates ought to be enabled and encouraged to preach in *both* tongues.[43]

Thus, in advocating the inclusion of English in Swedish immigrant education, Hasselquist did not necessarily wish to encourage the rapid abandonment of Swedish.[44] Finally, in his old age, Hasselquist may have pushed for a more ethnic educational policy. It was his Augustana graduates who staffed the parttime Swedish religious schools that appeared at the end of the century. Although the synod never established a parochial school system, it affirmed its right to do so just prior to Hasselquist's passing in 1891.[45]

* * *

Added proof that Hasselquist had an active role in building a Swedish American community and did not merely hasten his followers' assimilation is his selection of the longtime editor for *Hemlandet* in 1869. That individual was his protege, Johann Enander. Only slightly less popular than his mentor, Enander directed this leading newspaper over the last third of the century. He became known as the "foremost layman in the Augustana Synod." He was someone who "exerted a vast influence on his fellow countrymen."[46] His objective, like that of other leaders, was to harmonize American and Swedish traditions, and his well-known method was to stress the similarity of the first Swedish colonists in America to contemporary non-Swedes. He focused repeatedly on the lives of his American group pioneers, saying little about the Swedes' European culture and civilization.

Enander came to the United States in 1869 to enroll in the Augustana Seminary and become a minister. But before he graduated, Hasselquist prevailed upon him to take over the editorship of *Hemlandet*. Enander agreed, apparently persuaded that he would have a wider audience if he were an editor, not a pastor. He bought the paper in 1872, and as journalist and publisher, author and talented speaker, he became a leading outspoken Swedish American.

In his writing, Enander did occasionally speak of preserving "special national ways," and he attempted to do this in the 1870s by setting up an exchange with a more assimilative newspaper, *Svenska Amerikan.*[47] But his major task, as he saw it, was to inform his readers about the group's heritage *in America*. Enander's often-cited, cherished examples were the Swedish pioneers in the American colonies. These settlers, he pointed out, already possessed the same fine psychological and personal characteristics of the first Anglo-Americans. He dwelled upon these commonly held traits in his popular five-volume *History of the United States Compiled for the Swedish Population in America,* which he wrote for the nation's Centennial and serialized in *Hemlandet* between 1874 and 1880. In this filiopietistic tome he reminded his readers of the fortitude and courage of the Norse sailors who first came to the New World, and he emphasized the affinity of character among the colonial Swedish settlers with the Pilgrims and the patriots of the 1770s. The work was so well received by readers that Enander was invited to reiterate his views orally at several notable Swedish American occasions in the next few years.

He spoke on these matters at numerous group gatherings: on Swedish Day at the Philadelphia Centennial in 1876; at Chicago's Golden Anniversary observance in 1887; at the most significant Swedish American meeting in Minneapolis in 1888, the commemoration of the 250th anniversary of Swedish American settlement; and at both the preparatory meeting for the Columbian Exposition in 1890 and the Fair itself.[48] On these two latter occasions, Enander, by then known as the "most Swedish of Swedes," understandably criticized the Fair's promoters for ignoring America's real discoverers, the intrepid Norsemen.[49]

The Minneapolis 250th anniversary assembly in 1888 merits particularly close attention because it was the most important Swedish American meeting up to and probably since that time, and because it had a memorable and telling impact on the immigrant community. As a result of Enander's numerous writings on his seventeenth-century predecessors, some kind of recognition of the group's arrival in 1638 was bound to take place in the major city of the most Swedish American state.[50]

A committee of two hundred prominent Swedish American citizens arranged the affair, which was held on September 14, 1888. A large parade was to precede the gathering, but inclement weather cancelled the procession. Still, the rain did not prevent a throng of fifteen thousand from filling the Minneapolis Exhibition Hall and watching and hearing the proceedings. The setting was quite visibly ethnic, as Swedish American fraternal banners and Swedish and

American national colors hung on the walls. Also, to symbolize the assembly's theme of honoring ancestors, a huge picture of the Old Swede Church (1638) of Wilmington, Delaware, looked down on the throng.[51] A 150-voice Swedish American chorus opened the meeting and, appropriately, the elderly patriarch Rev. Tufve Hasselquist, just two years before his death, gave the invocation. Others offered speeches, and a poetry reading completed the observance.

Enander's address was given in Swedish (hence for his own countrymen), and was totally predictable; it was a paean to the group's colonial, not European, ancestors. He reminded his listeners that the Swedes had been in the land about as long as any other non-English-speaking group. These pioneers of the seventeenth century were much like his audience two and a half centuries later, "hard-working, industrious self-sufficient . . . farmers and craftsmen" who had a "fear of God," a warm "love of freedom," and a vigorous "sense of nationalism." The nationalism he referred to was not to Sweden but to their "beloved *adopted* fatherland."[52] He concluded by praising the Swedish American community, who knew its rights as citizens:

> As it has been done up to now, we shall do in the future our
> duty as American citizens, but as such we shall also insist
> upon our rights down to the smallest detail, maintaining in all
> areas the honor and reputation of the title 'Swedish America'
> until this becomes . . . a title of honor which denotes every-
> thing that is great, noble, true, and genuine.[53]

* * *

Also conspicuous at the Minneapolis celebration of Swedish American beginnings was another leading figure in the immigrant community of that time, and perhaps the most influential, Colonel Hans Mattson. If Enander provided the philosophical rationale for the gathering, with his frequent speeches and writings on the group's earliest American pioneers, Mattson was chiefly responsible for its being held at all. In short he was the Swedes' primary organizer.

This well-known adopted Minnesotan had always been a man of action more than one of words. He had achieved prominence as the group's major colonizer, its chief guide and political figure. In a number of occasional publications he explained to his audience the basis for his varied activities. Like Hasselquist and Enander, he, too, paid special tribute to those first Swedish emigrants who had brought with them certain, selected qualities that were most like American qualities. Hence, being already similar to natives, he concluded, Swedes did not need to establish a totally separate ethnic community. They were already Americans. In fact, Mattson's advice to his assimilated people in America was that they ought to have a particular impact on Sweden: to remake the old country into a society just like that of the United States!

Mattson's life to the time of the Minneapolis celebration illustrated his influence and his philosophical position on assimilation. He left Sweden in 1857 as a youth of 18 without his family but with a boatload of countrymen. He decided to emigrate because of his firm adherence to liberal ideals—an intolerable position in his homeland and one which made him uncomfortable in that stiff, conservative society. Forced to serve in the army in 1849, for example, he chafed in particular at the accepted principle of inherited class differences. He felt that success ought to be based on one's individual worth, not on one's name or title.[54]

Thus, his attraction to America, a more democratic society, was understandable. Settling in the heavily Swedish region of northern Illinois, Mattson quickly learned English and assumed almost immediately the role of directing friends and countrymen to what would be a major group colony in Goodhue County, Minnesota, in 1853. He acquired both personal wealth and political influence by a number of successful real estate ventures and by energetically promoting the region among newcomers.[55] The early colony at Vasa, near Red Wing, was popularly known as Mattson's settlement.

Partly because of his great facility with English, he decided to become a lawyer, and his profession enabled him to act as his people's intermediary with non-Swedes. Mattson continued to promote Swedish colonization in Minnesota with considerable success. His appeals to countrymen to come to the North Star state appeared regularly in the Swedish American press in the 1870s. Also, as agent for the railroads and the state, he even made recruiting trips to his homeland. He personally escorted at least one contingent of emigrants from his native region in Sweden in 1873.[56]

As a result of these various efforts, Mattson achieved a certain status in the eyes of both Americans and immigrants. He gained even more authority in various office holding capacities—as justice of the peace at Vasa in 1858, as state immigrant agent and member of the emigration board from 1865 to 1867, and as Minnesota's secretary of state in 1870. Thus, Mattson was no aloof group leader; he attained his place, as had other social leaders, by providing services for immigrants before, during, and after the Civil War.

At the beginning of the conflict in 1861, Mattson decided to recruit a regiment of Scandinavians for the Union Army, and in so doing he openly offered a rationale to his group to support the Northern cause. His public address appeared in the major Swedish paper, *Hemlandet*. As he put it, his audience must work to safeguard the group's newly acquired liberty and equality within the Union because its law was good. It protected foreigners and natives alike. As a result, about one hundred Swedes and Norwegians followed him to Fort Snelling, Minnesota, where Mattson became captain of the only company in the Union made up exclusively of northern Europeans.[57]

It was in his memoirs, originally published *in Swedish* just prior to his death, that Mattson showed more specifically the place and role of Swedes in America. The statement was clearly not intended to rationalize to Anglo-Americans his own or his group's actions from their arrival in the 1850s. He placed an unusual responsibility upon his Swedish-speaking audience. He said that Swedish immigrants, having the privilege of American rights, also had an obligation to improve the life of their countrymen in Europe, that is, to bestow on them the virtues of American security. He opened his description by saying that Swedish immigrants ought to regard their adopted homeland positively, as a place with wealth and religious freedom, and without European class privilege. He condemned Sweden because the working class grievously suffered there under medieval, anachronistic restrictions. Thus, it was up to immigrants in America to write to their cousins in Sweden to teach them about the advantages of a free land. In effect he was telling newcomers to initiate the Americanization of Europe!

Although he was heralding the New World, Mattson was not totally naive to America's social problems. He candidly admitted that the new land did have its faults, too. It was a democracy, but an imperfect one. It had, for example, an inequitable tax structure that favored the wealthy. Also, corporations here exploited their workers, and nativism occasionally rose to cause immigrant discomfort. Nevertheless, comparing overall European and American attributes, he believed the evils of the United States were minor. Scandinavians assimilated quickly because, as Enander often pointed out, from the first Norse explorers and the colonial Swedes down to the latest newcomer, all have upheld the cause of the Revolutionary patriots and the Union army. The Swedes now were rooted here. They were a solid, stable, farming population of property owners, with no radicals, no anarchists, and as he put it, no Clan-na-Gael. They ought to be and were in fact grateful for American citizenship.[58]

Norwegian and Swedish spokesmen, then, were stressing the ideological contrast between a worse life in the Old World and a better life in the New. Anderson, Hasselquist, and Mattson were certainly aware of the hardships encountered by their fellows in Europe as they came to America; they knew of the economic and cultural gaps that their fellow newcomers would have to transcend. In his most sweeping statement in his *Reminiscences,* Mattson listed some of the hardships that caused physical and material suffering. But the new land still offered the Scandinavians more important compensations—spiritual freedom and values that had been denied them in the old country.

* * *

A recent and important work on the Scandinavian immigrant experience merits consideration here because it, too, treats that transformation of northern Europeans who became Americans. *The Divided Heart: Scandinavian Immigrant Experience through Literary Sources* by Dorothy Burton Skardal arrived at a much different conclusion than the one this study has suggested, the dovetailing of the two identities. Skardal primarily felt that the fiction of Scandinavian writers was a more accurate reflection of the sentiments of the masses than the non-fiction works of historians. The historical scholar, she contended, conveys the feeling of exceptional, not ordinary individuals. After a long survey of the creative literature of her group over two generations, she concluded that the psychic adjustment of the immigrants was traumatic. Cultural shock was "central" to the experience of all:

> When [the ordinary] person leaves the culture in which his personality was formed and plunges into a society whose ways are strange to him but where he intends to stay, the confrontation will force him into a painful change.[59]

Certainly, Skardal showed how the Scandinavians' imaginative writing conveys the rich human drama of foreigners attempting to gain a foothold in new surroundings. Writers render the experiences of strangers with great sensitivity. In particular she reviews the classic assessment of immigrant life that was beautifully revealed by the greatest Norwegian American novelist, Ole Rölvaag. His careful drawing of family life suggested that the coming to America was a pathetic tale of homesickness and tragedy. Skardal quoted Rölvaag's own opinion on the experience. "We are strangers to the people we left behind and we are strangers to the people we came to. We gave up the fatherland which was our heritage for a thousand years and we of the first generation can never find another."[60]

Nevertheless, much of Skardal's other literary evidence and, in fact, the absence of additional proof suggests a less upsetting transition than the one Rölvaag so movingly depicted. Skardal never really explains away the built-in bias of immigrant literature toward feelings of stress and tension resulting from cultural differences. The effects of modernization, generational differences, and nostalgia for the Old Country are classic, real themes that immigrant authors use. Still, the universality and representivity of this trauma for all arrivals remains questionable.

Skardal also admitted that the literary evidence suffers from another weakness—its limited time span. It deals almost wholly with later immigrants and not with the life of the early pioneers who settled in America before 1870. And as we have seen, it was that generation of early immigrants who first confronted the issue of their two identities and decided they favored the new one.[61] In Rölvaag's story, Per Hansa's family came to America after 1870 and settled in the Dakotas. But Skardal points out that most of the real immigrants who came to the United States arrived before 1870 and settled in northern Illinois, southern Wisconsin, and southeastern Minnesota, areas with gentler natural environments and denser populations than the area of the Dakotas. So the story is not representative. This region, not the more formidable Great Plains, was the formative core of Scandinavian America.

Finally, virtually all of Skardal's fictional examples that refer to the immigrants' feelings about American culture are also set rather late in time. Her literary illustrations were written in the period between 1895 and 1932, giving the faulty impression that group members did not consider the identity question before then.[62] A weakness, then, in using fiction for historical evidence is that fiction draws upon memory and experience and requires time for reflection and for dwelling upon tension and confict, so it often lacks immediacy and it can be biased.

One must admit that for most northern Europeans coming to the upper Midwest at any time, before or after the 1870s, life was hard. The immigrants sacrificed much in getting settled and obtaining an adequate income for themselves and their families. But ordinary Scandinavian Americans knew of the lives and thoughts of men like Hasselquist, Enander, Anderson, and Nelson because they read *Hemlandet* or heard about its contents, and they attended church or voted in elections. So they understood that their Swedish or Norwegian identity was not necessarily incompatible with their American identity. It is likely that they did not suffer the kind of cultural shock described so movingly by Skardal and the literary figures she discusses.

5

The **JEWS**

Students of history might expect that the Jews, of the six immigrant groups under study here, would be able to work out most easily the difficulty of retaining their ancestral heritage in a new land that was known as an immigrant asylum. Such an acceptable adjustment might come about for them because of their long history of being almost everywhere an oppressed minority. With the Diaspora of ancient times, they had scattered to many countries throughout the gentile world, particularly in Europe. Natives occasionally treated them hospitably, but more often they were treated as pariahs, and they encountered both covert and open discrimination and persecution. Hence, more than any other immigrant group, they could and did look upon America as their ideal sanctuary, a place to alleviate their long suffering without having to surrender their identity.

Almost from their very first arrival in 1654, with a few exceptions, America has offered the Jews considerable religious toleration. It has permitted them to carry on their spiritual life relatively undisturbed. Indeed, the image of America as an asylum has been common in the minds of most European Jews in the nineteenth and twentieth centuries. It was, in their eyes, the "Goldene Medina," the land of milk and honey. Evidence of that romantic vision of an economic and religious haven existed in the ideas and theories that articulate members developed concerning group identity and the retention of ethnic culture. They believed that the maintenance of group identity was possible in America because the national philosophy fostered it.

The best-known Jewish social thinker to hold the view that the tolerance of cultural persistence was integral to the philosophy of the United States was Horace Kallen. His major work, *Cultural Democracy in the United States* (1924), was a reaction to the heavy pressure native-born American gentiles were putting on Jews to assimilate in the early 1920s. In the book, Kallen argued that the true meaning of the nation's pluralistic democracy, is that America should protect the integrity of its ethnic groups. Similar but less well known positions on the durability of Jewish culture were held by other Jewish philosophers, including Israel Friedlander, Judah Magnes, and Louis Brandeis. These men, too, wrote that American principles sanctioned a persistent ethnicity.[1]

Thus, the idea that a person can have a dual group identity, one reference within a larger one, was widely accepted by Jewish intellectual leaders in the early twentieth century. The issue to be discussed here is how close the Jewish masses, the poorer and more provincial immigrants from the ghettoes and shtetls of eastern Europe, were to such thinking. Could those immigrants, the so-called "greenhorns," be sophisticated enough to comprehend the compatibility of being both Jewish and American, and if so, how soon after their arrival did they accept that concept?

To be certain of the existence of such an awareness of a dual identity, one must know who the Jews were in America at the time of their mass immigration in the late 1800s. These people were not a homogeneous collectivity. They had come from all over Europe, from both east and west, and had retained rather distinctive denominational, intellectual, and linguistic differences. Some writers even suggest that these internal divisions, among Jewish Americans at the beginning of the twentieth century, especially those between the Jews who had come from western Europe and those from eastern Europe, caused hostility and tensions that were as severe as the anti-Semitism from gentiles. Hence, we must look more closely at the community at the time of the first major influx of later arrivals in the 1880s.

Most of American Jewry already living in the United States in the third quarter of the century had come from central Europe and had immigrated by the middle of the 1800s. Constituting the overwhelming majority who had entered continuously over the previous two centuries, these western and central Europeans were generally a homogeneous, well-to-do element who had been assimilating rather easily into American life. Their religious philosophy, which readily accepted the majority culture, eased the process. Being liberal Reform Jews, they had followed the modernist tenets of the Haskalah, the Jewish enlightenment of Europe, which urged congregants to conform to and even use many of the gentile forms of worship. By 1880 these assimilationist elements constituted a large portion of the Jewish American community of 250,000. Over the next thirty years, the Reform Jews could confront, with some fear and hostility, the incoming flood of far more conservative eastern European Orthodox

Jews, who numbered between two and three million by World War I.

This chapter will not deal in much detail with that older, German Jewish contingent who were successfully integrating their lives into American society. Rather this section will concentrate on the later-coming masses from eastern Europe, because it was this latter group who appeared less assimilable. They were poorer and more foreign in their ways. They brought with them a distinctive and less familiar folk culture of their own, Yiddish, as well as a differing denomination, Orthodoxy. They observed traditions carried over from their highly segregated eastern European settlements. They therefore seemed to have greater difficulty in making the necessary adjustment. The critical matter to examine here is how these more foreign people could conceive of themselves as both Americans and Jews. It was their own leaders, rising to prominence long before the bulk of the masses came in the early 1900s who provided a resolution rather early on. They referred to a continuing but evolving traditional culture.

One commonly cited denominator that highlights the similarity of Jewish and American cultures was the idea known as Hebraism. This view stressed that some of the ancient religious values found in the Torah and in Talmudic law closely resembled, and thus rein-forced, American humanistic, democratic principles. More signifi-cant, though, was the assertion of some eastern European leaders that the folk culture, Yiddish, was acceptable in America. These spokesmen felt that the adopted nation in fact offered a favorable environment for Yiddish.

Four well-known individuals who were influential and esteemed among ordinary immigrants helped to clarify how the masses could continue their folk tradition as they learned to be Americans. These were the Orthodox pioneer Kasriel Zvi Sarasohn; the educator and social worker Rabbi David Blaustein; the lexicographer Alexander Harkavy; and of course the best-known leader of Yiddish-speaking people, the journalist Abraham Cahan. In the late nineteenth cen-tury these men and others helped to transform the popular ver-nacular from a spoken to a written language. To understand the significance of that change in America and to see how that process made these men ethnic mediators necessitates a short historical re-view of the Yiddish tongue.[2]

* * *

Yiddish first emerged before the year 1000 in southwest Germany as a form of communication of numerous linguistic elements, Hebrew, Aramaic, Greek, Latin, and most especially, Middle High German.

The language soon spread all over eastern Europe in later centuries as the Jewish people migrated there. It did begin, however, to decline in the West in the 1700s, particularly when Reform leaders like Moses Mendelssohn condemned it as a corrupt Germanized tongue. He urged Jews to abandon it and employ instead the language of the gentile majority, retaining Hebrew for religious study. These appeals, however, part of the liberal philosophy of the Haskalah (Jewish enlightenment) made few inroads in the east. The Yiddish tongue continued to flourish in that region, however, not in one uniform pattern of speech but in multiple local dialects in Lithuania, Russian Poland, Austrian Galicia, the Ukraine, Rumania, and elsewhere.

This persistence of Yiddish among the Jewish masses of eastern Europe created a problem for the *maskilim,* the contingent of progressives and supporters of the Haskalah. They had sought to educate the lower classes so that they would give up the folk tongue. But with the stubborn refusal of the masses to do so, some of the maskilim were forced to employ the hated speech themselves. They felt they had no alternative but to use it as a means to achieve their original goal, the moral uplift of the *shtetl* dwellers. Intellectuals, then, in employing a folk tongue that they despised, raised the stature of Yiddish from a simple vernacular to a more refined tongue, and even produced belles-letters. They were transforming it into a vehicle for fine literature.[3] Plays in particular comprised much of the published communication because the maskilim regarded that literary form as the most popular and effective genre to reach and therefore educate the masses. Two well-known Yiddish dramatists in particular were the German Isaac Euchel and the "Father of the Yiddish Theater," Abraham Goldfaden.

Besides disputing among themselves as to whether they should dignify Yiddish, the maskilim encountered an additional problem in their effort to enlighten the shtetlach—how to reach the masses effectively, overcoming their audience's extraordinary regional diversity and geographical dispersion. The Jews lived in many lands, not only in eastern Europe but also, increasingly in the late 1800s, throughout the world, especially in America. Trying to contact a widely dispersed and highly fragmented population certainly compounded the task of educational reformers.

The massive emigration of eastern European Jews to the New World had resulted chiefly from the heightened discrimination of the Austrian and Rumanian authorities, and especially from the Russian authorities after the assassination of Czar Alexander II in 1881. The Russian government imposed harsh anti-Semitic economic and political restrictions, particularly in its repressive May Laws of 1882.

The oppressive conditions and ensuing hostility forced many to flee the resulting violence, pogroms, and property destruction, all of which seemed to be condoned by the officials.

This new exodus came largely to the United States and rose in great numbers in the 1880s. It reached over two hundred thousand by the end of the decade, numbered half a million by the turn of the century, and continued to be high until the start of World War I. Because their poverty limited their movement, and because there were work opportunities in the port cities where they arrived, most of the Jews congregated in America's largest East Coast centers, primarily New York's Lower East Side. Although they were concentrated there in a small area, they were still a highly fragmented community, identifying themselves according to their European origins and continuing to speak their Old World Yiddish dialects— Polish, Lithuanian, Galician, and the others. Then, and for many years thereafter, the New York City area comprised about one half the nation's Jewish population and was America's, in fact the world's, Yiddish capital.[4]

* * *

One Jewish intellectual in particular, Kasriel Sarasohn, accompanied the early Yiddish-speaking immigrants in the 1860s and 1870s and from that time onward tried to forge his heterogeneous eastern European countrymen into a single audience so they could receive his communications. A careful review of his life in the last quarter of the century proves that, until his death in 1905, Sarasohn, like a few other colleagues, worked continually to provide an ideology to facilitate the immigrants' adjustment.

Some recent research has begun to question the conventional view that Orthodox Jews were virtually leaderless and unprepared for life in America before 1900.[5] One historian has shown that even some conservative traditionalists did advocate some assimilation, and Sarasohn clearly was one of them.[6] Although he was not fully successful in reaching many of the Yiddish-speaking masses in the 1880s through his first newspaper, Sarasohn was able later, through his writings in other journals and his various humanitarian efforts, to command the attention of many eastern European newcomers and to inform them that America was indeed their home.

Sarasohn's early life evinced both a desire to improve the life of ordinary Jews and a firm adherence to their traditional faith as an Orthodox believer. Born a rabbi's son in Suwałki, Poland, in 1835, he grew up steeped in conservative religious practice. In 1859 he married the daughter of a famous Talmudic scholar. But his brother-in-law, with whom he was close, was a leading maskil, and since Sarasohn lived in the Vilna district of Lithuania, a region particularly subject to German Jewish thought, he was affected by the progressive ideas of the Haskalah.[7] Favoring the religious life, Sarasohn contemplated a rabbinic vocation, but wanting to travel to broaden his education, he postponed an ecclesiastical career for a mercantile one. He became a merchant and visited the United States three times, in the late 1860s, in 1871, and finally in 1874. By the latter date he had decided to settle in the United States and pursue his original goal, religious study. He was ordained an Orthodox rabbi and soon after served a congregation in Syracuse, New York.

The Orthodox Jewish settlement in New York City in the 1870s was a challenge to Sarasohn. He considered the immigrants of the time to be only minimally equipped for life in America, and he wanted to help them reestablish their religious traditions. He especially hoped to mobilize them into a unit and to help them become involved American citizens. A barrier to that goal of participation, and his people's first major problem, he believed, was their social fragmentation. As noted above, they had settled in small, disparate neighborhoods based on their Old World localities. Some began to organize into formal self-help, mutual aid societies called Chevras or Anshes, which probably are related to the better known *landsmanschaften* of later years.[8]

To reach and mobilize the immigrants, Sarason decided to begin a newspaper. Such an enterprise was not an easy task. Oddly enough, the Jewish masses were really unfamiliar with, and therefore uninterested in, the printed medium. Few had ever read newspapers in Europe, so Sarasohn could not just weld together a fragmented audience, he had to create one.

His several initial efforts to communicate with the arriving immigrants in the 1870s were unsuccessful. The failure may have been due largely to his choice of language. He chose to write his paper in the less familiar, more elitist Germanized Yiddish, known as *daytsmersch*. Finally, after other difficulties, chiefly financial ones, Sarasohn was able to begin a weekly in 1881 and later was more successful with the *Yiddishes Tageblatt* in 1885. This latter organ, known in English as the *Jewish Daily News*, became familiar to the Lower East Side as the world's first Yiddish "daily." It lasted nearly half a century.[9]

Although he was a pioneer journalist, Sarasohn remained basically an Orthodox leader who adamantly asserted the primacy of ancient Talmudic law in everyday Jewish life. Under that philosophy he fought bitterly with left-wing secularists in his later years (close to 1900). Still, this rather conservative journalist was not averse to advocating change, and he even favored a partial integration of Jews into gentile society. He was concerned with the successful, pragmatic adjustment of his readers to American life.

For example, contrary to what one might think would be the standard Orthodox position favoring social isolation, Sarasohn was decidedly opposed to ghettoization. He wanted Jews to be involved in American affairs. Further, while seeking to mobilize and organize newcomers, he was willing initially to accept and even recognize the diffuse nature of the early settlements. He actually encouraged the formation of *landsmanschaften,* which he thought would provide the necessary financial and social security. He did hope, however, that the Jewish masses would build upon these small social bodies later and make a larger, more united community.[10]

Further, Sarasohn's use of the less popular *daytsmersch* was not dogmatic but really flexible. In fact, he tolerated and finally accepted the printing of the more colloquial Yiddish despite the heated opposition of some of his colleagues and even Jewish newsboys who, prejudiced against that folk speech, refused to distribute his paper.[11] He had occasionally allowed Yiddish in advertisements as early as 1882 and had published an article by Alexander Harkavy in the popular immigrant dialect as early as 1886.

As stated, Sarasohn's greatest difficulty was to overcome the public's apathy and even hostility toward reading any periodical, religious or secular in the late 1880s and early 1890s. He did, however, eventually overcome that problem, too.

Available circulation figures to about 1895 bear out the masses' initial aversion to, but later acceptance of, the printed medium. The supporting statistics, however, deserve more analysis because they quite likely underestimate Sarasohn's influence. The *Tageblatt* did grow slowly in its early years, averaging from just under four thousand issues annually soon after it began to about thirteen thousand copies in 1895.[12] This expanding but still small circulation really minimizes the widening impact of Sarasohn's newspaper and his personal esteem on the Lower East Side.

For example, a contemporary observer stated that Sarasohn's newspaper articles of around 1890 were well known and popular. Even though the pieces were more instructive than entertaining, many Orthodox Jews looked forward to them.[13] In addition, the *Tageblatt's* audience was really much larger than statistics suggest because it included "listeners" as well as readers, always more than those who purchased copies. While some ordinary immigrants themselves would refuse to buy the paper, they avidly sought out others who read the articles to them or who could relate the content. Sarasohn's efforts in providing news on the occasional European pogroms were particularly successful in retaining for his paper a large audience at the end of the century.[14]

Hence the low figure of thirteen thousand readers of the *Tageblatt* in 1895 was only a small part of the number who looked up to this journalistic pioneer as their adviser and teacher.[15] At any rate the newspaper's audience did grow very quickly after the mid 1890s, reaching forty to seventy thousand by 1900, double that of the *Jewish Daily Forward*. It probably had the largest circulation of the several New York Yiddish papers in the decade prior to Sarasohn's death in 1905.[16] All this suggests, then, that Sarasohn was a man with a considerable social following at the end of the century, an individual not without enemies or competitors, but certainly one of the most influential Orthodox figures on the Lower East Side.

Since he held that position of power in the community, it is necessary, then, to examine in detail what Sarasohn told his readers specifically about the place of Jews in America. Of course, as one might expect, like the earlier Irish and German American newspaper men, he, too, viewed the United States rather favorably as a desirable place for his people to live. For his oppressed fellow Jews in particular, Sarasohn emphasized that the new land offered economic justice, equitable taxation, and most important, personal safety. And in finding such a sanctuary, Jews also had taken on a responsibility. As other writers told their groups, Sarasohn stated that in return for this freedom, Jews, too, had an obligation to become citizens and to uphold the political system they found. His advice to ex-residents of the shtetl and ghetto—that they should foster some social and political integration—must have sounded unusual coming from a prominent Orthodox Jewish leader. That kind of guidance would have been unthinkable in eastern Europe.

Sarasohn's dual role as an Orthodox Jew and an Americanizer was unconventional and even paradoxical. Yiddish editors were usually far less enthusiastic about life in the United States for ordinary immigrants. Some viewed every day existence in the tenements as difficult and discouraging, and they even occasionally raised the possibility that Jews should return to Europe. The editor of the *Tageblatt* felt differently; he never lost faith that the new land was the appropriate asylum for the group. His opinion, expressed often, was that Jews should above all understand the principles of democratic self-government and plant firm roots in the New World. As he put it:

We always wrote that the greatest crime of our [Yiddish-
speaking immigrant] people was [not] to remain in the
land . . . they must once and for all make up their minds [that]
it is harmful and detrimental in all respects for everyone when
a Jew comes to America with his only goal to make money and
not to live here [and when he comes to America] with the
intent to return to Poland unaware of the freedom in America
and the children's future.[17]

Rather surprisingly, then, Sarasohn sounded like a Reform Jew, despite his Orthodox beliefs, because he urged political Americanization. The Reform Jews had also been urging group members to join
American institutions. Sarasohn and the liberals were in agreement
over a wide area of immigrant guidance.

This similarity of views was also evident in Sarasohn's extensive
philanthropic work. Although he was like the wealthy German Jews,
this eastern European Orthodox rabbi also provided substantial help
for his less fortunate Russian coreligionists. He, too, wanted them to
appear less foreign and to contribute to American society. As a result
of Sarasohn's efforts in the 1890s, amazing as it may seem, he became a respected figure among eastern European Orthodox Jews
and German Reform Jews, two communities that had considerable
social differences. For example, he was widely esteemed as the person chiefly responsible for establishing and fostering the Hebrew
Sheltering House Association in 1889 and the institution that succeeded it, the better-known Hebrew Immigrant Aid Society (HIAS).
These organizations provided shelter and employment for poor Jews,
particularly immigrants. HIAS itself began in 1902, and Sarasohn
was its president at the time of his death in 1905.[18] He also promoted
religious education for children and was prominent in raising money
for the refugee victims of the Kishinev massacre.[19]

The events surrounding Sarasohn's funeral tell as much about
his stature among Orthodox and Reform Jews as do his journalistic
and humanitarian activities. The massive attendance and, more importantly, the identity of those who took part in the ceremony and the
things they said all suggest rather strongly that many Jews viewed
Sarasohn as an ethnic mediator, not only between Orthodox Jewry
and gentile America, but also between the older German and newer
Russian Jewish communities.

The attendance at the patriarch's funeral in mid January, 1905,
was unexpectedly large. The huge crowds of spectators reminded
reporters of the occasion, when masses of Jews came out to see the
funeral of Chief Rabbi Joseph some months before.[20] Fearing the

outbreak of another riot like the one caused by a grief-stricken mob after Chief Rabbi Joseph's death, the police deparment rushed two hundred extra officers to the scene to supplement the one hundred already there. Much to the relief of the authorities, the reinforcements were not necessary because the people were generally peaceful, showing only occasional displays of intense emotion. Officials remained somewhat uneasy, however, because of the extensive "weeping and wailing" of the vast "throng" who surrounded the synagogue where the services were taking place.

In a *New York Post* reporter's condescending description of the scene outside the building, he referred specifically to Sarasohn's stature among the masses:

> In front of the synagogue the struggle of the crowd to get [in] was so fierce that whenever anyone with a permit passed the gate, two policemen and four caretakers had to fall bodily on the poor old men and women who tried to slip in behind. These eager but unwelcome mourners, shaggy in rags and whining for admittance, testified pathetically to the affection with which the poor regarded Sarasohn.[21]

The ensuing procession to the cemetery across the river in Brooklyn was another indication of Sarasohn's exalted place among ordinary immigrants. Twenty cars preceded about two thousand walkers as they traversed the Williamsburg Bridge. Participants paid their last respects in a final honor at the Orthodox leader's grave, which was just to the right of that of the venerated Rabbi Joseph.[22]

The responses of the rest of the American public in general, and of Reform Jews in particular, to Sarasohn's passing still further reflected the patriarch's influence. The publicity given to his passing was nationwide. Over 165 newspapers, largely English-language journals in 118 cities across the country, from Augusta, Maine, to San Diego carried news of his death.[23] And the attendance and statements of several major German Jewish leaders also indicated how well his own people of widely varying persuasions thought of him.

Jacob Schiff and Louis Marshall, for example, well-known Reform Jewish leaders with many Orthodox enemies, were honorary pall bearers.[24] Schiff's eulogy was especially noteworthy. It was an expectedly laudatory and complimentary address, not just for a departed colleague, but for Sarasohn *as an intermediary* between the Reform and Orthodox communities and as a traditional progressive. "Conservative as he was in his own views," Schiff observed, Sarasohn "understood well how to equalize the contrast which generally exists between the old and the new in the [Jewish] community."[25]

The absence of some Jewish leaders at the funeral was just as significant as the presence of others. Certainly the Jewish socialists never considered Sarasohn their interpreter. He and his paper had fought the anticlerical left wing in the 1890s, so neither Abraham Cahan nor any other Jewish radical was at the service.

Still, Reform Jews continued to hold this Orthodox leader in high regard after the ceremonies because of his efforts at Americanization. A month after his death, for example, the Educational Alliance, one of the major liberal group institutions, held a memorial service in his honor.[26] And in an overall assessment, a major Reform newspaper heralded his work. He promoted, it said, a "wholesome American patriotism," and he always had a "friendly attitude toward reasonable assimilation."[27] Other papers emphasized his legacy of Americanization. They referred in particular to the influence of his newspaper, *The Tageblatt*, and his use of Yiddish. Joseph Jacobs, the editor of the *American Hebrew* wrote about the matter on the *Tageblatt*'s twenty-fifth anniversary in 1910:

> For those of our brethren who spoke only Yiddish and arrived too late to acquire facility in English reading [they] might never have been made acquainted with the news of the day in its relation to American feeling and sentiment. It [the Yiddish Press as a whole but Sarasohn in particular] has thus performed a highly important function in helping to Americanize the new arrivals.

Maurice Weidenthal of the *Jewish Independent* was more precise. Since its founding, he said "*The Jewish Daily News* . . . taught the immigrants the ways and manners of our country and inspired them with citizenship ambitions."[28]

In sum, Sarasohn was a pioneer journalist who sought to transform the disparate Jewish immigrants into politically active Americans who would be Orthodox in faith and Yiddish in culture. At about the same time, three other influential interpreters also assumed that task of advocating both tradition and progress. They were David Blaustein, Alexander Harkavy, and Abraham Cahan.

* * *

Blaustein knew the older patriarch, Sarasohn, and had been conspicuous at his funeral. He spoke briefly at the occasion and, like the others, referred to the deceased's mediating influence.[29] The younger speaker was a prominent Jew in his own right; he was superintendent of the Educational Alliance, a group welfare agency, which later honored Sarasohn. Blaustein held that position from 1898 to 1907.

Wealthy German Jewish "barons" had organized the Alliance in 1893 from earlier institutions, the Hebrew Free School Association and others, to facilitate the assimilation of the more alien "Orientals." They wanted these poorer, more foreign-looking people to adjust quickly, so they provided instruction in the English language, American history, civics and government, and industrial education. As the organizers stated at the agency's founding, their goal was "the Americanization of the downtown population."[30] The objective was not entirely unselfish. One historian has suggested that in helping their poor "cousins" to assimilate, the older Jewish leaders also tried to retain social control and hegemony over them.[31] Undoubtedly, a very large number of immigrants attended the Alliance's many classes and programs—several thousands weekly at the turn of the century, and 166,000 in 1904.[32] Thus, it is certain that Blaustein administered an institution that affected many newcomers.

While the formal objectives of the Alliance were totally assimilationist, the effect of the daily programs was mixed, at least in most of the nine years when Blaustein was superintendent. His social philosophy was definitely more conservative than that of the Alliance's founders. He was able to modify institutional policy so that, particularly after 1899, its programs respected religious and even folk traditions, while helping immigrants to adjust to American life.

Blaustein's early life, like Sarasohn's, was itself an amalgam of both old and new. He grew up in the Vilna district of Lithuania in the 1860s and 1870s, not far from Sarasohn's home. He fled to Germany in 1883 to avoid conscription. He embarked for America three years later and, unlike Sarasohn, who was Orthodox, he became a Reform rabbi in 1892, going on to serve a Rhode Island congregation. While there he was chosen to run the Alliance.[33]

This Russian-born liberal Jew coming from the center of European Yiddish culture had a high regard for both past and present. In his philosophy, the Jewish family was the foundation of his people. He thought it essential to maintain the family and its integrity, and to that end he accepted and sought to accommodate both tradition and change.

The major problem for immigrants, he believed, was the generational division between the older foreign-born and their more American, assimilationist offspring. Hence, Blaustein conducted affairs at the Alliance to ensure that young people respected the religion and customs of their parents. At the same time he also felt that the elders should understand their children. In that sense—by his stressing the identity of the old and the new, European and American Jews—group leaders remembered him, too, as a mediator.[34]

The director of the Alliance, then, viewed his institution not just as a place to assimilate the immigrant but, more importantly, as a place for the group to maintain kinship ties. As he himself put it, the program of instruction was definitely two-sided, "progressive in spirit and yet conservative; conservative yet progressive. It speaks to the older generation to consider the future and addresses . . . the rising generation to have regard for the past . . . [it] reconciles the heart of the parent with the heart of the child."[35]

The religious services held at the Alliance were central to Blaustein's theme of reconciliation. He did distinguish *among* the traditions of the incoming masses, esteeming their Hebraic legacy above the Yiddish. Hence, the Alliance offered a program in Hebrew education. Yet Blaustein could not ignore the folk culture because it, too, was within the family tradition. Like the maskilim, he, also, contributed to transforming Yiddish into a form of written communication. He wrote a Yiddish guidebook for the eastern European immigrants. Further, at the Alliance, he subscribed to Yiddish-language periodicals and encouraged visitors to read them. He even held courses there in the folk speech.[36] In general, then, he modified the original assimilationist goals of the Alliance.[37]

Always sensitive to psychological stress in the cultural adjustment of the family, Blaustein was really more of a social worker than an educator. He wanted to assure harmony in kinship relationships even though some change in roles for parents and offspring was bound to occur in the freer, more individualistic environment of the new land. But Americanization did not mean the complete abandonment of the past. Becoming American did "not demand the sacrifice of one's racial character and religious faith" or a total transformation of culture, nor did it mean "the mere acquisition of [English] and the ability to ape the salient customs of the country. To [Blaustein] it meant above all the preservation of the home as an American institution and the gradual uplift of the family as a unit." This process was slower than some would have liked, but it "entailed less sacrifice and a more even distribution of benefits." Cultural change would and should occur, but always within the framework of family stability and continuity. In his view, then, his task at the Alliance was to help elders understand progress and to help their offspring respect tradition.[38]

Both Sarasohn and Blaustein believed that maintaining Yiddish speech would have some stabilizing influence on the immigrants because it would serve as a means of adjustment, that is, it would promote political involvement or keep harmony between the generations. Two other Jewish intermediaries, Alexander Harkavy and Abraham Cahan, thought that maintaining Yiddish was essential to the adjustment of the Jewish masses. Harkavy was an ethnic lexicographer who, through his use of Yiddish and his demonstration of its English equivalents, revealed the similarity of both Jewish and American cultures. He deliberately employed the folk tongue in many of his writings in order to help readers understand their adopted nation's history and values.

*   *   *

Like Sarasohn and Blaustein, Harkavy was well acquainted early with the new immigrants. He settled in the same Yiddish region as his colleagues, leaving his native village, Novogrudok, for Vilna, where he grew up. He fled Lithuania in 1882 at the age of 19, like most of the Jewish masses, because of Russian persecution. He therefore arrived in the New World under conditions similar to those of other Jews. His first days in America were difficult because he suffered economically. He was unskilled, and he obtained only occasional employment, working at temporary, odd jobs in a factory, on the docks, and in a bakery. His earnings were minimal, generally two to five dollars per week.[39]

He was, however, exceptional at the time of his arrival in America because he was already a published writer and an accomplished linguist. He had written several articles in Yiddish, Hebrew, and Russian, and he was well acquainted with German and English.[40] He returned to Europe briefly, probably because of financial hardship, but he reemigrated once again, this time moving between Canada and the United States until he finally settled in New York in 1891.[41]

Harkavy was also a person of exceptional idealism. He originally supported the Am Olam movement, which viewed America as an agricultural haven for Jews. But he changed his philosophical goals in the late 1880s, deciding to help the masses through his writing. He sought to transmit "a knowledge of English and an understanding of America to the new arrivals."[42] Few writers were more successful at this kind of instruction than Harkavy. He produced numerous articles, tracts, and books on English and America for the masses, some of which became well known. Probably the most influential was one of his earliest, *The English Teacher* (1891). It was believed to have had an unparalleled impact on the 250,000 pupils who used it.[43]

Another manual, only slightly less popular, was the *English Let-*

ter Writer (1892), which instructed its readers not only on how to write the most personal correspondence, such as love letters, but also on how to become American citizens.[44] Representative titles of his many other works were *The English Alphabet* (1892); *Columbus: Discoverer of America* (1892); *Washington: A Biography* (1892); *The Complete English-Yiddish Dictionary* (1893), which appeared in many editions; and *The Constitution of the United States* (1897).[45] It was in these Yiddish-language publications that Harkavy functioned as an ethnic mediator. He did far more than provide his readers with the tools they needed for assimilation—English-language instruction and Yiddish translations of the adopted nation's founding documents. He, like Sarasohn, portrayed America as the highly desirable destination for shtetl refugees.

A typical example of his dual educational and acculturative goals was the theme of his Yiddish-language biography of America's founding father, George Washington. Harkavy not only recounted for his immigrant audience the virtuous life and grand achievements of the Father of the Country, traits with which American Gentiles were familiar. He also rendered the national hero in terms that would endear him to eastern European Jews in particular.

He actually made Washington into a *Yiddish* American figure. He did so in two ways. First, he used numerous indigenous Yiddish terms and phrases, nearly untranslatable references that only emigrants from the shtetl could understand. Some of the words really had no English equivalents. In addition, Harkavy conceived of the great American in qualities with which pious Jews could identify. For example, Harkavy's account of the nation's first president was not just a tale of a military leader and statesman. He transformed the man into a folk figure with a large mass following. Harkavy stressed that Washington had freed his people from British oppression, a liberation particularly meaningful to the poor immigrant refugees who had only recently escaped Russian persecution. The analogy of Washington to Moses leading his people out of bondage, while not cited openly, still was so strongly implied and so striking that it could not be missed. In fact, Harkavy did connect the great American to the Jewish masses, stating explicitly that by relieving America of British tyranny, Washington freed not only his generation but also all later immigrants fleeing oppression, including Russian Jews: "Washington should be thanked not only by the underprivileged and oppressed people of the United States but also by today's oppressed people of [many] lands who are present in this republic he built. It is a haven where people can attain freedom and the good life."[46]

In showing the close similarities between the guiding philosophies of Americans and Jews, Harkavy, like so many others, still respected his group's Old World traditions. He retained a deep attachment for his own Russian Jewish roots, and he hoped his readers would do the same. Although he was not much involved in the structured Jewish community and its institutions, as were Sarasohn and Blaustein, he still encouraged the formation of *landsmanschaften* and wrote a lengthy nostalgic account of his return to his native Russian village in 1921.[47] He cherished the folklore of the Jews, marveling in particular at the creativity within Yiddish tradition. He published two more Yiddish dictionaries toward the latter part of his life—a word lexicon in the mid 1920s and a folk dictionary in the mid 1930s.[48]

It is certain that Harkavy regarded himself as an interpreter of both the past and present, for he openly and proudly identified himself as a marginal figure. In his autobiography he announced to his readers that, although he was essentially a Hebrew, he was also half Russian and half American.[49]

Harkavy conveyed his ideas about bonding Jewish tradition to an American identity not only in his writings but also in person. It was probably his wide reputation as an interpreter that persuaded the Hebrew Immigrant Aid Society to use him as a translator and counselor for the Jewish immigrants at Ellis Island. They also employed him as a legal advisor for the foreigners at that major immigrant reception center from 1904 to 1909. He undoubtedly developed as a man of influence among the Jewish masses because these years were near the flood tide of Hebrew immigration.[50] Harkavy described how his clients could adjust to the new environment at this time.

> The Russian Jew is expected to adapt himself to American
> conditions of freedom and democracy, but America does not
> demand of him that he forget the ties that bind him to his
> mother country, no matter how cruel she may have been or
> that he forget his race no matter how prosperous or how
> wretched that race may have become.[51]

Thus, in addition to speaking to his audience in his many popular publications, Harkavy also stood literally at the nation's gate and told immigrants what pluralism meant in the new land.

*   *   *

Of all the Jewish leaders of the immigrant generation and beyond, the one who had the largest audience and therefore unquestionably made the greatest impression was Abraham Cahan, the longtime editor of the group's most popular newspaper, the *Jewish Daily Forward*. Although he had little personal charisma, he certainly had influence. He knew and understood the Yiddish-speaking masses intimately, like no other.[52] One biographer assessed Cahan's impact on his group in these terms, "Of all his contemporaries who had a hand in the settling and the cultural pattern of the Jewish community in this country, Abraham Cahan was easily the most outstanding."[53]

Cahan was a person of supreme social influence, but he was not precisely the same sort of intermediary as Sarasohn, Blaustein, and Harkavy. He attained his position somewhat later than they, after the arrival of the first eastern Europeans. Although he had held the post for a short time before the turn of the century, he did not assume editorship of the *Forward* permanently until 1903. Still, he retained notions of cultural continuity and change that were similar to those of his predecessors, especially Harkavy. He, too, consciously promoted Yiddish and helped to substantially remake Yiddish culture in America. All the while, he urged his audience to conform to certain majority values.

Cahan had come to the United States with the first interpreters in the early 1880s, but some time passed before he assumed his powerful mediating role. In the two decades after his arrival he found that in order to appeal effectively to the Jewish masses he would have to moderate his original radical philosophy. Upon his arrival in the United States, he found he would have to put off the socialist revolution that he had expected to work toward immediately. This rightward shift involved him in growing disagreements with his left-wing colleagues. He insisted that before the new collective commonwealth could be achieved, the masses' psychological and material security would have to be built up. Only on such a basis could they truly advance in the gentile world.

It was Cahan's background and early goals that enabled him to become intimately acquainted with the Orthodox immigrants and ultimately to become an effective interpreter. He, like Sarasohn, Blaustein, and Harkavy, grew up in the Yiddish area of northeastern Russian Poland and Lithuania, and he reached the United States in 1882. Even before he left, he was already comfortable in and involved with cultures other than his own. He was no close adherent to the Jewish faith early in life, and he became drawn to Russian language and literature. He particularly admired those literary realists who felt an empathy for the masses. They were to be his models in America. He left Russia, like Harkavy, as a firm supporter of the Am Olam movement, and he learned English quickly soon after he came to

America. He arrived as a committed radical, a crusading socialist who sought to enlist the masses in the cause.

Cahan decided to evangelize his audience by lecturing and writing in Yiddish. Like Sarasohn he, too, decided to begin a newspaper and, after some failure, he finally helped start a working-class journal, the *Arbeiterzeitung,* to carry the revolutionary message in 1890. It became popular in the same decade, partly because Cahan decided to write it in the immigrants' own language.[54]

The young Jewish journalist encountered difficulty with the paper, however, because critics and even some of his own associates objected to his growing subordination of socialist ideology in the publication. Cahan had already begun to drift away from the revolutionary ideology. He did not reject socialism fully, but he increasingly placed the proletarian commonwealth much further in the future. His primary goal was to help his working-class readers meet more immediate problems of life and work in America.[55] His involvement in 1897 with another left-wing paper, *The Jewish Daily Forward,* resulted in the same controversy. Some socialist critics condemned Cahan for advising readers on their immediate needs when they felt he should have been persuading them to accept socialism. As a result of these objections, Cahan left the paper to write for the gentile, English-language press. He did return to the *Forward* in 1903, when the owners finally agreed to give him a freer, more powerful hand in running the paper.[56] It was at this point, when Cahan was editor, that the *Forward's* circulation boomed and he became the leading immigrant interpreter. The paper's mounting circulation figures indicate Cahan's emerging dominance among his Yiddish constituents—19,500 copies in 1900 to 52,000 in 1905, to 122,500 in 1911. It was then the largest immigrant newspaper in America and likely the largest in the world.[57]

Two factors account for Cahan's journalistic success: his sensitive and intimate knowledge of the lives and needs of his readers, and his uncanny ability of communicating with them in their own American Yiddish dialect. He had been well acquainted for some time with the three cultures his readers had known, Jewish, Russian, and American. After growing up in the first two, he quickly mastered the third, writing articles in English and teaching the language to countrymen as early as the 1880s.[58] The experience he had prior to 1903 as an English-language journalist further enlightened him to American values. This immersion in three cultures gave Cahan an acute understanding of immigrant life in America and a special ability to know how his audience could improve their minds and develop their intellectual abilities[59] They would do so, according to Cahan, with him as their teacher. This "education" would be accomplished by accepting and adopting some of the traits of the host society.

Above all he believed that, for their own good, the immigrants must learn English. Not to do so would be a severe handicap to their progress. Furthermore, they should adopt American standards of decorum, etiquette, and hygiene and should participate as informed citizens in civic and political affairs. A famous and representative appeal to his audience was a 1909 editorial directed to parents. It asked, "Has Your Child a Handkerchief in His Pocket?" Cahan also wrote a history of the United States in Yiddish and, like Harkavy, he frequently translated and explicated the American Constitution and the Declaration of Independence for his readers. Finally, he wrote numerous biographies of famous Americans, and he often serialized the best English-language classics.[60]

Yet, while Americanizing his readers in this manner, in keeping with the goals of the other traditional progressives, Cahan did not advocate that his audience abandon Yiddish culture.[61] On the contrary, he did openly what Sarasohn did indirectly—raise the status of Yiddish as a written medium. In fact, he helped build an appreciation of the folk culture that the immigrants were creating in America. Cahan's papers really became outlets for, and promoters of, the many good but little-known *American* Yiddish authors, Peretz, Aleichem, Rosenfeld, Asch, and others.[62] In short, Cahan helped to construct a communal self-confidence, a kind of reference point for immigrants, to help them to become involved in American society.

Recently, the function of "ethnic intermediary," which Cahan and the others performed, has begun to attract the attention of a few Jewish American historians. One examination of the small Jewish community in Atlanta, Georgia, identified that settlement's ethnic interpreter as a Reform rabbi of the second, not the first, immigrant generation. The historians concluded that he found himself in a "disagreeable dilemma." Living in an atmosphere more anti-Semitic than that of larger northern cities, both outsiders and his own group members attacked him for being in league with others. Hence the historians concluded, the rabbi's mediating function was tension-filled and uncomfortable.[63]

The dilemma they describe may have been real, but it was probably exceptional rather than broadly representative. The authors do not cite any eastern European as a group mediator in Atlanta, and by asserting that community leadership in the larger settlements in Northern cities was highly diffused among Orthodox, Socialist and Zionist factions, they imply that no recent arrival after the 1880s could play that role.[64] Certainly my account of four New York leaders suggests the contrary. Admittedly the two most powerful figures, Sarasohn and Cahan, were not dominant over the entire Lower East Side. The area was indeed a very complex and divided community. But this multibiographical account has shown that the recently arrived foreigner could be an effective intermediary, if only for certain segments of the settlement. This kind of leader could give immigrants a rather sophisticated understanding of the compatibility of their American and ethnic identities without themselves laboring under "disagreeable dilemmas".

6

The **POLES**

In a number of ways the coming to America of Polish immigrants resembled that of most of the Jews. Both groups departed under similar circumstances (many Jews left Polish-speaking regions); both groups moved largely after 1880, the number of immigrants increasing yearly until World War I; they favored America's urban and industrial centers; and both groups sought unskilled employment. Finally, both the Jews and the Poles left lands ruled by others; neither had their own independent state.

Yet while their migration was similar in many respects, the two peoples did differ in culture, so the Poles' experience of Americanization, the acquisition of an American loyalty and identity, was unlike that of the Jews. In fact, the experience for these Slavs was distinctive compared to all other immigrant groups. The two salient features of the Poles that most affected their identity as Americans were their fervent adherence to Roman Catholicism and their growing ethno-nationalist enthusiasm to establish an independent Polish homeland. They worked for both church and homeland not only as Poles but also as Americans. It was some early group leaders, active before 1910, who showed the masses how to achieve those goals and thus to acquire and live with their dual identities.

The complete process of obtaining such a binational bond was not a rapid one for this eastern European group; it was probably a slower transformation than for all other immigrants. Most Polish immigrants, especially those who had lived in Russia and Austria, gained a sense of being Polish in America from a traumatic disagreement among themselves over the ownership and control of their Catholic parishes.[1] Thus, until that conflict reached a climax with the emergence of Independent Polish Catholicism in the 1890s, few individuals, leaders or followers, really thought much about obtaining an American identity. It was only in the last decade of the century that Polish nationalists were able to effectively persuade their own clerics to be more consciously Polish even if they remained Catholic. In doing so, they were also able to sensitize the rank and file to their ties to the United States.

Surprisingly, it was long before 1890 that Polish nationalists began stressing that immigrants could best contribute to the resurrection of the homeland and Polish independence, *as loyal Americans*. Such a dual bond was not just possible, it was desirable. In an argument similar to that of the Irish leaders, they asserted that working for national independence and Polish freedom was an effort not in conflict with any American principles. In fact, Polish nationalists essentially claimed that American and Polish identities were *uniquely* compatible when compared to all other immigrant groups. Thaddeus Kościuszko, the Polish national hero, was also a Polish American hero. He fought for Polish freedom in Europe after he fought for American freedom in America. Other foreigners like the Germans, the Jews, and the Irish, also participated in the Revolution, including Von Steuben, Salomon, and some others, but no other Europeans could claim these to be *homeland* heroes as well. In fact, the Poles had two, if one includes a cavalryman who died in the War for Independence, Casimir Pułaski.

The 1890s was an appropriate time for Polish immigrant leaders to educate their people about this distinctive tying of American and Polish identities. The Polish immigrant community, the *Polonia*, was by then large and mature enough to publicize and dramatize the heroes' stories at centennial observations of the historic attempts to free Poland in the 1790s. In 1910 the group held its grandest spectacle, tying their traditional and adopted loyalties at the unveiling of the Kościuszko and Pułaski statues in the nation's capital, Washington, D.C.

Historians of Polish America have recently paid some attention to the question of their subjects' marginal condition, the impact of trying to be both Polish and American. Their general conclusion is that the tension did exist, but that it really did not become a cause for concern in the community until the advent of World War I or just after, when Poland came into existence. When the issue did appear, most immigrants had difficulty confronting that duality. According to the historians, the group suffered from this marginality because they were uncertain and undecided as to whether they could be both Poles and Americans.

The best-known general survey of the group asserts that while Polish immigrants could easily support the American drive to free Poland in the world conflict in 1914, the rebirth of their homeland, its reality and existence, caused "hesitancy, changing moods, and mixed patriotic emotions. . . . Previously, Polish immigrants had been oriented only towards Poland and had ignored American local problems and needs." Thus, in a rather dramatic and upsetting shift, the Polonia now committed itself to becoming a loyal American community.[2]

The standard work on the political behavior of Polish immigrants assumes a similar position, pointing out the dilemma of clashing loyalties in the interwar period. Until World War I, the author concludes, Polish immigrants avoided an active role in politics because most considered themselves to be foreign visitors, not Americans. In his view, only with the onset of the conflict did they begin to change their old national ties, especially as they raised their American-born children. Still, the shift to becoming American, which actually took place in the early 1920s, was uncomfortable: "Polish Americans [after World War I] were suspended in a state of maximum tension between a Polish past they had largely rejected and an American future they were not yet able to grasp fully." The author concluded that the Polonia as a whole suffered from this duality, "a divided self image was fundamental to Polish American life."[3]

The most recent detailed history of Polish Catholicism in Chicago cites the same uncertainty among the people of the same time. The conventional notion of the relationship of the American Polonia to the homeland was to view it as the fourth part of Poland, the other three having been divided by the partitioning empires in the eighteenth century. Thus, whereas Polish Americans had once considered themselves as simply an extension of the nation in Europe, now with the rise of their European state, they found it difficult, according to the writer, to be both Polish and American:

> Despite her remarkable overall contribution to both the Polish and American governments during the war, [the Chicago Polonia] was to enter the 1920's still somewhat ambivalent about the entire complex of questions and issues dealing with Americanization and Polonization. This uncertainty and hesitancy must have been widespread.[4]

It is very possible that both the establishment of the Polish state on the one hand, and the oppressive climate of cultural conformity the United States in the early 1920s on the other, put pressure on Polish Americans to review their status as foreigners in America. All immigrant institutions encountered a pervasive intolerance in those times, and Europeans in the New World might well have had to reassess their ethnic and national ties in a difficult and sometimes painful reexamination.

Still, the implied assumptions of all these works—that the pre-war immigrant community regarded itself as only Polish and not Polish American; that the issue of dual bonds did not occur to members until the end of World War I or after; and that when the issue did come up, it caused widespread confusion—all seem unjustified. In previous research, I found that the Polish Americans' role during the worldwide conflict, their motivations and goals, suggested that they felt a dual commitment as Americans and Poles, but that they may have favored America. Certainly, from the very beginning of the war in 1914, the community acted as a conscious part of the United States.[5]

For example, after Sarajevo, Polish nationalism was the primary goal of most Polish immigrants in America. When Wilson initially declared American neutrality at the outbreak of hostilities, the major Polish American federation of fraternal associations followed his lead. A Polish National Council did function in America, but only as an agency to raise funds for war relief, not for military aid until 1916. Also, the one Polish organization which did train and equip recruits from America for the Polish Army was being raised in France prior to America's entrance in the war and did not fare well. About five times as many Polish Americans entered the American military service as the 38,000 who joined General Haller's Polish army in Paris. In fact, American Secretary of War Baker specifically cited the fervent Polish American support of the American, not the European, armed services. And the group's contribution in money matched its generosity in manpower. Polish Americans purchased an impressive quarter of a billion dollars overall in Liberty Bonds. On the other hand, the support for strictly Polish causes, a Polish American Army and the Ten Million Dollar Fund, lagged.

A final indication of Polish Americans' commitment to their adopted nation in the conflict can be seen in the statements made by the leading Polish nationalist when he was traveling through the country. Ignace Paderewski was the American group's most popular symbol of the Polish national movement in the early days of World War I. On the several occasions when he traveled through the immigrant colonies to raise money and support for the Polish cause, he insisted that his listeners should restore the homeland as part of their responsibility as loyal Americans, not as Poles.

Although Paderewski was a European, he was well acquainted with the United States and its people by the time the year began. He was a close student of our society, and he had been here numerous times between 1891 and 1909 on concert tours. He even became something of an American himself, purchasing a ranch in California in 1913.

As far back as 1893 he told his audience that he loved the new land because "hundreds of thousands of Poles are living [in America] freely and enjoying liberty." Thus, for his own sake and that of his transplanted countrymen, he welcomed and respected their selection of a new home.[6]

Until America joined the fray in 1917, Paderewski apparently approved of the Polish American role in providing relief rather than military assistance. When the United States finally did enter, he openly dealt with the issue of divided allegiance with his audience. His fullest comment on the subject came at the height of his influence among Polish Americans at the group's major congress during the war, in Detroit in late August 1918. There, before one of the largest indoor assemblies of Polish immigrants, he addressed one thousand representatives of nearly every Polish American faction. He told his listeners that the process of becoming American need not trouble them. The potential dilemma of dual identities was not a problem for the Poles. As he put it, "The Poles in America do not need any Americanization. It is superfluous to explain to them the ideals of America," because they already know them. He concluded by saying what Polish Americans should and could do in the struggle to restore homeland independence, "Bądźie więc najlepszymi Amerikanami ale pomożcie Polonia (Be therefore the best Americans, but also help the Polish community)."[7] When this personal symbol of Polish nationalism told Polish Americans that there was no conflict between the two identities, he certainly must have convinced many.

Paderewski's speeches, however, were still more the reflection than the source of the Polish immigrants' feelings about being American. The transformation involved in their becoming a part of their adopted community began long before Maestro Paderewski spoke to his countrymen during World War I. Their Americanization had originated in their devotion to Roman Catholicism.

The piety of the Polish masses and their attachment to the Universal Faith is legendary. This Slavic people accepted Roman Catholicism in the early Middle Ages, and although their history does show instances of conversion, no other religious movement, certainly not the Reformation, ever made such an impact on Poland. By the nineteenth century, when many departed for America, the peasants carried with them a deep devotion to their traditional religion. Unlike that of the Czechs and the Italians, the coming of the Poles to the New World did not weaken their affiliation to the church or cause any "leakage." Most of these Slavs retained their religious traditions and assiduously reestablished their place of worship in America. That earnest reconstruction of parish life was in itself a way of encouraging the Americanization process. Despite the emergence of Independent Polish Catholicism in the early 1890s, Polish Americans continuously accepted the authority of the *American* Catholic hierarchy rather than that of their homeland. Although they may not have realized the transfer consciously, living as Polish Catholics in America really meant living as Americans, not as transplanted European congregants. All their religious leaders, the exalted non-Polish elite as well as their own Polish clergy, followed the rules and dictates of the American hierarchy, who themselves adhered to American law and nationality. Thus, the religious devotion and piety of Polish immigrants really facilitated their becoming American.

* * *

The lives and work of the two leaders who were the most important to their group illustrate that new, emerging bond. These men, like others we have seen, were as influential with their people in the early years as they were representative of them. The figures are layman Peter Kiołbassa and the Reverend Vincent Barzynski, both of Chicago.

Chicago, of course, is and was the nation's premier Polish American city, and it held its preeminence from the founding of the very first parish in the mid 1860s. Certain urban centers do play a paramount role in shaping the entire immigrant community, and such was the case with this Midwest metropolis. In terms of numbers, Chicago attracted by far the most Poles—about four hundred thousand by 1920. Other Polish centers that had become important by the turn of the century were Buffalo, Milwaukee, and Cleveland.[8]

Peter Kiołbassa was the man responsible for establishing and maintaining the city's first Polish parish, St. Stanislaus Kostka. He was clearly the most influential Polish Catholic layman of his time, a man of considerable ethnic power who functioned as his group's leading interpreter of the American community.[9] His life is well known. He came with his family to America in 1855 from his native Polish Silesia as a teenager and went to the Poles' pioneer American settlement, Panna Maria, Texas. His military service in the Civil War brought him to Chicago, where he became friends with the major settler, Anton Schermann. By 1864 the small Polish colony elected Kiołbassa president of its parish society. Three years later he became a policeman, and thereafter, he began his long political career. By the

early 1870s he had advanced to desk sergeant and had become the
undisputed Polish lay leader. It was Kiołbassa who convinced Chicago's bishop to bring in the Polish religious order, the Resurrec-
tionists, to staff the new group church, over the objections of a smaller, more nationalist Polish minority.

Kiołbassa gained more power thereafter both in Polonia and in
mainstream America. As leader of the Polish Republicans in those
years, he served in the customs house and was elected to the state
legislature. Simultaneously, he was an officer of one of the group's
major religious societies, the Polish Roman Catholic Union. The
height of his influence came in the early 1890s, when he headed that
fraternal association, and despite his switching parties, he was elected city treasurer of Chicago. Thereafter, others came along and challenged his position until his death in 1905, but his role as ethnic
community leader always remained preeminent.

Kiołbassa, then, certainly had a substantial immigrant following. In the 1870s he, like others in the next decade, established a
notary office, which made him a kind of community guide and teacher. Many newcomers sought his personal advice and information on
adjustment. As one biographer described the newly-opened office on
the northwest side, it was the "headquarters to which Polish people
[came] for advice and help when in all sorts of trouble because
[Kiołbassa] was ready to listen and take pains in their behalf."[10]

Kiołbassa's life appears to have had three important goals, all of
which were aimed at rooting his countrymen in the new land. First
was his intention to provide settlers with a viable, secure parish life, a
Polish Catholic environment with their own ethnic pastor to hear
their confessions and minister to their other spiritual needs. Despite
the opposition of some more nationalistic countrymen, he always
worked under the authority of the non-Polish bishop to establish the
city's mother Polish church, St. Stanislaus, in the late 1860s and
early 1870s.

A second objective was to assure political representation for the
Poles and encourage their participation in civic issues. He committed
himself to a career in local politics by the early 1870s and rose within
the Republican party. But he switched to the Democratic party later,
when he decided the Grand Old Party was too elitist, too nativistic,
and too anti-immigrant. That particular transfer was critical because
it made Kiołbassa urge his followers, for their own welfare, to become
politically involved and hence to function as American citizens.

An example of this Chicagoan's thinking, his potent effect on the
American Polonia, and his Americanist instruction, was his ap-

pearance at a large rally in Buffalo, the Poles' second city, during the 1892 presidential campaign. There at the height of his power, having just been elected city treasurer of Chicago the previous year with strong community support, he went to western New York to promote Grover Cleveland and the Democratic ticket. The local newspaper viewed the gathering at the Poles' major hall as a "Great Polish Demonstration," a "monster" rally where three thousand had jammed into the twenty-two-hundred-seat facility.[11] With Kiołbassa's introduction, the crowd broke into loud cheers as the honored speaker held them "enthralled" by his endorsement of the Democratic platform. Under numerous signs reading "Four More Years of Grover," and others supporting tariff reform, Kiołbassa told his audience in Polish that they should be grateful to live in a land that was unlike Europe in that the nobility and the rich could not oppress them. The effect of his appeal was to instill greater American patriotism.

He implored his listeners to be good American citizens, to support education, and to be wary of anti-Polish who, in fact, were anti-American Republican plutocrats. As a reporter relayed Kiołbassa's speech,

'In this land of the free, there were no nobles or counts to
oppose [us] as in Europe. All were free and equal under the
law . . .' he counseled them not to be led away by fellows
[Republicans] coming around wearing high hats and kid gloves
ostensibly to teach [Poles] manners and politics.[12]

Combining this class appeal with democracy and Americanism was a political strategy that he used in Chicago to good effect as well. That city's Poles strongly endorsed Democratic candidates between 1893 and 1907. About 70 percent of their vote went to that party in that period, while only about 26 percent voted for the Republicans.[13]

A third objective in Kiołbassa's treatment of followers was to contrast the civil advantages his constituents held as *Americans* in the New World with the mistreatment of less fortunate countrymen in the Old, much like the Irish leaders noted earlier. That theme was obvious in another Polish gathering in Chicago in 1892, the same year that Kiołbassa spoke on the same subject in Buffalo. The meeting was called to protest the abuse and oppression of their European relatives by the Russians. Before a throng of two thousand Chicagoans, Kiołbassa drew the inevitable comparison:

We are gathered here as a free people in a free country who
desire to see the preservation and promulgation of democracy.

It is not wrong for us to express our opinion and protest against something which is undemocratic. We as free born citizens have a right to ask for assistance and moral support of *other* free citizens of this country.[14]

Clearly Polish Americans *are* Americans.

* * *

A close acquaintance of "Honest Pete" (as Kiołbassa was called) who had a similar impact on the Polonia then was the major cleric of that time, the Reverend Vincent Barzynski. As with Kiołbassa, Barzynski was well known; in fact, all historians agree that in influence he towered over all Polish American clergy in that century. Hence, it is unnecessary to review his life at length here. Nevertheless, although they have said that he was born in Poland in 1838, that he joined the Resurrectionist Order just before he went to Texas in 1866, that he appeared in Chicago in 1874 and that his great struggle was with lay nationalists and Independent Polish Catholicism in the 1890s, these writers have neglected his Americanizing influence on parishioners.[15] Barzynski himself was probably unaware that he was helping people to assimilate, but nevertheless, such was the outcome of his efforts to have immigrants retain their faith. More than Kiołbassa, Barzynski was dedicated to keeping his people as churchgoing Roman Catholics who had to abide by the authority of their American, not European, bishop.

Barzynski's loyalty to his non-Polish diocesan superiors in Chicago, first Bishop Foley and later Bishop Feehan, was unwavering. Not only did ordinary church government structure demand that allegiance, but so did a formal contract. Barzynski's own authority over his flock depended in part on the immigrants' acceptance of and obedience to diocesan authority. His Resurrectionist Order had made a pact with the bishop in 1871 that in return for the Order's administration of all Polish parishes in Chicago for 99 years, it would hand over the church deeds to the diocese.[16] Hence, to protect that contract over his long, quarter-century tenure at the city's mother Polish church, St. Stanislaus, Barzynski continually defended the bishop's authority down to 1899. From the Third Convention of the Polish Roman Catholic Union in 1875 to the 1896 Buffalo Polish Congress, he and his supporters forced through resolutions reaffirming their obedience to American, not European, hierarchical authority.[17] Thus, by assuring dutiful and durable Polish parishes, clerics were encouraging permanent residency for parishioners. This in turn promoted, even if subtly, an American consciousness.[18]

Barzynski recognized hierarchical control, but he was not simply a pale reflection of his non-Polish superior. Like Kiołbassa, he considered himself a Pole and as time passed, he became more openly a group nationalist despite his continued feud with the Polish National Alliance. So, like Kiołbassa, he considered himself to be an American in the 1890s.

One must remember that Barzynski did display his Polish identity early; he was a refugee of the abortive 1863 Polish Insurrection in Russia, and he participated in numerous nationalist observances in the 1890s. For example, he chaired a meeting of all his parish societies in 1891, and they jointly resolved to help Polish victims of the Prussian atrocities of that year. The formal statement they issued undoubtedly expressed the patriarch's own gratitude to America: "The lips of our countrymen in our native land are sealed by bayonets but here in America we are at liberty to speak."[19] Also, the Resurrectionist newspaper, *Dziennik Chicagoski,* which was inaugurated and guided by Barzynski himself, maintained a decidedly patriotic editorial policy. It advocated loyalty to the adopted country, and it "prided itself on its firm allegiance to the Constitution . . . and asked its readers to become politically active in the democratic process."[20]

The mid 1890s were indeed difficult years for the American Polonia; it was a time when the clash between nationalist and clerical forces spread throughout the group's settlements. Ethnic nationalism was winning new converts, and many religious leaders believed it was undermining the faith. To Barzynski's dismay, Independent Polish parishes began to spring up in many colonies in Chicago, Buffalo, Cleveland, Omaha, and the coal-mining districts of eastern Pennsylvania. Later, the dissent intensified when many of these schismatic parishes coalesced to form a competing Polish body, the National Catholic Church.

Thus, Polish ethnic consciousness rose to new heights in that decade. It was further promoted by particular commemorative events, including the elaborate Polish Day at the Columbian Exposition of 1892 and the centennial observances here and abroad recalling the abortive efforts of Kościuszko and the final Partition of the Polish state. But despite this increased ethnic awareness and an envigorated Polish nationalism within the American Polonia, the sentiment always remained tied to an American identity.

Even at its inception in America, Polish nationalism was depicted by its proponents as being consonant with the adopted nation's basic principles. Kościuszko's heroic role in *both* the Polish and American revolutions provided much of the basis for tying common national goals. His name had always bound the two peoples. For example, one of the earliest Polish political associations arose in Philadelphia in 1871 and encouraged civic involvement, and it was called the Kościuszko Club. One of its goals was clearly assimilationist—the club sought to prepare new members for American citizenship.[21] A short time later it sponsored the appearance of clothed human models of Kościuszko and the other Polish and American martyr, Casimir Pułaski, at the great American Centennial Exposition in Philadelphia in 1876. Pułaski died at the Battle of Savannah in the American Revolution in 1780.[22] Furthermore, just after the Polish National Alliance (PNA) was created by the merging of several local bodies in 1880, a Chicago meeting inaugurated a longtime PNA policy of urging members to become American citizens.[23]

While early nationalists fostered an American loyalty among ethnic group members, occasionally the clerical camp—Kiołbassa, Barzynski, and other clerics—did the very same thing, especially in the 1890s. The centennial celebration of the Polish Constitution, which was held in Chicago in 1893 was a rare joint effort. Thus, both the PRCU (Polish Roman Catholic Union) and the PNA came together to commemorate the occasion, although they were normally hostile groups. This event included decorating the group's major residential district with Polish and American flags and holding an elaborate parade.

The scene suggested a rare harmony by showing the two identities of Polonia. The procession, which had moved along the streets, entered the Central Music Hall, which was decorated with pictures of the revered triumvirate, Kościuszko, Pułaski, and Washington. With some pride a speaker, Zbigniew Brodowski, expressed the sentiment many felt. With their revered liberal Constitution of 1791, it was the European Poles who first brought the principle of freedom to the Old World, and it was freedom "for which both Washington and Kościuszko fought."[24]

Another popular sign of the immigrant community's dual Polish and American identity was an attempt to realize a permanent memorial to Thaddeus Kościuszko in Chicago. Barzynski and Kiołbassa played conspicuous roles in the attempt. They did not originate the idea; apparently a group of clerics and nationalists introduced the project of erecting a statue to the "Hero of Two Continents" as early as 1886. But when a committee to raise funds was organized in 1892, Barzynski apparently approved.[25] His newspaper, Dziennik Chicagoski, immediately assumed patronage of the project. It urged its readers to "show how much we love and respect the . . . man who in addition to defending his own native country was instrumental in the success of the American forces."[26] Within a few days the paper announced the financial contribution of Kiołbassa and reported that he and Barzynski had been appointed as fund officials.[27]

State promoters had hoped that the memorial would be unveiled by the time of the Columbian Exposition in 1893, especially on the day designated as Polish Day. But the monies were insufficient, and social leaders like Kiołbassa and Midowicz had to content themselves with a more subdued remembrance, a parade in which about 25,000 Poles participated, many coming from outside Chicago. By then Kiołbassa was regarded as the Polonia's first citizen, and he served in the procession as chief marshal. In the float behind him rode statues of Kościuszko and Washington dressed in colonial uniforms. At a rally following the spectacle, a PNA leader reminded his listeners of the close ideological tie between the Declaration of Independence and the Polish Constitution, a link that would be described often.[28]

The drive for funds for the memorial lagged after the Fair; only $4,000 to $6,000 of the $25,000 needed had been raised by 1895. But the *Dziennik Chicagoski* stated that lag was due not to any lack of group interest but to the press of other financial obligations on readers in the midst of hard times, the Polish Day expenses, and the drain of other Kościuszko celebrations, especially the exposition of Lwów in 1894.[29] The campaign continued and was completed in 1904.

*   *   *

The transition that Barzynski and the Chicago Polonia experienced in the 1890s from a primarily defensive concern for cultural survival to a more assertive involvement as nationalists and Americans took place in other group settlements as well. The experience of Michael Kruszka, a formative figure in Milwaukee, suggests a similar personal and communal transformation.

The Milwaukee Polonia grew more slowly than the one in Chicago, and it began to level off sooner, but it did begin about the same time, in the mid 1860s. It differed from its larger southern neighbor in that it had no truly longterm dominant intermediary like Kiołbassa. Michael Kruszka, the closest candidate, did not appear on the scene until the early 1880s. Like so many Wisconsin Poles, he grew up in Prussian Poland, in the Poznań district in the 1860s. He became a writer, was jailed for opposing the Kulturkampf of the 1870s, and arrived in New York in 1880. He settled in Milwaukee three years later.[30]

He turned almost immediately to writing and politics, starting a number of newspapers and becoming widely known among the Milwaukee Poles. Because of the strong group support he received, he was elected to the Wisconsin Assembly by 1890. Two years later, another Polish following raised him to a seat in the state senate. He was then at the pinnacle of his influence and was regarded as the state's foremost Polish representative and spokesman.[31]

This popular Pole spoke often about his constituents' identity. The comments he made before the 1890s concerning the relationship of his groups' Polish, Catholic, and American ties were similar to the position taken by Kiołbassa and Barzynski. In his newspaper writings he conveyed the same gratitude for American democracy and freedom, and he, like them, stressed the need to adhere to Catholicism, and the need to win political independence in Poland. At first, Kruszka put more emphasis on the religious endeavor, but by the end of the century, he had clearly shifted the priority of his goals for the group, subordinating Catholic affiliation to political work for an independent Poland.

For example, in 1885, in the opening issue of his briefly successful paper, *Krytyka,* he reminded his audience that they ought to glory in what their American asylum provided for them—freedom to cultivate their group heritage. As he said, "in the New World we have the best opportunity to exist as Poles . . . to feel Polish . . . to establish Polish societies, to have Polish priests, to pray in Polish . . . [and on the whole to practice our] nationality and religion."[32] He stressed the role of the Polish press, saying that the immigrants' newspapers ought not to be simply partisan—they should be the objective educator of the masses.

Continuing that theme three years later in his more successful journal, *Kuryer Polski,* he dealt with the question of his readers' religious identity. The conflict between the nationalists in the PNA and the religionists in the PRCU over group goals had intensified to such a point that Kruszka had to offer "Nasze Stanowszka" [Our Position] on the controversy. He stated that newspapers ought to be independent and nonpartisan, but he appeared more sympathetic to the religious interpretation of Polish American identity. Thus, like Kiołbassa and Barzynski, he tied Poles to Catholicism. Poles, he said, must respect the American church by rooting fraternal associations partially but undeniably in Catholic principles. He asserted that it was the church in America that contributed "most to the mainstream of customs and the Polish language," and he was certain that most Polish immigrants held that view.[33] It was in the new decade that Kruszka began to alter his position and emphasize the immigrants' national and political obligations more than their religious ones.

In the early 1890s he started to stress the political responsibility of newspapers to preserve European culture. For example, with his election to the Wisconsin state legislature in 1890 and 1892, he sought through statute to have the Polish language taught in the Milwaukee schools. Although he failed at this, he succeeded in gaining other legal recognition of his group's ethnic heritage. He forced through legislation authorizing the translation of local municipal statutes in Polish.[34] Just a year or so later, by 1895, political matters concerning the homeland began to supersede cultural matters in the priorities he listed for his audience. He, along with many others, began insisting that the paramount objective for the group was to achieve the political resurrection of the native land.

A further indication of Kruszka's more nationalist leanings in the later 1890s was his outright condemnation of Polish American clerics. He became very dissatisfied over the insufficiently Polish character of their parochial school curriculum. In 1896, condemning religious instruction as inferior to secular education, he set up the Polish Education Society to try to force public schools to offer his people's language on a par with German. Because of his increasing criticism of both Polish Catholic and American church authorities, by the turn of the century legal suits resulted, and ultimately the church placed *Kuryer* under interdict.[35]

Kruszka's clearest statement of the new political role he felt Polish immigrants ought to play was in an 1895 editorial appropriately titled "Patriotysm i Americanizm." In a surprisingly sophisticated comparison with other groups, he said that Poles throughout the world had a particular mission. Some newcomers to America, like Swedes, Germans, and Italians, he commented, would indeed assimilate easily, because they had left independent states to carry on their traditions. But American Poles did not have that luxury. His readers' task, since they were wealthier, more intelligent, and freer than "their countrymen across the sea," was to work hard in solving the Polish question in Europe.[36]

So the goals Kruszka laid out for his readers were clear—the Polish Americans were to help reestablish the homeland, using American institutions to do so. The journalist leader said nothing about returning to Europe once Poland was restored; his audience, he assumed, was an integral part of American society.

Kruszka spoke directly about the issue of Polish Americans' dual identity sometime around World War I. Regrettably, it is impossible to determine precisely when he made his comments on the matter, because they appeared as random reflections in his papers after his death in 1918.

He stated unequivocally that his people did have such a multiple bond and that he himself and, by implication, all Polish immigrants could and should be comfortable with both Old and New World allegiances. He put it directly, "Jestem gorącym Polakiem a zarazem Amerykaninem. I nie widzę aby jedno drugiem w czemkolwiek się sprzewiało." (I am an enthusiastic Pole and at the same time a [loyal] American. I do not see where one contradicts the other).[37]

* * *

In addition to Chicago and Milwaukee, another Polish center where leaders dealt with the issue of combining traditional and adopted affiliations was Buffalo, New York. This western terminus of the Erie Canal network had been another magnet for incoming Poles rather early, in the late 1860s. The group numbered only a few hundred when their first parish was founded in 1873, but, drawn by the growing industrial needs of this burgeoning city, more Poles arrived there in the later years of the century. Shortly after 1880 the Polish population was about ten thousand, and by 1915 it was well over one hundred thousand. Buffalo was second only to Chicago in the number of Polish Americans for most of that time.[38]

From outward appearances, the Buffalo Polonia did not seem to have gone through as traumatic a transition in the 1890s as did the other colonies, although Independent Polish Catholicism had been present there, too. Sufficient evidence on group leadership is available on two preeminent lay figures, the early settler Jacob Rożan and the later, younger physician, Dr. Francis Fronczak. Both were active in local politics and, although Rozan was more an openly partisan Democrat, in the 1890s both presided over a Polish community that was determined to work for its interests as American as well as Polish citizens. Thus, these individuals, too, as both leaders and followers, appeared to have a clear idea of their ethnic and adopted loyalties.

Rożan was the older of the two commanding figures, and he assumed his position as immigrant leader before Fronczak. Born in Poznan in 1866, he came to Buffalo two years later and grew up at the mother Polish parish. By 1890, he had become an eminent ethnic personality. He was a teacher at St. Stanislaus, the mother church, a director of a musical society, the grand secretary of the city's major Polish fraternal association, a bank official, and the president of the Polish Democratic Club. His constituents, largely Polish, also rewarded him in the early 1890s with an elective position as supervisor of the Fifth Ward.[39] It was in that position of community influence that Rożan (as noted, p. 112) mobilized the 1892 rally of countrymen to hear Peter Kiołbassa of Chicago speak on why Polish Americans ought to be better Democrats than Republicans.

During the next year, Rożan reassembled his constituents at a similar gathering that once again clarified the group's dual ethnic and adopted ties. This rally was actually a protest meeting. It was a response to a Protestant minister's condemnation of the area's Polish immigrants. He had charged them with being poor, illiterate clods who had no principles and who sold their franchise to the Democrats. Under Rożan's direction these immigrants gathered once again at the parish hall to affirm their role in politics as *both* American and Polish. In their concluding resolutions the protesters said they considered the minister's remarks insulting to a "patriotic" people whose "paramount duty of allegiance to their adopted country is ever proclaimed and manifested."[40]

The outbreak of the Spanish American War in 1898 a few years later tested the immigrants' American patriotism and gave them a chance to express it. By that time Rożan shared community authority with Francis Fronczak, but he did not yield it fully to him. Fronczak undoubtedly dominated the local Polonia for most of his life—from the turn of the century to his death in the 1950s.[41]

Fronczak rose to leadership by a number of solid accomplishments before 1900. By then, he was in his mid twenties and he had become the first Polish American to receive an M.D. degree from the local medical school in 1897, and he won a law degree two years later. In the meantime he maintained a close rapport with his countrymen, operating a thriving medical practice for Poles, serving as the first group state legislator, and becoming Buffalo's public health commissioner, a post he held for nearly half a century.

Fronczak saw the outbreak of the war with Spain as an excellent opportunity to demonstrate Polish American devotion to the Stars and Stripes. He encouraged, and might have initiated, a group demonstration to express that sentiment. The local Polish American newspapers had advocated holding a community rally to counter discriminatory charges of Polish apathy to the national cause. The young physician led the meeting, and his specific goal was to recruit his constituents for the conflict. Although he was disappointed that the American authorities had rejected his hopes for a separate ethnic military unit, he must have been pleased at the spirit of his people at the meeting, which was held in April, 1898. Community attendance at the patriotic rally was overwhelming. About twenty-five hundred Poles packed the parish hall, and hundreds more were waiting outside.[42]

Fronczak used the opportunity of the meeting advantageously. He gave the principal address, reminding his listeners that the fight for Cuban freedom, the goal of the inhabitants there was no different for Poles than for non-Poles. All could and ought to join the American army to work for their common goal, freedom. As he put it succinctly, "Poles loyal to Poland must be loyal to America."[43]

Specific incidents at the rally indicated the overwhelming support that Fronczak had. A man raised a vocal objection to the sense of the meeting. He charged that Poles were *not* obliged to serve the American nation, because the latter abused and exploited the immigrants. The man's outcry, however, provoked the crowd's ire, "a thousand angry hisses," according to one observer. At the conclusion of the ceremonies the eagerness to enlist was so great that when the authorities asked recruits to step forward, hundreds rushed up. Panic ensued and the stage collapsed.[44]

In later years, too, before World War I, Fronczak, like so many other immigrant leaders, referred occasionally to his group's dual identity. In a Buffalo Historical Society talk in 1905, he told his audience that his community would like to be regarded as "good Poles and good Americans."[45] And in an interview in Lwów in 1910 in the Austrian Polish sector, the doctor insisted that Poles could be even *more* Polish in America than in Europe because of the high regard for freedom in the New World. People can, for example, sing "with equal fervor . . . American National Hymn as well as Boże Coś Polske (God Bless Poland)"[46]

Long before World War I, then, in three of the group's major colonies, Chicago, Milwaukee, and Buffalo, prominent Polish individuals offered a solution to that potential dilemma of deciding which of two nations to identify with. They told their followers that they could be both Polish and American because the two nations' goals were either the same or mutually reinforcing. In particular, this eastern European people felt a unique personal relationship to the new land because of the symbolism of the group's two Revolutionary heroes, Kościuszko and Pułaski. Not only did individual colonies continually memorialize these men, but Polish nationalists also saw that these military leaders were recognized by Americans as well. The outcome of their efforts came at a major event in 1910. It was in that year that the statues of these soldiers were unveiled in the nation's capital at the well-known Polish American Congress. Polonia must have felt more comfortable as a result of the ceremony because both Americans and Poles honored these individuals as truly Polish American heroes.[47]

7

The **ITALIANS**

While the Jews and Poles seemed to accept and even welcome "Americanization"—that is having dual ethnic and American identities—the Italians appeared to be much more resistant. They were a huge contingent of over five million who left Italy, chiefly the southern regions, for America up to World War I. According to some observers, they arrived in the United States ill-equipped to go through such a consciousness-raising process, or apathetic about it, and in fact, many did not do so.[1] This apparent rejection of a New World identity is suggested by the high number of transient arrivals. Many of the Italians were sojourners; more than half returned to Italy in the two decades before 1914.

Religion played a role in the migration of Italians, but not in the same way as with the Jews and the Poles. Religious oppression was evident, but the chief reason for movement was material need, economic security, not the desire to escape a foreign faith. Although nearly all were Roman Catholic, religion did not provide a cultural anchor in the New World for the Italians as it had for the Irish and the Poles. For the latter two groups, parishes offered spiritual continuity and a cooperative base for meeting the vagaries of life, but the institution of the Universal Church was no such comfort to the Italian peasant-migrant.

In both Europe and America these southern Europeans were very suspicious about and cynical toward their priests and the hiearachy of the church. Moderately anticlerical, the Italian peasants traditionally viewed their clergy as an arm of the exploitative upper class. In addition to this historic suspicion of religious officials, these southern Europeans found the American church run by unsympathetic Irish leaders, so Catholicism in the United States did not offer Italians the means for adjustment to America that it provided for others. These and other cultural characteristics (such as close family ties, coolness to outsiders, and intense regional loyalty among the peasantry, the contadini) tended to inhibit people from becoming groupwide, dominant Italian immigrant leaders. All of these features tended to produce a highly fragmented alien society in America in the early immigrant years.

Still, despite this apparently impermanent, transitory, and highly atomized social existence in America, certain individuals emerged in the pioneer stages of Italian settlement to transcend those immigrant localisms and win widespread support from the alien masses. Contemporary group sources often referred to these figures by the term "pappa," or "pappa della colonia." Curiously, Italian American historians have neglected these important social leaders as a type, so the full cultural significance of the leaders must await future study. But without question these pappas commanded considerable esteem among the ordinary immigrants. They did not get the same kind of respect given to the ordinary *prominenti* in Europe and America; rather, they held a place of warmth and affection. These were individuals to whom immigrants could go for help with their many personal needs.

Many of these beloved advisors and guides were "padrones" or "padrone-bankers;" their position emerged with the arrival of the southern Italians. The padrones were evident in nearly every Italian concentration, especially in the larger colonies of New York, Philadelphia, and Chicago, as well as in the smaller settlements in upper New York state, Connecticut, New Jersey, and elsewhere. They were ubiquitous in the early years before the turn of the century because they had the important function of mobilizing and recruiting immigrant workers. Although this kind of labor system existed in other immigrant settlements, chiefly in communities of southern and eastern Europeans in the United States, it was identified as chiefly Italian.

These labor agents provided an important cultural and economic function in the early immigrant period. They occupied the critical marginal position of mediator between their own people in Little Italy and the American society outside. The role of the padrone was attractive because it could be very lucrative for an aggresssive group member. As recruiter and supplier of labor, he commanded significant influence within and without the colony. A few of the more successful padrones, those who won the trust and affection of their clients, became known throughout the immigrant and native communities as pappas.

Over the years the role of the padrone has attracted considerable attention from both popular and scholarly writers. Beginning in the late 1800s, with the discovery of this type of labor recruitment, jour-

nalists and reformers generally condemned the system for exploiting
the aliens. They charged that the aliens were totally dependent on
padrones, who were usually venal. More recent interpreters, however, have been somewhat less critical of the system. These modern
observers have stressed that the padrones helped the immigrants to
gain appropriate employment.[2] Oddly, despite all the extended debate over whether these middlemen exploited or helped their clients,
few have seriously studied and assessed the padrone's impact on the
immigrants' cultural adjustment. Virtually nothing has been suggested to explain how these labor agents or "pappas" affected the
newcomers' acquisition of an American consciousness.

Recent study of Italian immigration has veered in another direction. It has focused on how the families' values changed during the
migration experience.[3] This matter of studying cultural change at
the personal level within the context of kin is certainly a worthwhile
and valuable exercise. But such an examination of the shifting family
ties tends to overlook the important developmental phases of southern Italian migration to America. It seems to have omitted that early
period of colony-building when numbers of men came to live in the
Little Italies *without* close kin. The padrone system at that time was
in part a substitute for the absent kinship networks. Until 1900, and
even for a few years afterward, most Italian men in America lived
without wives and children and depended on padrones and pappas.[4]
It was the pappas who influenced immigrant thought on being
American. Examples of these individuals in the pioneer days were
Luigi Fugazi of New York, Paolo Russo of New Haven, the Pelletieris
of Utica, Thomas Marnell of Syracuse, and Charles C. Baldi of Philadelphia. These immigrant leaders were first padrones and later pappas, that is colony-wide social leaders.

*   *   *

To understand how these men acquired their mediating role in their
cities requires a brief and careful review of the origins and function of
the padrone in the New World. Certainly much confusion, my-
thology, and misunderstanding surround this institution because
critics blamed the padrones for much anti-Italian sentiment. The
role began in Europe with the Italian peasants' need for personal
protection in the middle of the nineteenth century. Italian society
then was definitely stratified, consisting generally of four classes: the
wealthy dons or *prominenti,* who were large estate owners or landed
gentry; the *artigiani,* the skilled craftsmen or businessmen; the
contadini, the small landholding peasants—the class of most Italian
emigrants; and the *giornalieri,* the poorest day laborers.[5] In this

milieu the masses not only lived very circumscribed lives in their villages, but they looked upon outsiders with great suspicion. The distrust of those outside the family and community extended in particular to the state and its officers.

In order to deal with officials in governmental affairs, the peasants had to look to intermediaries or interpreters. The situation in Sicily was especially critical because brigandage was common, heightening the need for security. Small landholders had to rely on power brokers and patrons to protect them and to provide the necessary link between the Sicilian village and the larger society.[6] In other areas of southern Italy, especially in Campania, a group of individuals existed who closely resembled the padrones in America—they were the *corporali*. These individuals were labor recruiters who mobilized agricultural work gangs, providing them with food and handling their compensation on a personal, face-to-face arrangement.[7] As a whole, in many areas of Italy the tradition of personal service was widespread among the contadini. One particular person commonly dealt with strangers as a representative of the peasants.

When the Italian vanguard came to America just prior to 1880, they had few intellectual and economic resources, so it was understandable that they would seek out and designate particular ethnic middlemen to provide them with employment. It is difficult to generalize about the padrones' operations and their arrangements with their clients, because they did not function in the same way in every case. But certain realities do belie the popular belief that the naive immigrant was totally subservient to the calculating padrone. For example, the padrones did not pay for their clients' transportation, nor did they enter into any labor contracts with arriving Italians. Nevertheless, located chiefly in New York and other East Coast cities, these intermediaries normally had networks of subagents who resided in their home province, district, or village in the Old World. These subagents probably encouraged fellow countrymen to use the services of the padrones from their home village or province when they arrived in America. Thus, it is likely that before 1900 a large number of immigrants associated with labor agents from their home in southern Italy.[8]

One cannot overestimate the importance of the padrone in the economic and social life of the early Italian immigrants when they arrived in the 1890s. One historian has judged that about two-thirds of the Italians in the largest colony in America, New York City, went through the system before 1905.[9] The padrone/bankers supplied their clients with more than work; in the early years they also provided housing in saloons or boardinghouses. They wrote letters for newcomers, provided steamship tickets, and acted as notaries and even marriage brokers. In other words, they functioned as immigrant advisers on a wide range of economic, social, and even political issues. Padrones may well have exploited their countrymen, but the latter continued to consult them for help up to the early 1900s.[10]

In examining the adjustment of Italians to America, any study must refer to their major colony in the New World, New York City. From 1890 to 1910 that city was the destination and home of about seven times as many group members as its nearest competitor, Philadelphia.[11] The New York City Italians congregated in and around the city's well-known Five Points district on the Lower East Side. There, for example, in 1913, over one hundred thousand Italians lived. Since New York was overwhelmingly the group's largest American settlement, it follows that their most influential and representative pappa should arise there, too. His name was Luigi Fugazi.

* * *

It was due to Fugazi's personality, his personal philosophy, and the many personal services he offered to the immigrants, that he was able to help them realize their new identity. In so doing he became the most highly esteemed pappa in America. He had a profound understanding of his clientele. He knew their need for employment and their strong desire for security. As their most respected pappa, he helped them to form numerous cooperative mutual aid societies, and in so doing, he brought a higher consciousness among them, making them aware that they were both Italian and American. To learn how he accomplished this extension of their identity requires a brief account of his life and activities in the colony.

Oddly, Fugazi was not from the region of most of the incoming Italians. He was born and raised in Liguria (in the Piedmont region of northern Italy) in the 1840s and 1850s. Still, his many considerable military exploits in the service of Garibaldi and King Victor Emmanuel gave him great status in the eyes of the New York Italians, despite the fact that many had little nationalist feeling in the late 1800s.[12] Almost immediately after his arrival in New York in 1869 he became the city's leading padrone/banker. He set up the colony's largest steamship agency, a labor office, and a money depository on the Lower East Side.[13] Of particular importance was his intermediary role with Anglo-Americans as the leading Italian American notary public. Many recent arrivals frequented his Bleeker Street home in the 1870s because they sought him out for help and advice in their dealings with the government. Hence his residence was not just a business address but also a lively social center. Newly arrived south-

ern Italians turned to him often as their legal adviser when he nota-
rized their mortgages, licenses, wills, and other formal documents.[14]

Fugazi, then, dominated the Italian Mulberry Bend area like no
other figure before 1900, gaining more influence from the high esteem that residents had for him than from the raw power he exerted
over them. A perceptive newspaper reporter observed in a long interview in 1896 that Fugazi was "the best authority on 'Little
Italy' . . . because he is the most honored and trusted among the
masses . . . he is without a doubt the one man [to] whom all Italians . . . look for advice and aid in personal affairs."[15]

Besides providing individual assistance and being influential on
a personal level, Fugazi also had an impact on the immigrants' organizations. He guided the formation of many of their mutual aid societies. Such bodies were not totally new in America; they had some
precedent in the Old World, especially among the artigiani. Whatever
their origins, these societies certainly grew rapidly in America. As
one authority estimated their proliferation in New York, the number
of societies grew from 15 in 1885 to 78 in 1890, to 200 in 1900, to
2,000 in 1910.[16] The first, consisting of mostly northern Italians,
were named for national figures like Columbus, Verdi, or Garibaldi,
while most of the later ones had titles of southern Italian geographic
localities.

Although Fugazi himself did not originate these self-help associations, he did provide members with administrative advice and
direction. He wanted the associations to provide economic security
and cultural continuity and to serve as an instrument to help them
adjust to and become involved in American society. Fugazi did initiate a leading mutual aid society called La Fraterna which became the
city's largest Italian organization by 1900; it then had about two
thousand members.[17]

The *New York Times* interview of May 31, 1896, revealed this
pappa's reason for promoting this organization, the 50 others over
which he "presided," and the 130 more for which he was the "leading
spirit."[18] Fugazi believed that these bodies were necessary not simply
to provide economic insurance in time of accident, illness, or death,
but also to raise members' consciousness as both Italians and Americans. Even if these social organizations were based on narrow provincial locality, he thought they ought also to participate in the celebration of Italian national occasions.[19] He sought to overcome the
intense localism of these mutual aid bodies by incorporating them
into a larger, New York City federation. The first article of the bylaws
of Fugazi's Italian Federation stated that this citywide organization
existed "to add to the [prestige] of the Italian name, to not scatter the

vital force of the colony and provide in all ways for the solemn formation of the Italians living in New York and environs."[20]

In his efforts to promote an Italian identity, Fugazi tried to make the newcomers realize that they were also Americans. He accomplished this not through any direct effort like what Harkavy did for the Jews or what Bishop Hughes did for the Irish, e.g., making direct references to the similar values of their groups. Rather, Fugazi encouraged the immigrants to regard the United States simply as their political and physical home. The mutual aid societies sought to encourage members to anchor and enhance their existence in America as involved citizens.[21]

Of course, Fugazi retained his own personal, political interests, but he did not force them on his followers. In urging arrivals to become active citizens in elections and to hold political office and the like, he deliberately avoided directing clients to his own partisan goals, or even suggesting which ones they should pursue. Fugazi was a Democrat, and he continually sought Tammany Hall recognition for his Italian group. Yet he eschewed involving others in party battles and strategies. Essentially, he advocated immigrant involvement in civic affairs but left to the aliens the specific choices of which parties and factions to join. Hence, because he urged involvement without giving specific direction, immigrants often regarded Fugazi as being above faction. Such an apparently Olympian position seemed to enhance and secure his role as an internal community leader.[22]

* * *

Probably no other New York Italian had greater influence than Fugazi in instructing immigrants about their dual identities. However, two other local padrones played a similar role by promoting an event that further encouraged Italians to think of themselves as Americans. One was Antonio Maggio, better known as James March, a political leader also from the Lower East Side, and the other was a newspaper publisher, Carlo Barsotti. The observance they staged was a spectacle honoring the great Italian discoverer Christopher Columbus. This celebration, held in New York in 1892, the four hundredth anniversary of the landing, and others like it in almost every other Italian American colony in and after the 1890s, helped all Italians to realize the stake they had in the New World.

The effect of the celebration was undoubtedly assimilationist, as was the Polish one held two years later to pay homage to Kościuszko, the "hero of two continents." The 1890s, then, seemed to have shown the Italians that their two identities were mutually reinforcing. Carlo

Barsotti, a member of the prominenti, had the inspiration for commemorating the great explorer's accomplishment. Although Barsotti
was not popular among the immigrant masses, the ex-contadini still
enthusiastically supported the event. The practice of honoring Columbus quickly became widespread throughout the country around
the turn of the century.

Since the celebrations had such broad appeal, it would be wise to
examine how they originated and spread throughout the many Little
Italies. The New York observance was clearly the brainchild of Barsotti. He had been a padrone himself, but he certainly was no pappa.
He did not have Fugazi's extensive following, although he soon
wielded considerable power in the colony. He had come to New York
from Pisa in northern Italy as a member of an upper-class family in
1870. Soon after arriving, he became a padrone/banker and a landlord, and he soon prospered. The immigrants of the time would have
said that he had "made America." In 1880 he founded the group's
largest newspaper in America, *Il Progresso Italo-Americano* and by
the end of the decade he used his newspaper to promote his pet
project, the commemoration of the quadricentennial of the discovery
of America. He set up a national committee consisting chiefly of
other prominenti to raise the necessary funds for a statue, which he
commissioned. The plan was to erect a monument at a prominent
city intersection that was to be, and in fact did become, the focal point
for annual celebrations.[23]

From 1892 down to the First World War, Italian colonies all over
the country held mass rallies and parades honoring the explorer as
both an American and a group hero, an individual in whose bold deed
they could anchor their dual identity. It was at the New York affairs
that both Fugazi and James March were prominent and where the
most elaborate memorial occasions took place.[24] For example, at the
tenth observance in 1909, just after the state legislature had approved a bill to make Columbus Day an official state holiday, thirty
thousand Italian Americans marched to the statue in Columbus Circle.[25] Actually the Empire State by that date was one of at least six
which had officially memorialized the famous Italian seamen. New
Jersey was probably the first to do so in 1902, followed by Colorado in
1905, California in 1909, and over thirty others by 1921.[26] A recent
historian has indicated the meaning of the 1892 celebration to the
San Francisco Italians. It was their sentiment that they should resolve their dual identity.

> [the] pageantry, color and excitement which these . . . Italian
> people brought to this gathering reflected not only their

attempt to recapture a way of life they had left behind in Italy, but to blend the old world traditions with the newness and individuality of their life in America.[27]

Columbus was used as a symbol throughout Italian America in the immigrant years.

*   *   *

The colony pappas existed in many other settlements in America and had a similar influence on the immigrants, although their precise impact did vary with each kind of colony and with the personalities of the individual leaders. The impact of Pappa Paolo Russo of New Haven resembled that of Fugazi. For example, he, too, considered social organizations and mutual aid societies to be facilitators of Americanization. Russo was as popular and formative a figure as his New York counterpart. Yet New Haven was a smaller city with a smaller Little Italy, and Russo appears to have had a more commanding influence on the people of his colony.

Russo's origins and his early popularity may have made that powerful impact possible. Unlike Fugazi, he was a southerner, as were most of the incoming Italians. His native town was Viggiano in the province of Basilicata. He arrived in New York in 1869, and settled in the southern Connecticut city in 1872 at the age of 13. Almost immediately after his coming to New Haven, the immigrants came to know and like him. His initial popularity was the result not of military exploits, as in Fugazi's case, but of a captivating musical ability. Many in the colony admired Russo's performances as a street violinist.[28]

In the 1880s the Italian community grew quickly. It numbered about a hundred in 1880 and reached five thousand by 1890.[29] Russo built on his early popular appeal by starting a grocery and bank which quickly became the major social center of the small immigrant community by 1882. Thus, it was in that decade of growth that Russo emerged not only as the major internal leader but as a pappa, the well-liked link with the non-Italian world. The musician-turned-businessman also became a policeman and court interpreter. His role in dealing with the authorities resembled Fugazi's role as a notary.

Russo added to his stature in the colony by being largely responsible for the city's major Italian Catholic parish and by founding the community's foreign-language newspaper. He was, in short, the one whom "many Italians had recourse to . . . for counsel and advice" and the one who "had the pleasure of saving them from a major disgrace [with the law]."[30]

He became known throughout the colony by the endearing term "papa affectuoso." His completing the Yale Law School in 1893 as the university's first Italian American graduate, and his becoming the city's first foreign-born attorney, added to his esteem in both the immigrant and native American societies.[31]

Like Fugazi, Russo regrettably left no extensive statement of his philosophy as an ethnic mediator, but his actions do indicate objectives similar to those of Fugazi. His support of fraternal associations was an example of his drive to at once mobilize and Americanize his followers. He established the first and probably largest Italian mutual aid society in the state, La Fratellanza, in 1884. Like his New York City counterpart, he wanted to facilitate immigrants' political involvement and promote American citizenship. Russo once briefly told a newspaper reporter his dual aim in rallying his constituents: "We organized mainly for the purpose of promoting our [American] citizenship and preserving at the same time a love for the [Italian] motherland."[32]

As regards balance then, Russo was as much of an assimilationist as a cultural pluralist. Additional evidence of his interest in helping Italian immigrants adjust to the new land include his efforts in teaching English to foreign adults in an evening class in the town of New Haven and his earnest support of Columbus Day as a symbol of Italian American identity. He and the members of his society, La Fratellanza, were conspicuous at the New Haven observance in October, 1892. Appropriately, it was Russo who unveiled the cornerstone of the statue of Columbus before a huge crowd assembled in Wooster Square, in the center of Little Italy, on October 2.[33]

Thus, by the end of the century this leading Connecticut pappa had illuminated the two identities of his people and had shown their compatibility. The immigrants had responded with considerable support.

*   *   *

In addition to New York City and southern Connecticut, another region of concentrated Italian American settlement included the several small upstate cities in New York. In this district, which also produced its own immigrant pappas, the flurry of late-nineteenth-century railroad construction along the water-level route to the west pulled in groups or gangs of unskilled immigrant workers. Italian colonies appeared in Syracuse and Utica, where there emerged the padrone/bankers Thomas Marnell and the Pelletieri brothers.

Sources clearly indicate that Marnell was personally responsible for the rapid growth of the Little Italy in Syracuse before the end of the century. Only three Italian families lived there in 1880, but the area had seven hundred Italian individuals in 1890 and about eight thousand by 1900.[34] Marnell had come to the upstate community in 1882 as a twenty-four-year-old gang foreman for the New York Central, which was then constructing its main line through the area. By the early 1890s this padrone had become the group's major internal leader. He had settled down permanently and had begun the group's familiar immigrant institutions, a bank, a saloon, a construction business, and an Italian Catholic parish. Like the other ethnic mediators elsewhere, he also initiated several religious and Italian national societies whose members displayed their membership by donning elaborate uniforms. In fact, he remained the city's leading fraternalist between 1886 and 1906, the last two decades of his life.[35]

Particularly notable, too, was his role as intermediary between the city government and the incoming foreigners; this role completed the pattern of the other pappas. Like Fugazi and Russo, he, too, served as translator for the police and the courts, and he continued in this function for the last fourteen years of his life. The position enabled him to get newcomers "out of [legal] trouble." And, like his ethnic colleagues in New York City and Connecticut, Marnell played important roles both within and without his colony. He was at once a traditionalist and an assimilationist. He was an active member of the Elks (a mainstream fraternal association) and, at the same time, a determined advocate of preserving the use of the Italian language. He accepted Americanization, but he believed it should be accomplished through the construction, not the elimination, of immigrant institutions.[36]

Salvatore and Elias Pelletieri of Utica held the same opinion. The older brother, Elias, was the founder of the Italian community there; he set up the group's leading social center, a saloon/boardinghouse, soon after he arrived in the early 1870s. The site served as the typical immigrant labor exchange. The standard group history refers to the Pelletieri home as "the first stopping place of nearly all the early Italian settlers."[37]

Elias grew wealthy over the next forty years from his services as padrone/banker, but it was his brother Salvatore who became the more influential city pappa. Interestingly, like Russo, his initial popularity rested on his musical talent. He, too, was known and admired by everyone as a colorful street musician. Later, in the 1880s, he built on that reputation to become a successful businessman and local politician.[38] Like the others, he was given nicknames by his followers. He became fondly known as "Pop Joe," or "Pop Pelletieri," or simply the "Grand Old Man." He gained some of this esteem by founding at least three ethnic mutual aid associations and by organizing the local parish. Finally, he was elected alderman of East Utica's Little Italy, and in that role he won even more popular support by opening a city bathhouse and playground in his area.[39]

Even when he was serving his ethnic countrymen and building Little Italy, "Pop Joe" did not neglect his other identity as an American. On the contrary, he had unusually well-developed ideas on how best to teach newly arrived foreigners about America's fundamental laws. His own knowledge of and intense devotion to both the Declaration of Independence and the U.S. Constitution were legendary among his constituents. Revering both documents, he believed the former in particular was nearly divinely inspired and that its republican principles and philosophy merited continual and serious study. He even cited the institution that should be responsible for that instruction, the public library. This tax-supported cultural center, he felt, ought to obtain American history books in particular and thus provide a place where the foreign-born could learn about their adopted nation's past.[40]

* * *

A final example of an early Italian community leader who helped acquaint his fellow immigrants with the American political mainstream was Charles C. Baldi of the large Philadelphia Italian colony. By 1905 that Italian settlement had become the second largest in America. Unfortunately, as with most of the other ethnic leaders, firsthand evidence of Baldi's goals fully expressed in oral, written, or published sources was unavailable to me. However, his preeminent status in Philadelphia's Little Italy and his service in many important posts in both the ethnic and mainstream American societies strongly imply his status as community leader and his conviction that one could be a member of both communities.

Baldi had come to the leading Pennsylvania city with some of his family, his father and brother, at the beginning of the Italian colony there. That was in 1877, just after the U.S. centennial. The group settlement at the time consisted of only a few hundred immigrants.[41] Shortly thereafter, Baldi returned to Italy, but in the mid 1880s he came back to southeastern Pennsylvania to serve as the traditional padrone. A railroad company in the anthracite coal region urgently needed a labor recruiter, and Baldi filled that position, acting as as an interpreter and organizer for the firm's foreign-born workforce. The experience not only gained him a position of influence among his countrymen, but it also enabled him to set up a lucrative business of his own in the City of Brotherly Love. He and some of his relatives started a coal company in the heart of the immigrant quarter, in South Philadelphia. Baldi soon expanded this enterprise so that it would serve other immigrant needs. Again, with the help of his extended family, he became an undertaker, fruit merchant, banker, real estate broker, and travel agent by 1903.

It was not surprising, then, that such a prominent Italian leader would begin the city's first Italian-language daily, *L'Opinione,* in 1906. By that time he had achieved a position similar to that of Fugazi in New York and Russo in New Haven. He was only slightly less esteemed in Philadelphia than his New York colleague, and it appears that his view about his role was amazingly similar to that of all the other social leaders covered here. He, too, initiated and led a number of mutual aid societies, heading three around the turn of the century, and grouping several into a city federation. He was also similar to the other leaders in that he served in the critical capacity as the Italian community's major, although not exclusive, liaison with mainstream society. He became the most important interpreter and legal adviser for fellow countrymen when they had dealings with local court authorities.

By about 1900, then, Baldi had gained the confidence of both the foreign-born and Anglo-American communities. An observer described his role in the community in terms similar to those we have seen: "No Italian considered that he could accomplish anything without coming to him, nor could any American get in touch with the Italian colony without recourse to his office."[42]

Baldi had achieved considerable status in the mainstream by the start of the century. He held membership in several important civic clubs, and he developed an extraordinary ability in American political activities. He served the Republican party in a number of important capacities. Baldi also took part in local professional and civic groups as an active member of the Philadelphia undertakers and a body concerned with promoting the city's public school system.[43]

Because of his deep involvement in highly partisan political affairs that created group opponents, Baldi does not appear to fit precisely the mold of the "pappa." He certainly did not command the nearly universal affection that Fugazi, Russo, or "Pop Joe" enjoyed. In fact, some younger Italian Americans led an open rebellion against him, objecting to his authoritarian manner. Nevertheless, Baldi still commanded the major influence over Little Italy in the *pioneer* years. The opposition to his position arose only later, in the period just prior to World War I, and in the 1920s when he began expressing strong, pro-Fascist sympathies.[44] Until that time he often received much community support as an immigrant leader who was both a loyal

Italian and a loyal American. For example, he became a citizen very soon after his arrival in the 1880s, which suggests an intense early commitment to becoming American. And, like all the other immigrant leaders listed here, he promoted Columbus Day. At the city's huge celebration in 1892, it was Baldi who led the Italian procession through the city streets.[45]

By that point Baldi's example must have been clear to the ordinary Italian immigrants in South Philadelphia who knew him as their contact with the larger society. They could see that a foreigner *could* play a significant role in mainstream political affairs in the new land, a land in which they, too, had a claim because of the voyage of the great hero. Although the Philadelphia Italians had become a complex and fragmented community by the time of Baldi's death in 1931, his funeral did indicate some of the respect that group factions had for the colony leader. Despite the rise of Italian American criticism of him in the last decade of his life, he was still the community's major figure to "thousands of humble folk whose lives [he] had . . . touched." The ceremony and procession were impressive. The cortege included members of over one hundred Italian fraternal societies and other Italians carrying flags and banners. There were also numerous symbolic expressions of condolences by non-Italians.[46]

* * *

Baldi, then, along with Fugazi, Russo, Marnell, and the Pelletieris, certainly showed the immigrant generation that they need not totally abandon their past in order to benefit from the present. These leaders not only established social organizations and ethnic institutions that provided some of the cultural continuity that their countrymen sought, but they also viewed those structures as opportunities for immigrants to participate in mainstream civic life. Christopher Columbus was the symbol that helped nearly every colony to harmonize the two cultures of Italian Americans. Although it was the prominenti and the internal leaders like Barsotti in New York who initiated the celebrations for the hero, members of all social levels of the group lionized Columbus, and the occasions were immensely popular. The many celebrations in the colonies in 1892 and afterward certainly transcended class lines. The parades really assumed the character of folk festivals, and numerous fraternal associations participated. And Italian communities as a whole pressured their state legislatures to make Columbus Day a legal holiday.

It is true that many, perhaps more than one-half, of the Italian immigrants who came to the United States returned to Europe. Also, most who stayed in America did not follow their leaders' exhortation to become citizens or to be politically active. A very interesting recent study of popular religion and folk life of a particular community, Harlem, concludes that the immigrants quickly became disillusioned with America. Having viewed America from Europe as an earthly paradise, as slum dwellers they found it to be oppressive and exploitative. Even the few who were successful, those who "made America," had to become American by denying their heritage. The results were strong "ambivalent feelings" about belonging to the new land and "alienation from America."[47] However, the author neglects the Americanizing effect of the popular mutual aid society that those Harlem immigrants from Polla established in 1881. In addition, he quotes a well-known Italian American writer who admitted that the appreciation for Columbus did ease the ambivalence of his dual identity.[48]

The prevalence of re-emigration and the apathy toward full political involvement do not necessarily mean that immigrants did not consider themselves "American" in the early years. And it is possible that some of those who moved back to the old country took a dual identity with them—being "Italian" and "American" simultaneously was still possible.[49]

A prominent and widely respected Italian American jurist, John Freschi of New York, spoke to that very issue of combined ethnic and national loyalties in 1916, the end of the era covered by this study. The period just before the entrance of the United States into World War I obviously forced the question of immigrants' ties and identity into national debate. While the outbreak of hostilities in 1914 produced the official American response of neutrality, leaders worried that the very large contingent of foreign-born, the "hyphenates," might embroil the United States in the quarrels of the Old World. As a result, conspicuous ethnic bonds bred suspicion and condemnation. Retaining Irish, German, or Italian ways in any manner was considered by many to be un-American.

Freschi watched the growth of these pressures for Americanization in the early days of the conflict and decided to illuminate the issue of American and Italian identities. Freschi, an esteemed jurist with a recent appointment to the New York City system, made his remarks at a meeting of fellow countrymen in Boston, one of the largest Italian American colonies. The speech was heard even more widely because a group journal later published his remarks.

Freschi rejected as unfair, discriminatory, and even un-American the heavy pressure upon his group to conform its culture to that of the majority. Speaking both for and to his fellow Italians, he pointed out that maintaining traditional ways was certainly acceptable and desirable, although such cultural preservation also entailed a group obligation. Italian immigrants ought, he said, to retain a "democratic affection for the institutions of [their adopted] country" as well as a knowledge of the laws that permitted such ethnic maintenance.[50] He strongly implied that such a juxtaposition of differing but complementary ethnic and national ties was distinctly American and not possible in Europe. In the United States, one could have two identities, but not dual allegiances.

Immigrants, then, did have rights under the American system, but they also had responsibilities. Freschi's assertion that privileges carried obligations was the very sentiment that pioneer leaders had been conveying to their people for years.

8

Conclusion

The aim of this work has been to determine to what extent and in what ways this nation's largest immigrant groups acquired an American identity in the nineteenth and early twentieth centuries. As I explained in the Introduction, most students of this topic have acknowledged that the process of gaining a new consciousness was indeed an important one for both leaders and followers. The conventional conclusion generally was that becoming American was for some a radical, thoroughgoing transformation, that is, a complete assimilation with no misgivings or reservations, while for others, probably the majority of immigrants, such a complete change did not occur. Rather, most scholars have believed that foreigners suffered in a marginal world, suspended awkwardly between their native and adopted cultures. Many chose to live in ghettoes or in clusters of their own people, but they were psychologically uncomfortable doing so. They were uncertain, confused, and even bewildered about their real identity. Observers believed that immigrants felt that to be ethnic was not to be American.

Certainly, much evidence exists that foreigners were under outside pressure to conform. Nativists in various eras, the Know-Nothings of the 1850s, the superpatriots of the 1890s and later Americanizers early in this century all insisted upon a speedy assimilation of the foreign-born. By theses demands, nationalists intensified the immigrants' fears and uncertainties about who they were and who they ought to be. The outsiders' insistence that foreigners shed their language and learn English, modify or give up their religion, and acquire majority customs quickly, must indeed have caused anguish in alien quarters. In addition, nativists felt that those newcomers from countries that were more recently under feudalism required special attention. To make the immigrants become worthy members of America's democratic society, the authorities would have to educate those aliens to American democratic principles. This concern accounts for the wide popularity of civics classes in the many social work institutions in U.S. cities in the early 1900s. The onset of the First World War and the entry of the United States in it in 1917 gave new urgency to Americanizing efforts.

Besides the superpatriots' worry over the many "hyphenated" Americans, more sober scholars have also been concerned with the foreigners' dilemma over their identity. They have cited the great psychological trauma that they believed their alien subjects had to endure; they felt that these newcomers must have found it difficult to accommodate their dual ties. Sociologists especially believed that the Irish, Germans, Poles, and others who entered our society in the last century had to transcend a huge gap in becoming American. The mere recognition of the cultural differences between their two homes, the Old World and the New, was painful. As a standard history of immigration puts it:

> Whether they came individually or in groups . . . immigrants
> faced the necessity of coming to terms with American life. . . .
> Even for those whose transplantation was accompanied with a
> minimum of economic and psychological buffeting, the process
> of adjustment was *painful* and *protracted*. For all immigrants
> immigration was a traumatic experience, resulting in a sense of
> alienation and isolation. It was nearly always the fate of the
> first generation to remain a 'marginal man' suspended between
> two cultures but belonging to neither.[1]

Another historian, Oscar Handlin, referred to a more specific crisis for foreigners. His observation that they came unprepared for involvement in the American political system is reminiscent of earlier scholars' views. But, according to Handlin, it was the naivete of the aliens that drew them into a situation that they clearly did not understand. As a result, the foreigners suffered from the manipulation of others. "With few exceptions [the immigrants] were complete strangers to the democratic process" because almost none had had the vote in the Old World. A few may have had an inkling of what self-government meant, but the "overwhelming mass rarely knew what to make of the circumstances they faced." Leaders, Handlin asserted, did arise who might have provided the foreigners with some direction, but that elite was unsatisfactory to the masses because they were frequently corrupt. Hence, immigrants simply could not comprehend their adopted society.[2]

A well-known sociologist who has written extensively on ethnicity has extended the idea of immigrant naivete even further, suggesting that the discomfort of marginality may not have existed at all.

Writing in the midst of the recent ethnic revival of the 1960s and 1970s, a time when many native-born Americans sought to recover their "roots," he observed that members of the first, incoming generation never really dealt consciously with the issue of dual group identities because they were so immersed in their own ethnic environment. It was only the third generation, that is the grandchildren of the immigrants, who had to define their group heritage in relation to others and therefore to make a choice. Identity-definition, then, was problematic only for descendants of the aliens, not for those who originally crossed the Atlantic.[3]

This notion that the second or third generation, rather than the first, encountered the major or more upsetting psychological issue of marginality may have some truth. But as my review of six immigrant groups has shown, the matter of how to relate the newcomers' traditional and adopted cultures was a subject widely discussed from the very birth of the ethnic community.

As a whole, this study agrees with many historians that the overall adjustment for immigrants was not an easy one. Certainly, for most foreigners, trying to earn a living in a strange setting with limited material resources in an unstable economy that fluctuated widely between prosperity and depression was a test that required great courage and fortitude. The occasionally severe but continually present discriminatory pressures and demands from hostile outsiders made the trial still more uncomfortable. The outcome for many may have been tragic; numerous immigrants did not achieve their aims in coming. Some had to return to their homeland as failures; others became victims of the business cycle, all amid official and unofficial apathy and even abuse.

Still, this work has indicated that the general trauma and discomfort felt by most arrivals was far more material, physical, and even emotional than intellectual or cultural. This review of the creation of the many ethnic settlements suggests that *most* of the immigrants, with the assistance of *some* of the popular leaders, did resolve that potentially thorny matter of group definition. The rise and influence of some members of the immigrant elite—the ones similar to the Italian pappas—did help substantially to provide an answer for that dilemma of identity which foreigners may have encountered when they thought of themselves as Americans.

One should note that every one of the six groups experienced a similar, but not precisely the same, Americanizing experience. Almost all of the leaders did refer to the American Revolution and the making of the American state to justify retaining their European culture. Harkavy for the Jews, Enander for the Swedes, Hughes for the Irish, Kiołbassa for the Poles, and others all found that they could be Americans and preserve their heritage by pointing out the compatibility of Revolutionary and immigrant ideologies. But there were differences as well among the six peoples covered here in this study of the Americanizing process. Because immigrant institutions were not as encompassing for the Swedes, the Germans, and the Italians as they were for the Jews, the Poles, and the Irish, the matter of identity definition affected fewer members, that is, a smaller percentage, of the latter. Also, because the Germans and Italians had the strongest local European ties of all the groups covered here, many more of them may have ignored the issue of competing national identities. I will not go so far as to assert that every member of the six immigrant groups had to face the identity-defining process described. Still, it was part of the experience for many, if not most, and it does appear that the groups' awareness of a new ethnic American identity was chiefly the result of the thinking of some of the group elite.

In trying to understand this new consciousness of followers by scrutinizing their leaders, this study is indebted to the findings of some of the most recent anthropological research. That research has suggested indirectly that American immigrant leaders should be viewed as social mediators. Anthropologists like Wolf, and Geertz have been concerned primarily with the less modernized societies of the Third World whose local chieftains and religious leaders have functioned as cultural brokers between the state's centralized power center and its provincial communities.[4] Thus, the relevance of their work to the American pluralistic society is only partial. Still, America's incoming groups did produce leaders who acted as cultural mediators and commanded a large following. Particular figures in the United States, as in the Third World, helped to interpret the larger culture for their group members.[5] So in both places individuals arose who achieved and maintained their position by supplying a vital service or essential product to the community in its formative period.

In addition, it is important to understand that this biographical survey has not concerned itself with judging the morality of the leaders' drive to success—many may well have gained their position by exploitation and intimidation, and they undoubtedly made enemies, even powerful ones. All, however, did have substantial grassroots support; they were not hollow, emblematic figures, holding their place in their communities solely or even largely by outside sanction.

These leaders sought to mobilize their followers to join associations that would encourage them to take an active role in the host society as well as their own. The result was the raising of the immigrants' consciousness as members of their adopted nation. Urging segregation *and* integration at the same time, these men of influence supplied a rationale for their people, ex-peasants, bonder, chłopi, contadini, shtetlach, and the like as to how they could carry over and reestablish their Old World culture and still be considered American. The answer to that potential problem was not only the early presence of heroic countrymen like Columbus, Kościuszko, and Pułaski, whom the the immigrants lionized, but more particularly the principles of the Declaration of Independence and the Constitution, which ethnic leaders insisted their groups shared. These guides were "traditional progressives," who disseminated those mutual values of self-determination and democratic self-government soon after their countrymen disembarked.

It was in the very inception of their ethnic colonies, then, that immigrants became more familiar with those political ideas underlying their host society than both contemporary observers or recent American scholars realize. Chiefly responsible for that education were the internal leaders reviewed here.

A Note on Bibliography

GENERAL COMMENT

This bibliographical essay will identify and review certain selected sources and archives that I consulted in my research. It is not necessary to list and assess all the important studies on the six immigrant groups I have covered. An extended inventory of secondary materials is superfluous, since the recent revival of interest in America's ethnically pluralistic society among scholars, academicians, and the general public has produced a considerable library of bibliographical articles and books on immigration and ethnic history. Among the more comprehensive and up-to-date essays on such sources has been the generally excellent series found in each issue of the *Immigration History Newsletter,* a semiannual publication of the Immigration History Society, edited by Professor Carlton Qualey since 1973 at the Minnesota Historical Society. These contributions have usually been written by the leading scholars of each particular group, and Professor Qualey is now engaged in publishing the entire series separately as a unit.

Until recently, also, immigration and ethnic history lacked good, general surveys, with the possible exception of the Maldwyn Allen Jones's work, *American Immigration,* mentioned in Chapter 8. Three of the better summary works that students should consult have come to light in the last few years. One is the overview by Thomas J. Archdeacon, *Becoming American: An Ethnic History* (New York: The Free Press, 1983), which, among other virtues, covers American history since colonial times. Another is Maxine Seller, *To Seek America: A History of Ethnic Life in America* (Englewood, N.J.: Ozer, 1977), superbly comprehensive; and a third, John Bodnar, *The Transplanted,* referred to in Chapter 1. Although it is limited to immigrants seeking American cities in the nineteenth and twentieth centuries, Bodnar's work improves upon Archdeacon's by drawing more upon the immigrants' Old World past and by illuminating the inner lives of foreign-born families and their communities.

In addition to the appearance of excellent interpretive texts, the last few years have also seen the publication of a monumental reference work on immigration and ethnicity, Stephan Thernstrom, et al., *The Harvard Encyclopedia of American Ethnic Groups* (Cambridge, Mass.: Harvard University Press, 1980). Published at the end of the ethnic revival of the 1970s, it filled a badly needed gap in the reference literature on American society. The encyclopedia provides general readers and students with succinct, introductory profiles for all of the major and minor ethnic groups in the United States. It brings together in one place brief but comprehensive historical essays on both well-known and lesser-known American minority groups and their leaders. In addition, by including several topical pieces, such as Higham's statement on leadership and other statements on identity, folklore, and the like, the *Encyclopedia* encourages and promotes comparative study, something the field has grievously lacked. Fortunately, too, all the contributions list other sources for further exploration

As I suggested in Chapter 1, chiefly non-historical scholars have increasingly become attracted to the study of elites in recent years. While anthropologists and sociologists have studied the relationship between the upper and lower classes, American historians must interpret their findings with caution. The conclusions of Wolf, Geertz, Blok, and others about traditional societies and the function of leaders as mediators or brokers between their constituencies and modern bureaucracies, for example, tell a great deal about their subjects. But American historians interested in marginality must remember that the setting in the United States is not entirely analogous. The association of an oppressed, indigenous people with central authorities in Europe or the Third World is not entirely the same as the contact between immigrants and the native majority in America. The newcomers' decision to move to the United States, especially when other choices existed, suggests that the newcomers and the established U.S. citizens had some values in common.

For the historian, any investigation of the elite has certain inherent advantages. It deals with persons who were well-known, so even if they were prominent among only the smallest communities of immigrants, virtually all will be on some written, even published record, authored either by themselves or by contemporaries. Hence, personal accounts by the individuals, their speeches, memoirs, and autobiographies, or just biographies about them are likely to be available. Of course, much of the literature written by others would be subjective, frequently laudatory and uncritical. At best these sources would be informative, but they would hardly be analytical and would probably not go beyond group boundaries in order to make comparisons.

THE IRISH

The most important work for this study on the Irish was clearly George Potter's *To the Golden Door* (New York: Macmillan, 1960). Although Potter did not employ the usual scholarly apparatus, I believe his study was enormously insightful. Far more than other authors cited here, including Handlin, McCaffrey, and Brown, he focused on the immigrants' folklife and conveyed effectively and sensitively many of the Irish arrivals' inner sentiments. The work suffers from poor organization and a rather conspicuous anti-English bias, but it has significant strengths. It is distinctive in that it is superb social history. It pays close attention to the matter of group identity among the ex-cotters and the place of the early Irish American social leaders in the community. Potter covers the Irish American political activity, as do the other writers, but his work has achieved better balance because he integrated pertinent cultural factors into his observations.

The most extensive single repository for anyone interested in the pioneer era of Irish America is the American Irish Historical Society in New York City. Its sizable collection of early documents and published material is mainly concerned with the leading revolutionary and journalistic figures of the late eighteenth and early nineteenth centuries. Gaining access to the papers and books, however, is difficult. The building is open only occasionally, the holdings are only partly catalogued; and over all it appears that the society has subordinated its research and library functions to its social and political activities.

Irish Catholic records are, of course, generally available at diocesan libraries around the country. I found the regional collection of the Boston area at the Boston College Library very helpful because it included certain ephemeral material. Especially valuable were the scrapbooks of printed newspaper and magazine articles on Mayor Patrick Collins located at the Boston Public Library. I made use of other good sources at the New York Archdiocesan Headquarters in Yonkers. It possesses a small but rather varied array of materials on Archbishop John Hughes which any biographer must consult.

THE GERMANS

The sources and depositories I consulted for the Germans were much like the group itself, fragmented and widely dispersed. One source was of particular value, that was the periodical, *Der Deutsche Pionier*. The journal contained a very rich array of biographical information on many of the group's luminaries, including some of my selected elite. The periodical was published in the several decades following the Civil War, and most of the articles I used appeared in the 1870s. They not only gave detailed accounts of the lives of leaders but, more importantly, they presented their views on leading political and social questions of the time. Several essays responded to criticisms of the German immigrants' cultural persistence, so they elaborated on the definition of being American.

The most fertile archives for me for this group was the Cincinnati Historical Society. It housed the papers of many of Cincinnati's ethnic leaders of the middle and late 1800s. Its several collections of prominent German figures regrettably did not include a separate file on Charles Reemelin. But the papers of the other leaders fortunately did include some of his letters and documents. In addition, Reemelin was articulate enough to have published a number of items offering his ideas on politics and the German American involvement in American civic life.

The most important German American of all those I reviewed was Francis Hoffmann. Active and prominent in several areas, most conspicuously as lieutenant governor of Illinois in the Civil War, Hoffmann has records at several archives. Some materials on him are at the Concordia Historical Institute in St. Louis and at the Illinois State Historical Library in Springfield. Both archives have marvelous Hoffmann scrapbooks that contain items on his life and his writings. Particularly revealing in these records are his many pieces of advice written for German immigrant farm families. He wrote these articles for a number of German papers the last quarter of his life under the very popular pen names of Hans and Grete Buschbauer, as I stated in the text.

The most helpful, single account of Missouri German leaders was the serialized set of articles by William Bek published in the *Missouri Historical Review* from 1923 to 1924. Having the general title "The Followers of Duden," they were highly informative descriptive profiles without the filiopietism and laudatory glorification one might expect in local life histories.

THE NORWEGIANS AND THE SWEDES

I employed most fully the rather large collection of Rasmus Anderson's papers at the State Historical Society of Wisconsin, and I drew upon the Minnesota Historical Society for its primary and secondary materials on former governor and senator Knute Nelson. Outside of the Augustana College Library and Archives, which had some records on its former president, Rev. Tufve Hasselquist, including copies of his well-known newspaper, *Hemlandet,* I could not locate many documents on the other leaders. Still, Hans Mattson's memoirs were rather revealing, as were the few items I found on Enander. For further references, I direct interested readers to two of my previous articles, "Ethnic Confrontations with State Universities, 1860–1920," in B. Weiss, ed., *American Education and the European Immigrant* (Champaign, Ill.: University of Illinois Press, 1982), pp. 189–207, and the more recent piece, "Swedish American Identity, 1850–1900: A Dilemma Resolved," in Odd Lovoll, ed., *Scandinavians and Other Immigrants in Urban America* (Northfield, Minn.: St. Olaf College Press, 1985), 123–39.

THE JEWS

Students interested in the Jews are fortunate because the research institutions covering this group are several and the amount of information is large and growing and of generally high quality. For the several leaders I chose here, the YIVO Institute in New York City, America's major Yiddish library, had the richest holdings of any archives. Because Alexander Harkavy was essentially a Yiddish lexicographer and a prolific writer, the number of works by him at YIVO was especially large. Included among that institute's many publications about him was a rare and extremely helpful biography-bibliography by Jacob Shatzky, *Harkavis Bio-bibliografye* (1933). Mr. Kenneth Rosett of Scarsdale, New York, the husband of a descendant of Sarasohn, was most gracious in allowing me to use his lengthy volume of documents, *Sarasohn and Son: A Scrapbook* (1984), on the pioneer Orthodox publisher and his family. The archives of the Hebrew Union College in Cincinnati supplied me with other records on Harkavy, Sarasohn and his newspapers.

THE POLES

There has been a revolutionary change in both the quantity and quality of scholarly research among students of the Poles over the last two decades. When I initiated my own investigation of Polish Americans a quarter-century ago, I knew of no other student of American history who was working on that group's past, although some students of European history and some non-historians were providing good studies. Since then the number of books and articles has multiplied because of the encouragement of the Polish American Historical Association and the increasing involvement of European historians, especially at the Polonia Institute in Cracow.

As those in the field know, the Polish Museum of America, which is connected with the Polish Roman Catholic Union in Chicago, remains the largest Polish American research archives; it is especially rich in Polish Catholic records and documents. It has, of course, much literature on the paramount Chicago Polish community. The staff at the State University College of New York at Buffalo was particularly generous in helping me find materials from their Polish collection, which was established with the help of Professor Walter Drzewieniecki. Especially valuable to this work was the rich collection of Fronczak Papers at the Buffalo and Erie County Historical Society. The scrapbooks on this local Polish American leader provided an excellent portrait of his life and community status.

Other materials that were indispensable to my work were the microfilm reels of the Chicago Foreign Language Press Survey, which contain translated excerpts of almost a century of that city's Polish papers; Anthony Kuzniewski's *Faith and Fatherland: The Polish Church War in Wisconsin, 1896–1918* (Notre Dame, Ind.: University of Notre Dame Press, 1980), a good example of the new Polish American scholarship mentioned above; and the microfilm file at the Milwaukee Public Library, which contains nearly every issue of the Milwaukee *Kuryer Polski* from its beginning in 1888.

THE ITALIANS

As with the Germans, one source stands out as the best compendium and biographical dictionary of Italian American leaders, and fortunately, it appeared at the start of the major immigrant influx, a most appropriate time for this study. That work is *Gli Italiani Negli Stati Uniti d'America* (New York: Italian American Chamber of Commerce, 1906). It is essentially a series of worshipful biographies, not a work of scholarship, but nevertheless, it was extremely valuable to me, and it was the major source from which I selected my internal leaders. It offered a good collection of rather informative profiles of elites. The directory also has a national, rather than local, focus. Most of the figures it describes were New Yorkers, but a large minority of others were from the hinterland and from Boston, Connecticut, Philadelphia, and even

San Francisco. Thus, the work really presents much of the nation's Italian American elite. In addition, the directory is like an encyclopedia, because it provides information on much of the group's daily life, discussing social organizations and institutions, the press, Columbus Day observances, and Italian American economic activities. Finally, the book contains many photographs which provide a valuable visual record of the immigrant community.

As I indicated in my notes, Professor Luciano Iorizzo of the State University of New York at Oswego directed me to the small set of documentary materials on Thomas Marnell at the Onondaiga County Public Library in Syracuse. The Balch Institute for Ethnic Studies in Philadelphia provided me with some rare works on that city's Italian colony, and I am grateful to Professor Richard Juliani for directing me to them. Sister Irene Fugazy at the New York Archdiocesan Headquarters in Yonkers generously called upon her knowledge about her grandfather for me. She graciously guided me to his letterbooks, which were very revealing about his bond with new immigrants. The Immigration History Research Center at the University of Minnesota, now the nation's major archives for that area, has just embarked on an ambitious endeavor—inventorying and preserving records of the Sons of Italy, the group's major fraternal association.

Notes

1. INTRODUCTION

1. William I. Thomas and Florian Znaniecki, *The Polish Peasant in Europe and America,* 5 vols. (Boston: Badger; Chicago: University of Chicago Press, 1918–1920); Lloyd Warner and Leo Srole, *The Social Systems of American Ethnic Groups* (New Haven: Yale University Press, 1945). Park and Wirth will be discussed at length below.

2. Oscar Handlin, *The Uprooted* (Boston: Atlantic, Little, Brown, 1951).

3. Nathan Glazer and Daniel Patrick Moynihan, *Beyond the Melting Pot* (Cambridge, Mass.: MIT Press, 1963), pp. 20, 310–11; and Milton Gordon, *Assimilation in America* (New York: Oxford University Press, 1964). Cf. the extended review of theories in Herbert J. Gans, "Symbolic Ethnicity," in Herbert J. Gans et al., eds., *On the Making of America: Essays in Honor of David Riesman* (Philadelphia: University of Pennsylvania Press, 1979), pp. 194ff.

4. Frederik Barth, "Introduction," in Frederik Barth, ed., *Ethnic Groups and Boundaries* (Boston: Little, Brown, 1969), pp. 9–10, 23–33, 38.

5. See, in particular, Stephan Thernstrom, "Reflections on the New Urban History," in Felix Gilbert and Stephen Graubard, eds., *Historical Studies Today* (New York: Norton, 1972), p. 328 and passim. Two contemporary historians who have focused on the immigrant middle class and therefore on leaders are John Bodnar, *The Transplanted: A History of Immigrants in Urban America* (Bloomington: Indiana University Press, 1985), chap. 4, pp. 214–15, and Olivier Zunz, "The Synthesis of Social Change: Reflections on American Social History," in Olivier Zunz, ed., *Reliving the Past: The Worlds of Social History* (Chapel Hill, N.C.: University of North Carolina Press, 1985), pp. 53–114. Although Bodnar presents the best interpretive survey on immigration history to date, I believe he still overemphasizes class differences within ethnic communities. He also defines Americanization in exclusively economic, rather than also ideological and philosophical, terms. Bodnar, *Transplanted,* pp. 117–19, 138–39. Zunz, on the other hand, in a careful review of recent works, concludes that his colleagues unjustifiably subordinate ethnicity to class, at least in their studies of the nineteenth century. Zunz, "Synthesis," pp. 87ff, esp. 88–90, 92–93.

6. Elizabeth Pleck, "Challenges to Traditional Authority in Immigrant Families," in Michael Gordon, ed., *The American Family in Social-Historical Perspective* (New York: St. Martin's Press, 1983), pp. 504–17, is a typical example.

7. A few examples may suffice. One informative and worshipful profile is Daniel S. Buczek's *Immigrant Pastor: The Life of the Right Reverend Monsignor Lucyan Bójnowski* (Waterbury, Conn.: Heminway, 1974), which stresses this important Polish community leader's problems and achievements. The cleric's mediating role is obvious from the work, but although his actions are cited by the author, they are not discussed at length or given much analysis. See chapters 1–4, and cf. pp. 147–48. Another example is the more critical study by Lloyd Hustvedt, *Rasmus Bjorn Anderson: Pioneer Scholar* (Northfield, Minn.: Norwegian American Historical Association, 1966). Hustvedt assesses Anderson's academic, intellectual, literary, and diplomatic activities as a Norwegian American but still only alludes to the man's intermediary role. One biography that does concentrate on an immigrant leader's duality is Jonathan Sarna's *Jacksonian Jew: The Two Worlds of Mordecai Noah* (New York: Holmes & Meier, 1982). But this work emphasizes Noah's adjustment in being a Jew in America more than it shows his influence on other Jews. This is because he lived a quarter-century before most of his people came here en masse.

8. My review here is taken from both Tom Bottomore, *Elites and Society* (New York: Penguin, 1966) and James Meisel, *The Myth of the Ruling Class* (Ann Arbor: University of Michigan Press, 1958).

9. Meisel, *Myth,* p. vii.

10. Ibid., pp. 360–61; Bottomore, *Elites,* pp. 10–11, 33–35.

11. Eric R. Wolf, "Aspects of Group Relations in a Complex Society," *American Anthropologist* 58 (1956):1076. He was speaking of American society, but he and others have applied his examination to other contexts. Cf. Anton Blok, *The Mafia of a Sicilian Village, 1860–1960: A Study of Violent Peasant Entrepreneurs* (London: Oxford University Press, 1974).

12. Blok, *Mafia;* Alex Weingrod, "Patrons, Patronage and Political Parties," *Comparative Studies in Society and History* 10 (July 1968): 377–82; Richard Adams, "Brokers and Career Mobility Systems in the Structure of Complex Societies," *Southwestern Journal of Anthropology* 26 (Winter 1977): 320–21; Marc J. Swarz, "The Political Middleman," in Marc J. Swarz, ed., *Local Level Politics: Social and Cultural Perspectives* (Chicago: Aldine, 1968), pp. 201–2.

13. Peter Berger and Richard John Niehaus, *To Empower People: The Role of Mediating Structures in Public Policy* (Washington, D.C.: American Enterprise Institute, 1977), pp. 3–7, 45; and Oscar Handlin, "The Social Structure," in Lloyd Rodwin, ed., *The Future Metropolis* (New York: Braziller, 1971), pp. 32–34.

14. Wolf, "Aspects," p. 1076.

15. Swartz, "Political Middleman," p. 200; F. G. Bailey, *Stratagems and Spoils: A Social Anthropology of Politics* (London, Schweken, 1969), p. 167; Weingrod, *Patrons,* p. 382.

16. Robert E. Park and Herbert Miller, *Old World Traits Transplanted* (New York: Harper & Brothers, 1921), p. 308.

17. Ibid., pp. 61, 120–25, 287–307.

18. Apparently the only release was in the second generation, among those born in the new land. His examples were Ludwig Lewisohn and Henrich Heine. Robert E. Park, "Human Migration and the Marginal Man," *The American Journal of Sociology* 23 (May 1928): 881–93, esp. pp. 890–93.

19. Louis Wirth, *The Ghetto* (Chicago: University of Chicago Press, 1928; paperback edition, 1956), pp. 284–85, 289–90.

20. E. V. Stonequist, *The Marginal Man* (New York: Scribner, 1937), p. 83.

21. Ibid., pp. 95, 201–2, 221.

22. According to William Carlson Smith in *Americans in the Making: The Natural History of the Assimilation of Immigrants* (New York: D. Appleton-Century, 1939), pp. 229–31, 242, the words quoted here are those of W. O. Brown, as found (by Smith) in American Sociological Association, *Race and Culture Contacts*, Edward Byron Reuter, ed. (New York: McGraw-Hill, 1934), p. 44.

23. Kurt Lewin, *Resolving Social Conflicts: Selected Papers on Group Dynamics* (New York: Harper, 1948), pp. 195–97. This book was the basis for his later contribution on minority leadership in Alvin W. Gouldner, ed., *Studies in Leadership* . . . (New York: Harper, 1950). See especially pp. 192–94.

24. Stonequist, *Marginal Man,* pp. 83, 87, 142, and esp. pp. 93–94.

25. My previous work, for example, on Polish and Lithuanian ethnic consciousness, indicates that a new kind of ethnic feeling developed among those immigrants when they were in America. *For God and Country* (Madison, Wisc.: Society Press, 1975).

26. Recent examples are Glazer and Moynihan, *Beyond the Melting Pot;* Gordon, *Assimilation;* Virginia McLaughlin, *Family and Community* (Ithaca, N.Y.: Cornell University Press, 1977) and Neil Sandburg, *Ethnic Identity and Assimilation: The Polish American Community* (New York: Praeger, 1974).

27. Paul Lazarsfeld, Bernard Berelson, and Hazel Gaudet, *The People's Choice: How the Voter Makes Up His Mind in a Presidential Election,* 3d ed. (New York: Columbia University Press, 1968), pp. vi, xxiv–xxv, 152–53, 155–56.

28. John Higham, "Leadership," in Stephan Thernstrom et al., eds., *Harvard Encyclopedia of American Ethnic Groups* (Cambridge, Mass.: Harvard University Press, 1980), pp. 642–46.

29. Ibid. My own work, *For God and Country,* supports this idea.

2. THE IRISH

1. A convenient recent summary is Patrick J. Blessing's "The Irish," in S. Thernstrom, *Harvard Encyclopedia* (see chap. 1, n. 28), pp. 524–45. Also extraordinarily helpful and suggestive to me were George Potter's, *To the Golden Door* (New York: Macmillan, 1960), esp. pp. 35–43, and Lawrence McCaffrey's, *The Irish Diaspora in America* (Bloomington, Ind.: Indiana University Press, 1976) pp. 60–70, another standard survey.

2. Oscar Handlin, *Boston's Immigrants* (Cambridge, Mass.: Harvard University Press, Belknap edition, 1969), p. 276; Lawrence McCaffrey, "Pioneers of the American Ghetto," *Illinois Quarterly* 34 (September 1971):31–42. McCaffrey later qualified this generalization, applying it only to the postfamine arrivals. See his *Irish Diaspora,* p. 67.

3. Brown offers only general, not specific, evidence. See Thomas Brown, *Irish American Nationalism* (Philadelphia: Lippincott, 1966), p. 23 and passim.

4. Ibid., pp. 24–26. Concerned more with the work of Irish American nationalists, Brown only alludes to the origins of that group association.

5. James Boyd, "Address Delivered before the Charitable Irish Society in Boston . . ." (Boston, 1837), p. 4 in the Irish Collection, Boston College, hereafter ICBC.

6. John D. Crimmins, *St. Patrick's Day: Its Celebration in New York* (New York: Author, 1902), pp. 5, 9, 17, 25.

7. See McCaffrey's good survey, *Irish Diaspora*, pp. 24–28, 31. See also Blessing, "Irish," p. 530.

8. Dennis Patrick Ryan, "Beyond the Ballot Box: A Social History of the Boston Irish, 1845–1917" (Ph.D. diss., Harvard University, 1979), pp. 140–41.

9. Blessing, "Irish," p. 527.

10. James Boyd, "Address," pp. 14–16. The list of presidents is in *Charitable Irish Society Founded 1737: Its Constitution and By-Laws . . .* (Boston, n.p., 1917), p. 21, which shows Patrick Donahoe in the leading office in 1851 and 1854. I cannot identify clearly any earlier president as Catholic.

11. My emphasis. Crimmins, *St. Patrick's Day, . . .* p. 37.

12. Cf. Boyd, "Address," pp. 9–12.

13. Crimmins, *St. Patrick's Day*, pp. 145–46.

14. Ibid., pp. 118–19.

15. Ibid., p. 111.

16. Ibid., p. 155.

17. Ibid., pp. 66, 68, 84, 89.

18. Although he was a Protestant, Boyd felt he commanded large Irish Catholic support. Boyd, "Address," pp. 29–36.

19. Potter, *Golden Door*, p. 94. Handlin also attributes the high susceptibility to the landlord's influence. See O. Handlin, "The Immigrant and American Politics," in David Bowers, ed., *Foreign Influences in American Life* (1944; reprint, New York: Peter Smith, 1952), p. 86.

20. Conrad Arensburg, *The Irish Countryman* (1937; reprint, Garden City, N.Y.: Natural History, 1968), pp. 160–62; Robert E. Kennedy, *The Irish: Emigration, Marriage, Fertility* (Berkeley and Los Angeles: University of California Press, 1973), p. 36; Owen Dudley Edwards, "Conclusion: Some Counterthemes," in David Noel Doyle and Owen Dudley Edwards, eds., *America and Ireland, 1776–1976: The American Identity and the Irish Connection* (Westport, Conn.: Greenwood, 1980), p. 320.

21. Biographical information is in Edward Preble, "William James Mac-Neven," in Dumas Malone, ed., *Dictionary of American Biography*, 20 vols. (New York: Scribner, 1936), 12:153–54; Deasmumhan O'Raghallaigh, "William James MacNeven" *Studies: An Irish Review*, no. 11 (June 1941):247–53; and Thomas Addis Emmet, Jr., *Incidents of My Life* (New York: Putnam, 1911), pp. 65ff.

22. R. R. Madden, *The United Irishmen: Their Lives and Times*, 2d ser. in 2 vols. (London: J. Madden, 1843), 2:224–28, 265, 287–88; Preble, "MacNeven," p. 154.

23. Emmet, *Incidents*, p. 65.

24. Ibid., 65; Madden, *United Irishmen* (1843), 2:264. The assertion of David Noel Doyle in *Ireland, Irishmen and Revolutionary America, 1760–1820* (Dublin: Mercier, 1980), p. 218, supports this observation.

25. Potter, *Golden Door*, p. 228. See also Doyle, *Ireland*, p. 226.

26. Quoted in Madden, *United Irishmen* (1843), 2:276–77; and R. R. Madden, *The United Irishmen* (London: J. Madden, 1893), pp. 274–76, by Thomas O'Connor, an associate of MacNeven.

27. From the *New York Freeman's Journal,* July 17, 1841, quoted in Madden,

United Irishmen (1843), 2:285–86. Other signs of public esteem are in the *New York Herald Tribune,* July 14, and the *Truth Teller,* Oct. 8, 1842, according to Thomas Addis Emmet, *Memoir of Thomas Addis and Robert Emmet . . .* (New York: Emmet, 1915), p. 244n.

28. Potter, *Golden Door,* pp. 208–9.

29. A good biographical sketch is in the account of his better-known son, J. C. Walsh, "Charles O'Conor," *Journal of the American Irish Historical Society* 27 (1928):290–91, 307–9.

30. *Shamrock,* Aug. 17 and Dec. 7, 1816.

31. Note the announcement in the *Shamrock and Hibernian Chronicle,* May 29, 1918, when O'Connor was editor of another paper, the *Military Monitor.*

32. *Shamrock and Hibernian Chronicle,* Dec. 15, 1810.

33. Ibid., June 18, 1814.

34. Ibid., Sept. 8, 1815.

35. Ibid., Jan. 4, 1817. His emphasis.

36. Thomas O'Connor File 9.2H.19. See file 9.2H.04 in the O'Connor Papers at the American Irish Historical Society, New York.

37. Ibid., File 9.2H.03.

38. The term is in Jay Dolan, *The Immigrant Church* (Baltimore: Johns Hopkins University Press, 1975), pp. 9, 45, 54, 56, 64, 164–65. Although admittedly only half of the city's Irish population attended church regularly, clerical influence may have been stronger due to larger attendance at Sunday mass, when pews were frequently full. In any event, Hughes's influence was sizable. See esp. p. 58.

39. Ibid., pp. 118, 144, 148; Potter, *Golden Door,* p. 403; Richard J. Purcell, "John Joseph Hughes," in Malone, *Dictionary,* 9:353. See the biographical sketches in Rev. R. H. Tierney, "John Hughes, Archbishop of New York," in C. E. McGuire, *Catholic Builders of the Nation,* 5 vols. (Boston: Continental, 1924), 5:68 and passim; and John O'Dea, *History of the Ancient Order of Hibernians and Ladies Auxiliary,* 3 vols. (Philadelphia: Keystone, 1923), 2:889. Rev. Andrew Greeley, in *The Catholic Experience* (Garden City, N.Y.: Doubleday, 1969), chap. 5, criticizes Hughes for his belligerence and consequent intensification of the Protestant Crusade, but he considers him a Catholic social as well as religious leader nevertheless. Note finally Richard Shaw's *Dagger John: The Unquiet Life and Times of Archbishop John Hughes of New York* (New York: Paulist, 1977), p. 223.

40. Tierney, "Hughes," p. 79; Lawrence Kehoe, comp., *Complete Works of the Most Reverend John Hughes, D.D.,* 2 vols. (New York: Author, 1864–66), 1:29, 31, 544–45; 2:149–58, 160ff.

41. Rev. Augustus Thebaud, *Three Quarters of a Century (1807–1882) . . . ,* 3 vols. (New York: United States Catholic Historical Society, 1904–13), 3:6–7; O'Dea, *Hibernians,* pp. 887–90; Tierney, "Hughes," p. 77; *Leaves from the Annals of the Sisters of Mercy . . . ,* 4 vols., (New York: Catholic Publication Society, 1889), 3:142, 151, 155; and Helen Sweeney, *The Golden Milestone, 1846–1896: Fifty Years of Loving Labor . . . by the Sisters of Mercy . . .* (New York: Benziger, 1896), pp. 6–7, 15, 20–21. Sweeney's work, which was dedicated to the Archbishop, is a history of a female community to protect Irish immigrant women.

42. From his letterbook in Rev. Henry A. Braun, D.D., *Most Reverend John*

Hughes, First Archbishop of New York (New York: Dodd, Mead, 1892), pp. 110–11.

43. Potter, *Golden Door,* p. 407.

44. Hughes was certainly no Catholic pluralist, as he was rather hostile to the ethnic demands of non-Irish communicants. See Dolan, *Immigrant Church,* p. 23.

45. John Hughes, *Naturalized Foreigners,* pp. 29–30, File R6 B12, Hughes Papers at the New York City Archdiocesan Archives, Yonkers, N.Y..

46. I am summarizing his argument, not evaluating his historical veracity. Note his comments in Kehoe, *Hughes,* 1:417, 419, 436; 2:102–3, 119.

47. "In Regard to What is called the Catholic Press in the United States," in Ibid., 2:696. Greeley, in *Experience,* p. 126, refers to Hughes's profound American patriotism but also to his dissatisfaction with the anti-Catholic circumstances before the Civil War.

48. Joseph and Helen McCadden, *Father Varela: Torch Bearer from Cuba* (New York: United States Catholic History Society, 1969), pp. 49, 99–104; Dolan, *Immigrant Church,* pp. 45, 113, 118, 164–65, 167.

49. From Donna Merwick, *Boston Priests, 1848–1910: A Study of Social Change* (Cambridge, Mass.: Harvard University Press, 1973), p. 5.

50. Ibid.; Blessing, "Irish," p. 531; Potter, *Golden Door,* pp. 134–37; and Ryan, "Ballot Box," p. 2.

51. Robert H. Lord et al., *History of the Archdiocese of Boston . . . ,* 3 vols. (New York: Sheed & Ward, 1944), 2:58; Potter, *Golden Door,* p. 177. His obituary is in the *Pilot,* Oct. 24, 1840.

52. Robert Francis Walsh, "The *Boston Pilot:* A Newspaper for the Irish Immigrant, 1829–1908" (Ph.D. diss., Boston University, 1968), p. 94.

53. Sister Mary Alphonsine Frawley, C.S.J., "Patrick Donahoe" (Ph.D. diss., Catholic University, 1946), p. 290.

54. Walsh, *"Boston Pilot,"* pp. 40–43; Frawley, "Donahoe," p. ix; F. J. Lally, D. D., "Patrick Donahoe," in the *New Catholic Encyclopedia,* 17 vols. (New York: McGraw Hill, 1967), 4:998. Potter, in *Golden Door,* p. 599, calls it the most important of all Irish Catholic newspapers.

55. It was, therefore, similar to Thomas O'Connor's paper. It came out with an *Emigrant's Guide* in 1851. Walsh, "Boston Pilot," p. 115.

56. Ibid., p. vi; Frawley, "Donahoe," p. 131; Lally, "Donahoe," p. 998; and *Pilot,* Mar. 30, 1901 and Mar. 8, 1930, p. 23.

57. Frawley, "Donahoe," pp. 291–92. An account of his elaborate funeral is in the *Pilot,* Mar. 23, 1901, pp. 1, 4. In recounting his benefactions, I do not wish to lionize Donahoe. Many of his contributions were made in his own self-interest. Still, he clearly was in contact with ordinary Irish who knew him.

58. The chronology of the early changes in the paper is in dispute. The frequent changes in name, ownership, and editor are listed in the *Pilot,* Mar. 8, 1930, sec. B., p. 22; *Boston Transcript,* Mar. 8, 1901; and Walsh, *"Boston Pilot,"* p. v.

59. See Donahoe's editorial, "Changing Names," *Pilot,* Mar. 25, 1839, p. 142.

60. Ibid., "Patrick and Bridget," Jan. 28, 1860, when Finotti was editor and Donahoe publisher.

61. "Progress of a New Policy," in the *Pilot,* July 19, 1845, p. 230; and ibid., "The Immigrant," Aug. 7, 1847, p. 6.

62. The titles of Donahoe's editorials are instructive themselves, ibid., "Social and Political Duties of the Emigrant," July 31, 1847, p. 6; "Political Obligations of the Irishmen in America," Aug. 15, 1847, p. 6; and "Get Your Citizenship and Know How to Use It," Nov. 3, 1849, p. 6.

63. Ibid., May 5, 1850, p. 5.

64. Ibid., May 11, pp. 2–3; May 18, pp. 2, 6.

65. Cf. Joseph Donahoe and Michael Jordan, "Patrick Donahoe," *Journal of the American Irish Historical Society* 23 (1924):130–31.

66. Sister M. Jeanne d'Arc O'Hare, C.S.J., "The Public Career of Patrick Andrew Collins" (Ph.D. diss., Boston College, 1959), pp. 16–18.; *Memorial of Patrick Collins, 1844–1905,* p. 5 in the Collins Scrapbook in the Boston Public Library.

67. O'Hare, "Collins," pp. 41–45; M. P. Curran, ed., *Life of Patrick A. Collins* . . . (Norwood, Mass.: Norwood, 1906), pp. 4, 17. *Memorial,* p. 94, says he joined the Fenians in 1861 at the age of 17.

68. O'Hare, "Collins," pp. 54–63.

69. Curran, *Life,* p. 23.

70. From an 1866 speech entitled "Advice to Irish Voters," in Ibid., pp. 23, 32.

71. Handlin, in *Boston's Immigrants,* pp. 222–25, identifies Collins as an example of unsatisfactory Irish American leadership because Collins left the community to achieve success in the wider American society.

72. Patrick A. Collins, *Autobiography* (n.p., 1893), in manuscript in Collins Papers, ICBC; *Memorial,* p. 7; and esp. O'Hare, "Collins," pp. 7, 75, 84, 115, 119.

73. Curran, *Life,* pp. 56–59, and O'Hare, "Collins," p. 165 (as quoted in the *Boston Globe,* Feb. 28, 1881 and the *Pilot*) and p. 184. Whatever the sincerity of this rationalization, it is more important to know what he wanted his Irish American and American audiences to hear.

74. Curran, *Life,* p. 24. The address had the partisan aim of winning over New York's Irish population, a critical test for Cleveland, whose stock among the Irish was not high. Democrats distributed copies of the speech widely under the title, "An Irishman Speaks for Irishmen." Whether Collins did so is less important here than how he rationalized the two identities. See O'Hare, "Collins," p. 223.

75. Curran, *Life,* pp. 63, 120. Note, too, his spirited nationalist address on St. Patrick's Day in 1899, upon returning home, a statement reminiscent of his early, radical days. Patrick A. Collins, "Ireland's Dream of Nationality," in Thomas B. Reed et al., eds., *Modern Eloquence* (Philadelphia: J. D. Morris, 1901–3), pp. 257–60.

76. His electoral majority in 1903 was unprecedented. See the editorial from the *Boston Globe,* Sept. 15, 1905, in *Memorial,* p. 35, and passim.

77. See the *Boston Sunday Post,* Nov. 11, 1943, and the *Boston Traveler,* Sept. 14, 1940 in the Collins Papers, ICBC, and esp. *Memorial,* pp. 5–7. An account of the broad public support for the statue, a photo of the monument, and an appropriate inscription are in William Muir Whitehill, *Boston Statues* (Barre, Mass.: Barre, 1970), pp. 72–73.

78. Note his indebtedness to, but disagreement with, Handlin's picture of

the Irish in Boston. Michael Funchion, *Chicago's Irish Nationalists, 1881–1890* (New York: Arno, 1978), pp. 83n, 131.
    79. Ibid., pp. 22, 131.

3. THE GERMANS

1. A. B. Faust, *The German Element in the United States,* 2 vols. (New York: Steuben Society, 1927), 1:584–89; Kathleen Conzen, "Germans," in S. Thernstrom, *Harvard Encyclopedia* (see chap. 1, n. 28), pp. 910–11; Walter Kamphoefner, "Transplanted Westphalians" (Ph.D. diss., University of Missouri, 1978), p. 12; Frederick Luebke, *Bonds of Loyalty* (DeKalb, Ill.: Northern Illinois University Press, 1974), p. 32.
2. Mack Walker, *Germany and the Emigration, 1816–1885* (Cambridge, Mass.: Harvard University Press, 1964), pp. 1ff, 70, 158ff, and passim.
3. Julius Goebel, "A Political Prophecy of the 48ers in America," *Deutsch Amerikanische Geschichtesblätter* 12 (1912):466–67.
4. Carl Wittke, *Refugees of Revolution* (Philadelphia: University of Pennsylvania Press, 1952), pp. 59–60.
5. Günter Moltmann, "German Emigration to the United States in the First Half of the Nineteenth Century as a Form of Social Protest," *Przegląd Polonijny* 6, no. 4 (1980):46, 51 (in Polish).
6. Ibid., p. 50; Günter Moltmann, "German Emigration during the First Half of the Nineteenth Century as a Social Protest Movement," in Hans Trefousse, ed., *Germany and America* (New York: Brooklyn College Press, 1980), p. 105.
7. Moltmann, "Emigration to the United States," pp. 46–47.
8. Moltmann, "Movement," p. 106.
9. From Karl Kiel, "Grunde und Folgen," *Mitteilungen des Vereins . . .- Osnabruch* 61 (1941):127–28; and Albin Gladen, *Der Kreis Teklenberg an der Schwelle des Zeitalters der Industrialisierung* (Munster: Aschendorff, 1970), pp. 141, 215–18.
10. In Kamphoefner, "Westphalians," pp. 94, 95–97.
11. Quoted in Walker, *Germany,* pp. 115–17.
12. Typescript, "An Immigrant's Letter," located and translated for me by Rolf Engelsing of the Free University of Berlin, Spring, 1981.
13. Koerner's remarks are quoted in John Hawgood's *The Tragedy of German America* (New York: Arno, reprint 1970), p. 41.
14. Wittke, *Refugees,* p. 14.
15. From Heinz Klaus, "German American Language Maintenance Efforts," in Joshua Fishman et al., eds., *Language Loyalty in the United States* (The Hague: Mouton, 1966), p. 229. The slogan is widely reprinted in the historical literature. See for example Merlin Timothy Tucker, "Political Leadership in the Illinois-Missouri German Community, 1836–1872" (Ph.D. diss., University of Illinois, 1968), pp. 81–82, and Luebke, *Bonds,* p. 48.
16. The best biography is William Yeaton Wagener's "General John Andreas Wagener" (Ph.D. diss., University of South Carolina, 1937), pp. 2ff. See also Heinrich Armin Rattermann, *General Johann Andreas Wagener: Eine Biographische Skizze* (Cincinnati: Mecklenberg and Rosenthal, 1877), pp. 6ff; G. D. Bernheim, *History of the German Settlements and of the Lutheran Church in North and South Carolina . . .* (Philadelphia: Luthern Book Store, 1872, reprint

1972), p. 530. One group begun several decades before Wagener's arrival had continued to speak German but had still assimilated. See Anton Eichoff, *In der Neuen Heimat . . . über die Deutschen Einwanderer* (New York: Steiger, 1884), p. 214; and George J. Gongaware, comp., *The History of the German Friendly Society of Charleston . . .* (Richmond: Garrett and Massie, 1935), pp. 1, 3.

17. Samuel A. Court Ashe, *Cyclopedia of Eminent and Representative Men of the Carolinas of the Nineteenth Century* (Madison, Wisc.: Brant and Fuller, 1892, reprint 1972), pp. 614–15.

18. Uwe Schnall, ed., *Auswanderung-Bremen-USA* (Bremerhaven: Deutsches Schiffahrtsmuseum, 1976), p. 77; Ratterman, *Wagener,* p. 7.

19. Apparently such multifaith institutions were not uncommon in early German American history. See Gustav Koerner, *Das Deutsche element in den Vereinigten Staaten Von Nordamerika, 1818–1848* (Cincinnati: A. E. Wilde, 1880), p. 387; Bernheim, *History,* p. 387.

20. From Eichoff, *Heimat,* p. 214.

21. My emphasis. Wagener, "Wagener," p. 17–18.

22. From *Der Teutone,* Aug. 13, 1844, quoted in Rattermann, *Wagener,* p. 12.

23. Gongaware, *Friendly Society,* p. 127. He participated in the Civil War and afterward became more of an American leader—he was a delegate to the state convention in 1864, later state commissioner of emigration, and finally mayor of Charleston in 1871. Ashe, *Cyclopedia,* p. 616.

24. George von Bosse, *Das Deutsche element in den Vereinigten Staaten* (Stuttgart: Belsersche, 1908), p. 237. The translated inscription reads, in part, "Next to all his love for his new fatherland his heart still also adheres to the old fatherland and his countrymen."

25. Statistics from Martin Davis, comp., *Historical Background of German Churches . . .* (typescript at the Cincinnati Historical Society) Rumelin Papers, Box 1, Folder 6, n.d.; Carl Wittke, "The Germans of Cincinnati," Historical and Philosophical Society of Ohio, *Bulletin* 20 (January 1962), p. 3; Alvin Harlow, *The Serene Cincinnatians* (New York: Dutton, 1950), p. 192; William Anthony Rengering II, "Early Germans in Cincinnati" (master's thesis, University of Cincinnati, 1950), pp. 26–27.

26. My sources are numerous but they eschew speculation. Cf. Carl Vetz, "Martin Baum, Pioneer Cincinnati Entrepreneur," Historical and Philosophical Society of Ohio, *Bulletin* 16 (July 1958), pp. 215ff; Harlow, *Cincinnatians,* pp. 26, 30, 181–82, 304; Wittke, "Germans," pp. 3–4; Rengering, "Early Germans," pp. 1–6, 20–21; and Edward Deering Mansfield, *Memoirs of the Life and Services of Daniel Drake, M.D.* (New York: Applegate, 1855, reprint, 1975), p. 133.

27. "Deutsche Bilder aus der Geschichte der Stadt Cincinnati: V. Martin Baum," *Der Deutsche Pionier,* Jahre 10, Heft 2 (May 1878), p. 45; von Bosse, *Element,* p. 155; Rengering, "Early Germans," pp. 3–4.

28. Some dispute exists over the degree of his support. Vetz, "Baum," pp. 232, 235; Rengering, "Early Germans," p. 6; "Deutsche Bilder," p. 46.

29. Reemelin's first and last names have numerous different spellings in sources: Charles, Carl, and Karl Gustav Reemelin and Rumelin. In my citations I list the names as given on the title page. I use only Charles Reemelin in the text to minimize confusion. *Koerner, Element,* p. 187; *Cincinnati und sein Deutschtum* (Cincinnati: Queen City, 1901), p. 79; Carl Gustav Rumelin, *Life of Charles*

Reemelin (Cincinnati: Weir and Daiker, 1892), pp. 1, 10, 14, 22–24, 29, 31, 35, 39–45; von Bosse, *Element,* pp. 156ff.

30. Reemelin was an "adviser" whom many trusted, according to *Cincinnati und sein Deutschtum,* p. 80; he was a "fearless" and "distinguished" "representative of *Deutschtum,*" according to Reinhold Scholl, "Karl Rumelin," *Schwabische Lebensbilder* 7 (1940):448. His Catholic criticism is mentioned in Rumelin, *Life,* pp. 94–95.

31. Henry Roedter, *Memoirs,* p. 2, in the Roedter Papers at the Cincinnati Historical Society, hereafter CHS.

32. Charles Reemelin, "Address to the Democratic Party of Hamilton County (1838–39)," in the Rumelin Papers, Box 3, CHS.

33. Rumelin, *Life,* p. 83.

34. Charles Reemelin, *Treatise on Politics as a Science* (Cincinnati: R. Clarke, 1875), pp. 138–39.

35. Karl Rumelin, "Amerikanismus," *Der Deutsche Pionier,* Jahre 17, Heft (1885), pp. 38–39.

36. Carl Reemelin, *A Critical Review of American Politics* (Cincinnati: Clarke, 1881), pp. 36–39, 42–47.

37. Carl Rumelin, "Die Zukunst des Deutschtums in America." *Der Deutsche Pionier,* Jahre 2, Heft 2 (January 1871), pp. 340–41, 344–46.

38. Hawgood, *Tragedy,* p. 275; Guido Dobbert, "The Disintegration of an American Immigrant Community: The Cincinnati Germans, 1820–1920" (Ph.D. diss., University of Chicago, 1965), p. 913.

39. The standard biography remains that of the Right Reverend Peter Leo Johnson, *Crosier on the Frontier: A Life of John Martin Henni, Archbishop of Milwaukee* . . . (Madison, Wisc.: Society Press, 1959), pp. 34–35, 173. See also Wilhelm Hense-Jensen, *Wisconsin's Deutsche-Amerikaner* . . . , 2 vols. (Milwaukee: Die Deutsche Gesellschaft, 1900–1902), 1:86; Koerner, *Element,* pp. 290ff; and Martin Marty, O.S.B., *Dr. Johann Martin Henni* . . . (New York: Benziger, 1888).

40. Joseph Michael White, "Religion and Community: Cincinnati Germans, 1814–1870" (Ph.D. diss., University of Notre Dame, 1980), p. 163.

41. Johnson, *Crozier,* pp. 51–53.

42. Ibid., p. 41. Henni's argument was similar to the appeal that Peter Paul Cahensly made decades later, and it even shrewdly went beyond it.

43. Ibid., p. 45.

44. Ibid., p. 49.

45. *Der Wahrheits-Freund im Weltlichen,* July 20, 1837.

46. Johnson, *Crosier,* p. 56.

47. The most convenient and reliable life history is J.H.A. Lacker, "Francis A. Hoffmann of Illinois and Hans Buschbauer of Wisconsin," *Wisconsin Magazine of History* 13 (June 1930):327–55. See also Rudolph A. Hofmeister, *The Germans of Chicago* (Champaign, Ill.: Stipes, 1976), esp. p. 25; Koerner, *Element,* pp. 184ff; and George Upton and Elias Colbert, *Biographical Sketches of the Leading Men of Chicago* (Chicago: Wilson and St. Clair, 1868), pp. 367–71.

48. From Charles J. Townsend, "The Germans of Chicago" (Ph.D. diss., University of Chicago, 1927), pp. 3–5, 7–9, 16, 24–26.

49. Von Bosse, in *Element,* p. 186, discusses Hoffman's charismatic qualities, as do Karl Kretzmann, "Francis Arnold Hoffmann," *Concordia Histor-*

ical Institute Quarterly 18 (1945):39; and Hildegard B. Johnson, "Adjustment to the United States," in A. E. Zucker, ed., *The Forty-Eighters: Political Refugees of the German Revolution of 1848* (New York: Columbia University Press, 1950), p. 61.

50. Kretzmann "Hoffmann," p. 47; Lacker, "Hoffmann," pp. 332–34; Hofmeister, *Germans,* p. 116.

51. Upton and Colbert, *Sketches,* p. 371.

52. Minna Hoffman Nehrling, "Memoirs, of Riverside Farm," *Wisconsin Magazine of History* 13 (June 1930): 358, 361.

53. Sharon Mallman, "The Brumders of Milwaukee" *Milwaukee History* 3 (Autumn 1980); 68–69. The Milwaukee *Germania,* in which the column first appeared, had a circulation of one hundred thousand alone. See also J.H.A. Lacker, "Francis Arnold Hoffmann," in Malone, *Dictionary* (see chap. 2, n. 21), 9:118–19; "'Hans Buschbauer' der deutsch-amerikanische Bauer in Wisconsin," *Neidersachlische Dorfzeitung* (Hannover), Jan. 8, 1890, in Hoffmann Papers, Illinois State Historical Library, Springfield, Illinois. This latter article calls Hoffmann an "endearing" (Beliebter) and "popular" author, and a "true and well-intentioned adviser" (truer and wohlmeinender Berather), of the German immigrant farmer in Uncle Sam's vast country. Ibid, p. 1.

54. According to his Milwaukee editor, George Brumder, in *Milwaukee Journal,* Jan. 23, 1903, p. 12. See also Emil Mannhardt, "Francis Arnold Hoffmann," *Deutsch Amerikanische Geschichtsblätter* 3, pt. 3 (1903), p. 61.

55. The anti-immigrant provision was dropped in the bill's final version. Lacker, "Hoffmann," pp. 338, 340.

56. His wife almost divorced him early in their marriage because of his insistence, according to his granddaughter. Nehrling, "Memoirs," pp. 354, 347, 359–60.

57. F. A. Hoffmann, "Deutsch," in *Die Germania,* Dec. 3, 1844. Note also Mannhardt, "Hoffmann," pp. 59, 61.

58. "German Celebration of the Fourth," in a Chicago(?) newspaper article in the Hoffmann Papers, Concordia Historical Institute. The German version is in *Illinois Staats-Zeitung,* July 6, 1855.

59. Cf. Von Bosse, *Element,* p. 187; Kamphoefner, "Westphalians," p. 119; and a reading of the 1850 census by Kathleen Neils Conzen, *Immigrant Milwaukee* (Cambridge, Mass.: Harvard University Press, 1975), p. 29.

60. "Dr. Franz Huebschmann," typescript in Huebschmann Papers, Milwaukee County Historical Society, hereafter HP-MCHS.

61. Eunice B. Bardell, "German Immigrants and Health Care in Pioneer Milwaukee," *Historical Messenger* of the Milwaukee County Historical Society, 33 (Autumn 1977):89.

62. Koerner, *Element,* pp. 284–85; "Dr. Franz Hübschmann, *Der Deutsche Pionier,* Jahre 12, Heft 2 (May 1880), p. 45; *Der Musikverein von Milwaukee, 1850–1900* (Milwaukee: n.p., 1900), pp. 1–2; H. Russell Austin, *The Milwaukee Story: The Making of an American City* (Milwaukee: Journal, 1946), pp. 140–41; M. Schoeffler to Huebschmann, letter of Feb. 11, 1844, HP-MCHS; "Dr. Franz Huebschmann," pp. 4, 8, HP-MCHS; Robert Wild, "Dr. Francis Huebschmann," in Ellis Baker Usher, ed., *Wisconsin: Its Story and Biography,* 8 vols., (Chicago: Lewis, 1914), 4:646.

63. The significance of the parade is recounted in Conzen, *Milwaukee,* p. 1.

See also Rudolph Koss, *Milwaukee* (Milwaukee: English edition, 1971), pp. 150, 170–72, 185, typescript at Milwaukee Public Library; Carl H. Knoche, "Dr. Francis Huebschmann's Political Career," *Historical Messenger* 28 (Winter 1972): 11ff.

64. Koss, *Milwaukee*, p. 190.

65. Huebschmann's speeches are in Milo Quaife, "Constitutional Convention of 1846," in Wisconsin Historical Publications, *Collections*, 27 (Madison: author, 1919): 231–35; and Hense-Jensen, *Amerikaner*, 1:96. The provision remained in the ratified document of the second convention. Knoche, "Career," p. 116.

66. Conzen, *Milwaukee*, pp. 173, 195–96.

67. Gottfried Duden, *Report on a Journey to the Western States of North America . . .* , eds., and trans., George Kellner et al. (Columbia: University of Missouri Press, 1980), pp. vii, xi–xvii.

68. William G. Bek, "The Followers of Duden," *Missouri Historical Review* 18 (1923–24): 418–19; Thomas J. McCormack, ed., *Memoirs of Gustav Koerner, 1809–1896*, 2 vols. (Cedar Rapids, Iowa: Torch, 1909), pp. 306–7.

69. Tucker, "Political Leadership," pp. 112, 421–43.

70. Ibid., pp. 421–43; Friedrich Munch, *Gesammelte Schriften* (St. Louis: Witten, 1902), pp. 124ff; Gerard Wilk, *Americans from Germany* (New York: German Information Center, 1976), pp. 33–34.

71. Wilk, *Americans*, p. 34.

72. Note a translation of his writings in Bek, "Followers," 18 (1923–24): 562–84, and ibid., 19 (1924–25): 345.

73. Munch, *Gesammelte Schriften*, pp. 386, 388.

74. Bek, "Followers," 19 (1924–25):346.

75. *History of Franklin, Jefferson and Gasconade Counties, Missouri* (Chicago: Goodspeed, 1888; reprint, 1970), p. 753.

76. Koerner, *Element*, p. 312; *History of Franklin . . . Counties*, p. 752; Bek, "Followers," 16 (1921–22):290–91.

77. From the translation of Bek, "Followers," 16 (1921–22):343–44.

78. Gert Goebel, *Langer als ein Menschenleben in Missouri* (St. Louis: Ritters, 1877), p. 170.

79. Luebke, *Bonds* pp. 48–50, states that this faith in both American and German cultures was held by German Americans, but he implies that it took a long time before they realized it—not until the dawn of the twentieth century. My contention is that this understanding came much earlier, even in the pioneering generation.

4. THE NORWEGIANS AND SWEDES

1. A succinct historiographic survey is Robert S. Salisbury, "Swedish American Historiography and the Question of Americanization," *Swedish Pioneer Historical Quarterly* 29 (April 1978):117–36.

2. A recent work on the topic is Dorothy Burton Skardal, *The Divided Heart: Scandinavian Immigrant Experience through Literary Sources* (Lincoln: University of Nebraska Press, 1974). It will be discussed at the end of this chapter.

3. A good summary of immigration and settlement patterns is in Peter

Munch's "The Norwegians," in Thernstrom, *Harvard Encyclopedia* (see chap. 1, no. 28), pp. 750–60.

4. The figures are from Olaf M. Norlie, *History of the Norwegian People in America* (New York: Augsburg, 1925; reprint 1973), p. 169, and Einar Haugen, "History of the Department of Scandinavian Language at the University of Wisconsin, 1869–1931," typescript in the University of Wisconsin Archives.

5. An explanation for the clerics' lack of popularity among the immigrants is in Munch's "The Norwegians," p. 755, and Theodore Blegen's *Norwegian Migration to America: The American Transition* (Northfield, Minn.: Norwegian American Historical Association, 1940), p. 246.

6. The standard biography is Hustvedt, *Anderson* (see chap. 1, n. 7), pp. 3, 5, 11. See also Einar Haugen, "Wisconsin Pioneers in Scandinavian Studies," *Wisconsin Magazine of History* 34 (Autumn 1950):29; and Rasmus Anderson, *Life Story . . .* (Madison, Wisc.: Author, 2d ed. revised, 1917), p. 58.

7. Haugen, "History . . . " p. 3.

8. Laurence M. Larsen, *The Changing West and Other Essays* Northfield, Minn.: Norwegian American Historical Association, 1937), p. 121.

9. Blegen, *Migration,* pp. 243–52, has the representative criticism.

10. Cf. Haugen, "Wisconsin Pioneers," p. 32.

11. Anderson, *Life Story . . . ,* p. 145. Italics mine.

12. Letter to Karina Anderson, May 11, 1885, quoted in Hustvedt, *Anderson,* p. 352; and citation in the newspaper *Skandinaven,* August 15, 1877, in Frank Nelson, "The School Controversy among Norwegian Immigrants," in Norwegian American Historical Association, *Studies and Records* 26 (1974):215.

13. Hustvedt, *Anderson,* p. 95.

14. See my article, "Ethnic Confrontation with State Universities, 1860–1920," in B. Weiss, ed., *American Education and the European Immigrant* (Champaign, Ill.: University of Illinois Press, 1982), esp. p. 196.

15. Blegen, *Migration,* p. 585.

16. Larsen, "West," p. 132, and Hustvedt, *Anderson,* pp. 55–56.

17. Hustvedt, *Anderson,* pp. 56, 102. See also Johnson's letter to President J. Bascom, February 12, 1876, in *Annual Report of the Board of Regents of the University . . . September 30, 1876* (Madison, 1876), pp. 24–25, and Nelson, "Controversy," p. 212.

18. Blegen, *Migration,* pp. 263–65.

19. Hustvedt, *Anderson,* p. 352. See also Larsen, "West," pp. 133–34, and Blegen, *Migration,* p. 267.

20. Haugen, "Pioneers," p. 30.

21. Blegen, *Migration,* p. 553.

22. Ibid., p. 554n.

23. J. Socke Lowell, "Norwegian Americans and the Politics of Dissent, 1880–1914" (Ph.D. diss., University of Iowa, 1979), p. 37. Aside from the Odland work cited below (n. 25), good biographical accounts are Jacob A. O. Preus, "Knute Nelson," *Minnesota History Bulletin* 5 (February 1924):329–47 and Solon J. Buck "Knute Nelson," in Malone. *Dictionary* (see chap. 2, n. 21), 7:418–19.

24. Nelson to Anderson, February 14, 1868, in the Anderson Papers, University of Wisconsin, hereafter cited as AP-UW. In "Nelson," Buck noted that "he had

the vote of his countrymen behind him in his early [political] career." In Malone, *Dictionary*, 7:419.

25. Martin Odland, *The Life of Knute Nelson* (Minneapolis: Lund, 1926), p. 7, 10–13, 33, 51–56.

26. Blegen, *Migration*, p. 555.

27. Cf. letters from Nelson to Anderson, August 19, December 4, 1882, and June 2, 1883 in AP-UW.

28. Speech of Nelson in the House of Representatives, March 27, 1888, in the Nelson Papers, Minnesota Historical Society, hereafter cited as NP-MHS. See also Odland, *Nelson*, pp. 294–95.

29. *Immigration . . . Speech of the Hon. Knute Nelson of Minnesota . . . May 14, 1896* (Washington, 1896), NP-MHS.

30. Odland, *Nelson*, pp. 229–30, 234, 316–17; G. Rudolph Bjorgan, "The Success Story of an Immigrant" (Ph.D. diss., University of Minnesota, 1967), pp. 177–78, 312.

31. Blegen, in *Migration*, pp. 69–72, 81, attacks the great Norwegian American writer O. E. Rölvaag for overdramatizing the trauma of immigrant identity. Blegen, a dean of Norwegian American historians, probably considered Rölvaag a man of talent, but he questioned the accuracy of his writing as a reflection of the lives of the ordinary immigrants. Norwegian Americans, in Blegen's view, fashioned a stable way of life largely from their avid interest in American politics.

32. Ulf Beijbom, "The Swedes," in S. Thernstrom, *Harvard Encyclopedia*, pp. 972–75.

33. E.g., H. Arnold Barton, ed., *Letters from the Promised Land: Swedish America, 1840–1914* (Minneapolis: University of Minnesota Press, 1975), p. 18.

34. George Stephenson, *The Religious Aspects of Swedish Immigration* (Minneapolis: University of Minnesota, 1932; reprint, New York: Arno, 1969), pp. 169–70; O. Fritiof Ander, *T. N. Hasselquist: The Career and Influence of a Swedish American Clergyman, Journalist, and Educator* (Rock Island, Ill.: Augustana Historical Society, 1931), p. 25.

35. Stephenson, *Religious Aspects*, p. 169; Ander, *Hasselquist*, p. 41–42.

36. Ander, *Hasselquist*, p. 224; Stephenson, *Religious Aspects*, p. 167; and Barton, *Letters*, p. 18.

37. Lars Ljungmark, *For Sale, Minnesota: Organized Promotion of Scandinavian Immigration, 1866–1873* (Goteborg: Laromedlsford, 1971), p. 67n.

38. Cf. Beijbom, "Swedes," p. 977.

39. Peter P. Peterson, "A History of Higher Education among the Swedish Immigrants in America" (D.Ed. diss., Harvard University, 1941), p. 110 and *passim;* Dag Blanck, "A Language That Does Not Die Easily," undergraduate paper, Augustana College Archives, dated February 5, 1978; Stephenson, *Religious Aspects*, p. 311; Ander, *Hasselquist*, pp. 225, 228–29.

40. Ander, *Hasselquist*, p. 27, also pp. 46, 160.

41. Barton, *Letters*, p. 68.

42. Ibid., p. 139.

43. Letter from Hasselquist to Rev. Henry Baugher, Paxton, Mo., October 8, 1863, Ms. 2, Box 2, Hasselquist Papers, Augustana College Library; Blanck, "Language," p. 6.

44. Peterson, "History," p. 110.

45. Stephenson, *Religious Aspects*, pp. 410–11.

46. Ulf Beijbom, "Historiography of Swedish America," *Swedish Pioneer Historical Quarterly* 31 (October 1980):264; Allen Kastrup, *The Swedish Heritage in America* (St. Paul, Minn.: Swedish Council of America, 1975), p. 377. An uncritical but still helpful review of Enander by his daughter is Hilma Enander's "Dr. Enander," in *Yearbook of the Swedish American Historical Society of America* 7 (1921–22):24–32.

47. Ulf Beijbom, *The Swedes of Chicago* (Chicago: Chicago Historical Society, 1971), pp. 296, 301.

48. Beijbom, "Historiography," pp. 269, 284n.

49. Kastrup, *Swedish Heritage,* pp. 378–79.

50. H. Arnold Barton's "Swedish American Historiography," *Immigration History Newsletter* 15 (May 1983):2, 5n6 strongly implies the event's historical significance to Swedish Americans and its impact on their identity. The details of the day are described in Hans Mattson, comp., *250th Anniversary of the First Swedish Settlements in America, September 14, 1888* (Minneapolis: Author, 1889), pp. 1–5 and *passim;* and Hans Mattson, *Reminiscences: The Story of an Emigrant* (St. Paul: D. D. Merrill, 1891), pp. 292–95; and Beijbom, "Historiography," p. 266.

51. Mattson, *Anniversary,* p. 3.

52. My emphasis, Ibid., pp. 3, 27.

53. Ibid., p. 28. The translation is by Professor Roy Swanson of the University of Wisconsin–Milwaukee, to whom I am grateful.

54. Mattson, *Reminiscences,* pp. 12–14. A superb biography is Luther Jaeger's "Hans Mattson," in A. E. Strand, ed. and comp., *A History of the Swedish Americans of Minnesota* . . . 2 vols. (Chicago: Lewis, 1910), 1:80–89.

55. John B. Rice, "The Swedes," in June D. Holmquist, ed., *They Chose Minnesota* (St. Paul: Minnesota Historical Society, 1981), p. 258, cites Mattson's unrivaled influence on Swedish settlement in the state. His leadership in other areas can be assumed.

56. Kastrup, *Swedish Heritage,* p. 335; Lars Ljungmark, *Swedish Exodus* (Carbondale, Ill.: Southern Illinois University Press, 1979), p. 63; Ljungmark, *For Sale, Minnesota,* pp. 267–68, 108.

57. Mattson, *Reminiscences,* pp. 60–61.

58. Ibid., pp. 296–313.

59. Skardal, *Heart,* p. 20.

60. Ibid., pp. 264, 328.

61. Ibid., pp. 18, 259–69.

62. Ibid., pp. 107, 117.

5. THE JEWS

1. Note the succinct discussion in Arthur Goren's "The Jews," in Thernstrom, *Harvard Encyclopedia* (see chap. 1, n. 28), pp. 586–87, a superb summary.

2. This survey is taken from a number of sources, esp. Max Weinreich, *History of the Yiddish Language,* trans. Shlomo Noble and Joshua Fishman (Chicago: University of Chicago Press, 1977), pp. 284–89; Samuel Niger, "Yiddish Culture," in *The Jewish People: Past and Present* 4 vols. (New York: Jewish Encyclopedic Handbooks, 1946–55), 4:264ff; Jacob De Haas, *Encyclopedia of*

Jewish Knowledge (New York: Behrman, 1934), p. 642, Solomon Liptzin, *A History of Yiddish Literature* (Middle Village, N.Y.: J. David, 1972), pp. 1–3, 17, 24–25; and Marvin Leon Singer, "A History of the Yiddish Theatre in New York City to 1892" (Ph.D. diss., Indiana University, 1960), pp. 8–9, 39–50; and Joshua A. Fishman, ed., *Never Say Die: A Thousand Years of Jewish Life and Letters* (The Hague: Mouton, 1980), esp. pp. 12–16ff.

3. Fishman, *Never Say Die*, p. 12n. ff.

4. A few Yiddish-speaking Jews had come to the city even before 1880. The first synagogue was established in 1852, and as many as thirty such congregations were located there two decades later. Bernard Martin, "Yiddish Literature in the United States," *American Jewish Archives* 33 (November 1981):184.

5. This conventional view was the conclusion of Irving Howe et al., *The World of Our Fathers* (New York: Harcourt, Brace, Jovanovich, 1976), pp. 116–17.

6. Jeffrey S. Gurock, "Resisters and Accommodators: Varieties of Orthodox Rabbis in America, 1880–1983" in *American Jewish Archives* 35 (November 1983):105–9. Curiously, Gurock does not mention Sarasohn. Note the statement by Sarasohn's granddaughter in Kenneth Rosett and Frieda Rosett, comps., *Sarasohn and Son: A Scrapbook* (White Plains, N.Y.: Authors, 1984, 2d ed.), Foreword.

7. The best biography is Moshe Starkman's, "Kasriel (Chasriel) H. Sarasohn: Sarasohn Memoirs About the Yiddish Press in America" in *Yorbukh Amopteyl* (New York: n.p., 1931), pp. 273–95 (in Yiddish). See also De Haas, *Encyclopedia*, p. 490; Rosett and Rosett, *Sarasohn*, pp. i–viii; and Solomon Liptzin, "Kasriel Hersch Sarasohn," in Cecil Roth et al., eds., *Encyclopedia Judaica* 16 vols. (New York and Jerusalem: Macmillan, 1971), 14:872–73.

8. One source cited over one hundred local societies formed in the city before 1900. Milton Doroshkin, *Yiddish in America: Social and Cultural Foundations* (Rutherford, N.J.: Fairleigh Dickinson University Press, 1969), pp. 230–36. There were undoubtedly many more. See also Howe, *World*, pp. 183–86.

9. Sarasohn's early trials are recounted in Starkman, "Sarasohn," pp. 3–5, 137; De Haas, *Encyclopedia*, p. 490; and Mordecai Soltes, *The Yiddish Press: An Americanizing Agency* (New York: Teacher's College Press, 1925), p. 15; and Martin, "Yiddish Literature," pp. 184–85.

10. Starkman, "Sarasohn," p. 26.

11. Sarasohn had to recruit gentile youth to distribute copies. Niger, "Yiddish Culture," p. 273.

12. Liptzin, *Yiddish Literature*, p. 156; Soltes, *Yiddish Press*, pp. 24–25; Liptzin, "Sarasohn," p. 873.

13. Moses Weinberger, *People Walk on Their Heads: Moses Weinberger's Jews and Judaism in New York*, trans. Jonathan Sarna (New York: Holmes and Meier, 1981), p. 67.

14. Starkman, "Sarasohn," pp. 36–37; Niger, "Yiddish Culture," p. 274.

15. Note the observation of a contemporary in Weinberger, *People Walk*, p. 67, and the assertion of *Congress Weekly*, Mar. 2, 1945, that Sarasohn was "the most powerful Yiddish newspaper publisher in the country" before the time of Cahan and *Jewish Daily Forward*, in Rosett and Rosett, *Sarasohn*.

16. Ayer's Directory for 1905 pegs the *Tageblatt*, the *Forward*, and the *Yiddischer Morgen Zhurnal* about the same, at about fifty thousand. Cited in Soltes,

Yiddish Press, pp. 24–25. But Liptzin, "Sarasohn," p. 873, and Martin, "Yiddish Literature," pp. 184–85, say the *Tageblatt* had seventy thousand subscribers in 1900. Note the high estimate of the Tageblatt's dominance given in the *American Hebrew and Jewish Messenger,* Jan. 13, 1905, p. 251. See also, Howe, *World,* p. 520; Hutchins Hapgood, *The Spirit of the Ghetto: Studies of the Jewish Quarter of New York* (New York: Schocken, 1902; paperback ed. 1976), pp. 179–80; and S. Margoshes, "The Jewish Press in New York City," *Jewish Communal Register* (1917–1918):602–3.

17. Starkman, "Sarasohn," p. 26; see also Martin, "Yiddish Literature," p. 185; and Charles A. Madison, *Yiddish Literature: Its Scope and Major Writers* (New York: Ungar, 1968), pp. 135–46.

18. Mark Wischnitzer, *Visas to Freedom: The History of the Hebrew Immigrant Aid Society* (Cleveland: World, 1956), pp. 16, 33; Starkman, "Sarasohn," p. 7.

19. A full list of his humanitarian and philanthropic activities is in *New York Evening Sun,* Jan. 12, 1905; *New York Mail,* Jan. 12, 1905; *New York Herald,* Jan. 13, 1905; and *American Hebrew,* Jan. 13, 1905, in Sarasohn Papers, American Jewish Archives, Microfilm 525, hereafter cited as SP-AJA; see also item in SP-AJA listed simply as *Jewish Encyclopedia,* p. 59.

20. Starkman, "Sarasohn"; "Thousands Watch Sarasohn Funeral" *New York Times,* Jan. 14, 1905, p. 9. Note in particular the account in "A Funeral as Grand as That of Moses," Portland (Oregon) *Evening Telegraph,* Jan. 12, 1905, in SP-AJA.

21. From *New York Evening Post,* Jan. 13, 1905, in SP-AJA.

22. Ibid.

23. Compiled from SP-AJA.

24. *New York Herald,* Jan. 13, 1905, in SP-AJA; *New York Times,* Jan. 14, 1905, p. 9, in SP-AJA.

25. Quoted in *American Hebrew,* Jan. 13, 1905, p. 251, and in his letter in the *Jewish Daily News,* Mar. 20, 1920, p. 2.

26. *American Hebrew,* Feb. 17, 1905, p. 400.

27. *American Israelite,* in SP-AJA, Microfilm 525.

28. From the *Yiddishes Tageblatt,* Mar. 20, 1910, English language section. See also the statement of A. L. Wolbaret, Ibid., p. 6. Cf. the conclusion of one scholar that Orthodox leaders were "politically wise. They understood the American style of politics." Arthur A. Goren, "Orthodox Politics, Republican and Jewish: Jacob Saphirstein and the *Morgen Zhurnal,*" in *Eighth World Congress of Jewish Studies, Panel Sessions, Jewish History* (Jerusalem, 1984), pp. 70–71.

29. "A great Americanizing influence among [the Yiddish coreligionists]." *American Hebrew* Jan. 13, 1905, p. 251; *The New York Evening Post,* Jan. 14, 1905, in SP-AJA.

30. *First Annual Report of the Educational Alliance, 1893* (New York, 1894), pp. 15–16.

31. Cary Goodman, "Recreating Americans at the Educational Alliance," *Journal of Ethnic Studies* 6 (Winter 1979):2–3, 10–14.

32. *First Annual Report,* p. 20; Yehezkel Wyszkowski, "The *American Hebrew* Views the Jewish Community in the United States, 1879–1884, 1894–1898, 1903–1908" (Ph.D. diss., Yeshiva University, 1979), p. 435.

33. Miriam Blaustein, arranger, *Memoirs of David Blaustein: Educator and*

Communal Worker (New York: McBride, Nast, 1913), pp. 18–28; "David Blaustein," *Encyclopedia Judaica*, 4:1078.

34. Note the comments of Edward Levine in 1912 and S. Lowenstein in 1913. Blaustein, *Memoirs*, pp. 271, 287.

35. Quoted in ibid., p. 43.

36. Ibid., p. 79. See also Moses Rischin, *The Promised City* (Cambridge, Mass.: Harvard University Press, 1962), pp. 101–2.

37. Cf. Howe, *World*, p. 231.

38. These are Blaustein's opinions, according to his wife. See Blaustein, *Memoirs*, pp. 48, 63, 157.

39. *New York Times*, Nov. 28, 1939; Alexander Harkavy, "*Chapters from My Life*," trans. Jonathan Sarna, *American Jewish Archives* 33 (April 1981):35ff, esp. 42–48.

40. Benjamin Richards, "Alexander Harkavy," *American Jewish Yearbook* 42 (1940–41):156–57. He had been employed as a printer's assistant in Vilna prior to his leaving Europe. Chanan Harkavy, *Stammbuch der Familie Harkavy* (New York: n.p., 1913), Yivo Library, New York. I am grateful to Mr. Paul H. Melrood of Milwaukee for his help with the translation.

41. Richards's "Harkavy," 153ff, is one of the best biographies in English. See also Jonathan Sarna, "Our Distant Brethren: Alexander Harkavy on Montreal Jews—1888," *Canadian Jewish Historical Society Journal* (Fall 1983):59. Although he was not an outstanding teacher, he was a community leader in Montreal from 1886 to 1888. Ibid., p. 60.

42. Richards, "Harkavy," p. 158.

43. Yudel Mark, "Alexander Harkavy, 1863–1939," *Jewish Book Annual* 26 (1968–69):102–3.

44. The manual went through several editions. Ibid.

45. Richards, "Harkavy," pp. 160–61; De Haas, *Encyclopedia*, p. 197.

46. A. Harkavy, *Washington: The First President of the United States Including the Declaration of Independence in English and Jewish* (New York: Kantrowitz, 1892), esp. pp. 15, 21. Available at Hebrew Union College Library, Cincinnati. My thanks again to my translator, Paul Melrood.

47. Richards, "Harkavy," pp. 163–64.

48. Mark, "Harkavy," pp. 106–7.

49. Alexander Harkavy, *Chapters from My Life* (New York: Hebrew, 1935), p. 3, (in Hebrew, *Perakim me-hayyai*).

50. Wischnitzer, *Visas to Freedom*, p. 41; and Thomas Pitkin, *Keepers of the Gate: A History of Ellis Island* (New York: New York University Press, 1975), p. 45.

51. *American Hebrew*, Oct. 25, 1907, p. 607, as quoted in Wyskowski, "American Hebrew," p. 495.

52. Although I will not verify it at length, the consensus of historians is that Cahan maintained a close acquaintance with his audience. Note the opinion of John Higham, "Abraham Cahan: Novelist Between Two Cultures," in J. Higham, *Send These to Me: Jews and Other Immigrants in Urban America* (New York: Atheneum, 1975), passim, esp. p. 98. The best biographical sketch is Moses Rischin's "Abraham Cahan," in John Garraty, ed., *Dictionary of American Biography, 1951–1955* (New York: 1975), supplement 5, pp. 95–97.

53. Melech Epstein, *Profiles of Eleven* (Detroit: Wayne State University Press, 1955), p. 51.

54. Hapgood, *Spirit*, p. 182.

55. Jules Chametzky, *From the Ghetto: The Fiction of Abraham Cahan* (Amherst, Mass.: University of Massachusetts Press, 1977), pp. 4–5, 7, 12. Some disagreement exists over precisely when Cahan subordinated socialist ideals to pragmatic aid. Moses Rischin, in "Abraham Cahan and the *New York Commercial Advertiser*," *Publications of American Jewish Historical Society* 43 (September 1953):35, says the shift came later, in the 1897–1902 period, when he was an English-language reporter.

56. Rischin, "*Commercial Advertiser*," pp. 10–13, 35; Epstein, *Eleven*, pp. 75, 79.

57. The exact figures are in dispute. Mine are from Ayer's, as cited in Soltes, *Yiddish Press*, pp. 24–25. See also Howe, *World*, p. 539. Again, as with the *Tageblatt*'s circulation, these numbers may well understate readership. At any rate, the primacy of the *Forward* under Cahan is undeniable. Theodore Marvin Pollock, "The Solitary Clarinetist: A Critical Biography of Abraham Cahan, . . ." (Ph.D. diss., Columbia University, 1959), p. 295, states that the paper began at an even lower point; it had dropped to 6,000 copies before Cahan resumed working on it in 1903.

58. Abraham Cahan, *The Education of Abraham Cahan*, trans. Leon Stein et al. (Philadelphia: Jewish Publication Society, 1969), pp. 238ff, esp. p. 262. Cahan's leading biographer cites his subject's further ability of linking the past with the present. He states that Cahan was a modern man who also recreated "in loving detail the most deeply felt religious emotions and expressions of his fellow Jewish immigrants." Moses Rischin, ed., *Grandma Never Lived in America: The New Journalism of Abraham Cahan* (Bloomington, Ind.: Indiana University Press, 1985), pp. xxx–xxxii.

59. Howe, *World*, p. 246.

60. Ibid., pp. 228–29; Pollock, "Clarinetist," pp. 300, 343, 409, 410.

61. Note his "lingering love" of Jewish tradition. Joan Zlotnick, "Abraham Cahan, A Neglected Realist," *American Jewish Archives*, 33 (April 1970):39–40.

62. Chametzky, *Ghetto*, p. 22. See also Cahan, *Education*, p. 280; and Howe, *World*, p. 246.

63. Mark K. Baumann and Arnold Shankman, "The Rabbi as Ethnic Broker: The Case of David Marx," *Journal of American Ethnic History* 2 (Spring 1983):51–53.

64. Ibid., pp. 51–53, 60–63.

6. THE POLES

1. Greene, *For God and Country* (see chap. 1, n. 25), pp. 173ff.

2. Joseph Wytrwal, *America's Polish Heritage* (Detroit: Endurance Press, 1961), pp. 236–38, 241.

3. Edward Kantowicz, *Polish American Politics in Chicago, 1888–1940* (Chicago: University of Chicago Press, 1975), pp. 97, 163.

4. Joseph J. Parot, *Polish Catholics in Chicago, 1850–1920: A Religious History* (DeKalb, Ill.: Northern Illinois University Press, 1981), pp. 163, 177–78.

Also see Adam Walaszek, *Reemigracja Ze Stanów Zjednoczonych do Polski Po Wojnie Światowej, 1919–1924* (Cracow, 1983), p. 178.

5. See Victor Greene, "Slavic American Nationalism, 1870–1918," in International Congress of Slavists, Seventh, Warsaw, 1973, *American Contributions*, Anna Cienciała, ed., 3 vols. (The Hague: Mouton, 1973), vol. 3, *History*, pp. 197–215, for my assertions in the following three paragraphs.

6. Quoted in Edward Algernan Baughan, *Ignaz Jan Paderewski* (New York: J. Lane, 1908), p. 51.

7. Quoted in The Polish Army Veterans Association of America, *Czyn Zbrozny Wychodźtwa Polskiego w Ameryce* (Chicago: Author, 1957), p. 639. See also ibid, p. 191; Joseph Borkowski, "The Role of Pittsburgh's Polish Falcons in the Organization of the Polish Army in France," *Western Pennsylvania Historical Magazine* 54 (October 1971):365; Josef Orlowski, *Ignaz Jan Paderewski i Odbudowa Polski* (Chicago: Stanek, 1939), pp. 83, 123; and Charles J. M. Phillips, *Paderewski* (New York: Macmillan, 1933), p. 220.

8. Detroit did not acquire its large colony until closer to World War I. Many Poles went there from other American cities.

9. The best biographical accounts are two articles by Helen Busyn, "The Political Career of Peter Kiołbassa," *Polish American Studies* 7 (January–June 1950):8–22; and Busyn, "Peter Kiołbassa: Maker of Polish America," 8 (July–December 1951):65–85. See also T. Lindsay Baker, *The First Polish Americans: Silesian Settlements in Texas* (College Station, Tex.: Texas A and M University Press, 1979), pp. 69–72, 165; Waclaw Kruszka, *Historya Polska w Ameryce*, 13 vols. (Milwaukee: Kuryer Polski, 1905–8), 3:131–32; Democratic Party, Illinois, *Blue Book of Cook County Democracy* (Chicago: Pettibone, 1902), pp. 126, 201; and Andrzej Kapostas, *Polski Slownik Biograficzny* (Crakow, 1966), T. XII/I, p. 409.

10. Busyn, "Political Career," p. 12; and Busyn, "Peter Kiołbassa," pp. 78–84.

11. *Buffalo Daily Star*, Sept. 17, 1892.

12. Ibid.

13. Kantowicz, *Politics*, p. 76. I am not suggesting that Kiołbassa alone was responsible for the Poles' Democratic vote.

14. My emphasis. Quoted in *Dziennik Chicagoski*, Jan. 2, 1892, microfilm roll 58, segment III H, Foreign Language Press Survey (herafter FLPS), copy in University of Wisconsin-Milwaukee Library.

15. Greene, *For God and Country*, pp. 103–21; Kantowicz, Politics, p. 51 and *passim*; Parot, *Polish Catholics*, pp. 52, 59ff, 124ff.

16. Parot, *Polish Catholics*, p. 49.

17. Ibid., pp. 132, 135, 144.

18. Ibid., pp. 41–42. Parot suggests that this created an inchoate and taxing dilemma for immigrants, but I believe he exaggerates the trauma.

19. Quoted in *Dziennik Chicagoski*, Dec. 29, 1891, roll 58, segment III H, FLPS.

20. Parot, *Polish Catholics*, p. 85. Note also the occasional endorsement of American cultural education for Poles in the resolutions made in 1875 and 1890 by the Polish Roman Catholic Union. Quoted in Wytrwal, *Heritage*, pp. 213–14.

21. Sister M. Theodosetta Lewandoska, "The Polish Immigrants in Phila-

delphia to 1914," *Records of the American Catholic Historical Society of Philadelphia* 65 (June 1954):83–84.

22. Stanisław Osada, *Historia Związek Narodowego Polskiego* (Chicago: Dziennik Zwiazkowy, 1905), p. 74.

23. Casimir E. Midowicz, "The Polish National Alliance of the United States," *Poland* 9 (August 1927):489–90.

24. Osada, *Historia*, pp. 315–16.

25. Ibid., p. 266.

26. *Dziennik Chicagoski*, Feb. 6 and 17, 1892, roll 58, segment III H, FLPS.

27. Ibid, Mar. 1, 1892, p. 30.

28. Osada, *Historia*, pp. 373–80.

29. *Dziennik Chicagoski*, Feb. 11, 1896, roll 53, segment II C, FLPS.

30. The best biographical accounts are Stefan Rachocki, "Michał Kruszka," in Kruszka, *History*, 5:38–51, and Lieut. Col. Jerome A. Watrous, ed., *Memoirs of Milwaukee County*, 2 vols. (Madison, Wisc.: Western Historical Association, 1909), 2:957–58.

31. Anthony J. Kuzniewski, *Faith and the Fatherland* (Notre Dame, Ind.: University of Notre Dame Press, 1980), pp. 30–31, 39–40.

32. Kruszka admitted, though, that little real progress had yet been made. *Krytyka*, Nov. 7, 1888, quoted in *Kuryer Polski*, June 23, 1913, p. 2.

33. *Kuryer Polski*, Oct. 16, 1889.

34. Watrous, *Memoirs*, p. 958; "Sprawy Polskie w Polnocnej Ameryce," *Kuryer Polski*, Dec. 30, 1893, p. 5; Howard L. Conard, ed., *History of Milwaukee County* . . . , 3 vols. (Chicago and New York: American Biographical Publishing Co. 1895?), 3:110–11.

35. Kuzniewski, *Faith*, pp. 36–38.

36. *Kuryer Polski*, Aug. 7, 1895.

37. Quoted in ibid., Dec. 15, 1918, p. 4.

38. Detroit took over second place, but not until the early 1900s. Francis Fronczak, "History of the Buffalo Polish Colony" (1925?), 1; and Francis Fronczak, "Polish Settlement in Buffalo and Its Importance," transcript of a speech given March 15, 1915, at Lincoln Hall, Buffalo. Both are in the Fronczak Papers, New York State University College Library.

39. Buffalo *Courier*, Oct. 18, 1894.

40. "Offended Poles," *Buffalo Evening News*, Dec. 9, 1893.

41. My estimate and most of my information on Fronczak comes from Stanisław Dabrowski, *Francis Eustachius Fronczak, 1874–1955: A Study in Cultural Dualism in Buffalo* (Buffalo: Author, 1980), pp. 8–38, 47–50. Of course, I believe the subtitle is apt. I am much indebted to Mr. Dabrowski of Buffalo for some of his other writings as well. Mark Goldman, in *High Hopes: The Rise and Decline of Buffalo, New York* (Albany: SUNY-Albany Press, 1983), pp. 184, 303n, refers to Fronczak's stature as that of a local folk hero.

42. Newspaper clipping, "Patriotic Poles," in Fronczak-Bukowska Papers, vol. 3, Apr. 3, 1898, in Buffalo and Erie County Historical Society, hereafter FBP.

43. He went on to Elmira, New York, a short time later with a similar message. Quoted in Dabrowski, *Fronczak*, p. 55.

44. "Patriotic Poles," and "Poles Would Enlist," newspaper clipping, April 25, 1898, in vol. 3, FBP.

45. Quoted in Dabrowski, *Fronczak*, p. 182.

46. Ibid., pp. 182–83, and esp. p. 64. See also his speech of April 27, 1913, at Holyoke, Massachusetts, given before the Allied Polish Societies of Central Massachusetts, "Poland and Its Historical Relationship to the United States: The November Insurrection of 1863" box 6, file 1, in FBP; and his "Poles in America," *Free Poland* 2 (June 1916):4.

47. The entire event was of great symbolic importance and merits a full study in English. See the brief references in Angela Pienkos, "A Bicentennial Look at Casimir Pułaski: Polish American and Ethnic Folk Hero," *Polish American Studies* 33 (Spring 1976):1–17; Wytrwal, *Heritage,* pp. 197–98. The contemporary account is Romuald Piatkowski, ed., *Pamiętnik . . . Kongresu Narodowega Polskiego . . .* (Chicago: Polish National Alliance, 1911).

7. THE ITALIANS

1. Leonard Covello, in the introduction to *The Social Background of the Italo-American School Child* (Leiden: E. J. Brill, 1967), conveys the standard interpretation.

2. Examples of the early condemnation of the practice are John Koren, "The Padrone System and Padrone Banks," *Bulletin of the Department of Labor* 9 (March 1897):113–27; Edward E. Hale, "The Padrone Question," *Lend A Hand* 12 (January 1894):449–51; and the articles in *Charities* 12 (May 7, 1904):454ff. Recent examples of the revisionist view are Robert Harney, "The Padrone and the Immigrant," *Canadian Review of American Studies* 5 (Fall 1974):101–18, and Charlotte Erickson, *American Industry and the European Immigrant, 1860–1885* (Cambridge, Mass.: Harvard University Press, 1957), 72–86. Humbert Nelli's "The Italian Padrone System in the United States," *Labor History* 5 (Spring 1964):153–67 is the most comprehensive recent examination, but he is more concerned with the system's practical effect than with its cultural effect. John Briggs, in *An Italian Passage: Immigrants to Three American Cities, 1890–1930* (New Haven: Yale University Press, 1977), pp. 187ff, does deal directly but briefly with the issue of cultural identity.

3. See Virginia Yans-McLaughlin, *Family and Community: Italian Immigrants in Buffalo, 1880–1930* (Urbana, Ill.: University of Illinois Press, 1983, reissue of 1971 publication), pp. 118–19, 121, 124–25, 130–31. Yans-McLaughlin does refer to the difficulty of forming mutual aid organizations for the immigrants. Donna Gabaccia, in "Kinship, Culture, and Migration: A Sicilian Example," *Journal of American Ethnic History* 3 (Spring 1984):39–53, only alludes to the families' growing confidence in Italian neighbors in America who were not kin. In the eyes of these authors, the impact of immigrant institutions other than the family seems minimal or unexplored.

4. John S. MacDonald and Leatrice D. MacDonald, "Chain Migration, Ethnic Neighborhood Formation and Social Networks," *Milbank Memorial Fund Quarterly* 42 (January 1964):86–87.

5. I use the categories used by George Pozzetta in "The Italians of New York City" (Ph.D. diss., University of North Carolina, 1971), pp. 3–5, which are most convenient.

6. From Blok, *Mafia* (see chap. 1, n. 11), pp. 5–7, 96, 172.

7. Edwin Fenton, "Immigrants and Unions, A Case Study: Italians and American Labor, 1870–1920" (Ph.D. diss., Harvard University, 1957; Arno Reprint, New York, 1975), 4.

8. I am combining the views of Nelli, "Padrone," pp. 155–57, and Anna Maria Martellone, *Una Little Italy Nell 'Atene D'America: La Communita Italiana di Boston dal 1880–1920* (Naples: Guida Editori, 1973), pp. 120–21; Fenton, "Immigrants," p. 89; Antonio Mangano, "The Associational Life of Italians in New York City," *Charities* 12 (May 7, 1904):431–32.

9. Pozzetta, "Italians," p. 322.

10. The distinction between "padrone" and "banker" exists, but it is unimportant here. The former was a labor recruiter and money handler; the latter, a job supplier. See Nelli, "Padrone," p. 157.

11. See Humbert Nelli, "Italians," in Thernstrom, *Harvard Encyclopedia* (see chap. 1, n. 28), p. 547, and Pozzetta, "Italians," pp. 105–7.

12. George Pozzetta, "The Mulberry District of New York City," in R. Harney and J. V. Scarpaci, eds., *Little Italies in America* (Toronto: Multicultural History Society of Ontario, 1981): pp. 11–12.

13. He was a subagent for the Bank of Naples. *Il Progresso Italo-Americano,* Feb. 2, 1892; *Gli Italiani Negli Stati Uniti d'America* (New York: Italian American Chamber of Commerce, 1906), p. 291.

14. The Fugazi Letterbooks, esp. vol. 11, 1877–1913, obtained with the assistance of Sister Irene Fugazi at the New York Archdiocesan Headquarters in Yonkers, New York, have many wills, mortgages, and other legal documents.

15. *New York Times,* May 31, 1896, p. 32., corroborated by *Il Progresso Italo-Americano,* Aug. 8, 10, 1930, and by *Corriere della Sera,* Jan. 4, 1912, who referred to him as energetic, honest, "esteemed," and "popular."

16. In Fenton, "Immigrants," p. 49. See also Pozzetta, "Mulberry District," p. 34, n. 49.

17. Ibid., p. 33, n. 48.

18. *New York Times,* May 31, 1896, p. 32. See also Fenton, "Immigrants," p. 98, and Pozzetta, "Italians," p. 248. I obviously do not agree fully with Samuel Bailey, "The Adjustment of Italian Immigrants in Buenos Aires and New York, 1870–1914," *The American Historical Review* 88 (April 1983):292–93. Bailey generally minimizes the influence of immigrant mutual aid societies in New York. Admittedly, they were small, poorly financed, and perhaps not well managed, as he suggests, but they did provide experience for operating a social organization for the immigrant, and they did have a disproportionately large impact on the total ethnic population. Letter to author from George Pozzetta, May 24, 1983. See also Robert Anthony Orsi, *The Madonna of 115th Street: Faith and Community in Italian Harlem, 1880–1950* (New Haven: Yale University Press, 1985), p. 51.

19. Fugazi's last name is spelled many different ways. I use the most common one. Fugazi to New York Superintendent of Police, September 22, 1897, Fugazi Letterbooks, vol. 2, p. 368; Fugazi letterbook marked "R Privato," p. 29. Note Fugazi's prominence in the *festa* of September, 1896, held to commemorate Garibaldi's march on Rome. *Eco d'Italia* (New York newspaper), Sept. 24, 1896.

20. Fugazi Letterbook, "R Privato," p. 30.

21. *New York Times,* May 31, 1896, p. 32. He even named one of his sons

Italo-Americo to show his dual loyalty. Letter from Sister Irene Fugazy to author, August 17, 1979.

22. *New York Times,* May 31, 1896, p. 32: *Il Progresso Italo-Americo,* Aug. 8, 1930.

23. *New York Times,* July 9, 1890, p. 8; July 11, 1890, p. 2; May 3, 1891, p. 9.

24. Factionalism marred the 1910 affair, but it was massive nevertheless. *New York Times,* Oct. 13, 1910, p. 2; Sister Irene Fugazy interview, November 2, 1979, New York City.

25. *New York Times,* Oct. 12, p. 4; Oct. 13, 1909, p. 7.

26. *New York Times,* June 6, 1909, p. 8; Alfredo Bossi, *Cinquant Anni di Vita Italiana in America* (New York: Bagnasio, 1921), pp. 408–9. Charles Speroni, "The Development of the Columbus Day Pageant in San Francisco," *Western Folklore* 8 (October 1948):331. The 1910 parade in New York, in which fifty Italian organizations participated, lasted four hours. *New York Times,* Oct. 13, 1910, p. 14. See also Charles Churchill, "The Italians of Newark: A Community Study" (Ph.D. diss., New York University, 1942), p. 41, and Josef Barton, *Peasants and Strangers* (Cambridge, Mass.: Harvard University Press, 1975), pp. 70ff. These authors cite Italian immigrant leaders as promoters of Columbus Day in Newark and Cleveland.

27. Deanna Paoli Gumina, *The Italians of San Francisco, 1850–1930* (Staten Island, N.Y.: Center for Migration Studies, 1978), p. 49.

28. G. Chiodi Barberio, *Il Progresso de Gli Italiani nel Connecticut* (New Haven: Maturo, 1933), p. 311; *New Haven Register,* May 6, 1942, p. 8; ibid., Mar. 19, 1961, p. 3.

29. *New Haven Register,* Mar. 19, 1961, p. 3.

30. The word "disgrace" is a generic, not specific, reference. *New Haven Sunday Register,* Feb. 16, 1920, sec. 5, p. 7. See also Morty Miller, "New Haven's Italian Community" (1979), pp. 72–87, undergraduate paper in typescript at New Haven Colony Historical Society. Barberio, in *Progresso,* p. 312, made him responsible for the entire colony's rapid growth before 1900. See also *New Haven Evening Register,* May 6, 1942, p. 8.

31. *New Haven Register,* Mar. 19, 1961, p. 3; *Gli Italiani . . . America,* p. 419.

32. *New Haven Register,* Feb. 16, 1930, p. 7; Miller, "Community," p. 25.

33. Note in particular the description in Miller, "Community," p. 35, and *Gli Italiani . . . America,* p. 419, and see Joseph Carlevale, *Who's Who Among Americans of Italian Descent in Connecticut* (New Haven; Author, 1942), p. 343.

34. *Syracuse Herald,* Jan. 27, 1889; *Syracuse Post Standard,* June 23, 1901, pt. 2, p. 1. I am deeply grateful to Professor Luciano Iorizzo of New York State University College at Oneonta for sharing his research and notes with me.

35. *Syracuse Herald,* June 5, 1906, p. 6, and June 6, 1906, p. 9; *Syracuse Post Standard,* June 23, 1901, pt. 2, p. 1; Local History Department, Syracuse Public Library, comp., "Obituaries and Bibliographical Clippings of Residents of Syracuse . . . 1860–1926," vol. 15, Ma–Mc (Syracuse, 1915–1926).

36. See in particular his statement in the *Syracuse Post Standard,* June 23, 1901, pt. 2, p. 1. Italians came from a wide area outside the city to attend his funeral. Letter from Professor Iorizzo to author, February 26, 1982, and *Syracuse Herald,* June 5, 1906, p. 6, and June 6, 1906, p. 9. See also Syracuse Public

Library "Clippings," passim, esp. *Syracuse Herald,* May 31, 1906, p. 7, which stated that Marnell "represented 90 percent" of the city's Italians.

37. George Schiro, *Americans by Choice* (Utica, N.Y.: Author, 1940), pp. 93, 95, 107–10; and Briggs, *Passage,* p. 141.

38. Salvatore and Elias convinced their people to support the Republican party. Schiro, *Americans,* pp. 110–13.

39. Ibid., pp. 113–14; "Pop Pelletieri is Claimed by Death," *Utica Daily Press,* Oct. 11, 1921, p. 5; *Utica Observer-Dispatch,* Oct. 10, 1921, p. 12.

40. "Pop Pelletieri," p. 5; Schiro, *Americans,* p. 114.

41. From Richard Juliani, "The Italian Community in Philadelphia," in Harney and Scarpaci, *Little Italies,* p. 89. I am indebted to Professor Juliani for sharing his research with me. Note also A. Francini, *La Colonia Italiana in Filadelfia* (Philadelphia: "L'Opinione," 1907?), p. 14.

42. Philip Rose, *The Italians in America* (New York: Doran, 1922), p. 82. Note also Francini, *Colonia,* pp. 19–21; Juliani, "Community," pp. 92–93; and Hugo V. Mailey, "The Italian Vote in Philadelphia" (Ph.D. diss., University of Pennsylvania, 1950), p. 126; *Philadelphia Inquirer,* Dec. 29, 1930, pp. 1, 4.

43. Ernest Biagi, *The Italians of Philadelphia* 2 vols., (Philadelphia: Carlton, 1967–73), 1:163–64; Mailey, "Vote," pp. 115–17, 127. The most complete list of Baldi's ethnic and civic activities and memberships, and his fullest biography, are in *L'Opinione,* Dec. 29, 1930. See also A. Francini, *Colonia,* pp. 20–21 and passim.

44. Baldi's decided Fascist sympathies in the 1920s probably caused protestors to bomb his home in 1923. Juliani, "Community," p. 212; Mailey, "Vote," pp. 126–28; *Philadelphia Public Ledger,* Dec. 29, 1930, pp. 1, 4; Rose, *Italians,* 82.

45. Francini, *Colonia,* p. 19; *L'Opinione,* Dec. 29, 1930.

46. *Philadelphia Inquirer,* Jan. 4, 1930, p. 6.

47. Orsi, *Madonna,* pp. 51. 150–51, 156–58, 160. Without designating the founders of the mutual aid society, Orsi says its goals were solely social and economic. Unfortunately, he does not discuss the other objectives of group leaders and padrones in Italian Harlem, nor does he examine their effect on immigrant marginality.

48. Orsi, *Madonna,* pp. 161–62. The author cites Leonard Covello's discomfort with an Italian in an American public school "which made [him] American by teaching him to be ashamed of [his] parents." Covello follows this remark with an interesting reservation: "except with reference to Columbus as a famous Italian." I would question that this crisis in identity in Covello, a second-generation Italian American, was shared by all early immigrants. The pappas, at least, did not show it.

49. European Italians referred to returnees from America as "Americani," a distinct group. My position here agrees with Briggs, *Passage,* ch. 6, esp. pp. 120–25, 136. His examples, however, are intellectuals; mine are internal social leaders. Note the description of, and the rather formal inscription on, the well-known statue in New York's Columbus Circle. J. Stanford Saltus and Walter E. Tisne, *Statues of New York* (New York: Putnam, 1923), p. 58. A second memorial was set up in Central Park. Ibid., p. 64.

50. John Freschi, "The Loyalty of Citizens of Italian Origin," *Il Carrocco* 3 (March 1916);150–54.

8. CONCLUSION

1. Maldwyn Allen Jones, *American Immigration* (Chicago: University of Chicago Press, 1960), p. 127. Italics mine.

2. Handlin, "Immigrant in American Politics" (see chap. 2, n. 19), pp. 85–87.

3. Herbert Gans, "Symbolic Ethnicity" (see chap. 1, n. 3), p. 203.

4. Clifford Geertz, "The Javanese Kijaji: The Changing Role of a Cultural Broker," *Comparative Studies in Society and History* 2 (October–July 1959–1960):228ff. The similarities and differences of his subjects to American immigrant leaders are obvious.

5. This argument does not contradict the "spectrum of leadership" thesis offered by Jonathan Sarna in "The Spectrum of Jewish Leadership in Ante-Bellum America," *Journal of American Ethnic History* 1 (September 1982):59–67. My category of "traditional progressives" is not exclusive.

Index

Forward, Jewish Daily (Forverts), 92, 101, 102–3
Founding Fathers: cited by Cahan, 103; cited by Henni, 54; esteemed by Salvatore Pelletieri, 133. *See also* American Revolution
French Revolution, 25
Freschi, John, 136–37
Friedlander, Israel, 86
Friendly Sons of St. Patrick of New York, 19, 22
Friends of Ireland, 25
Fronczak, Francis, 119; education and stature, 120; mobilizes Poles in Spanish American War, 120–21; on Polish American identity, 120–21
Fugazi, Luigi, 124, 130; early life, 126; as immigrant organizer, 126–27; on Italians as Americans, 126, 128; prominence, 126, 129
Funchion, Michael, 40

Galesburg, Illinois, Swedish Lutheran parish in, 76–77
Geertz, Clifford, 141
German Democratic Association, 60
German emigrant ballads, 43, 44
German Pioneer Society, 50. See also *Der Deutsche Pionier*
German redemptioners, 48
Giessen Emigration Society, 61
Gillespie, Edward, 28
Glazer, Nathan, 2
Gobel, Professor David, 62–63
Gobel, Gert, 46, 61; on being German in America, 63; early life and family, 61–62; as German community leader, 62–63
Goldfadden, Abraham, 88
Goodhue County, Minnesota, Swedish colony in, 81
Gordon, Milton, 3
Grays, 42–43
Greens, 42, 43, 44

Handlin, Oscar: on immigration history, 2; on insecurity of foreigners, 139; on Irish immigrants, 18
Hansen, Marcus, 2
Harkavy, Alexander, 87, 95, 140; early life and arrival in U.S., 98; on Jewish American identity, 98; success as Yiddish author, lexicographer, 99–100; on Washington, 99
Haskalah (Jewish Enlightenment), 88, 90
Hasselquist, Reverend Tufve: arrival in U.S., 76; critic of Swedish Lutheran Church, 76–77; on Swedish American identity, 77–78; at 250th Swedish American anniversary observance, 80
Haugean movement, 68
"Der Haus and Bauerfreund" (Hoffmann's articles), 56–57
Hebraism, 87
Hebrew Free School Association, 96
Hebrew Immigrant Aid Society (HIAS), 93, 100
Hebrew Sheltering House Association, 93
Hemlandet (Homeland), 77–79, 82, 84
Henni, Reverend John Martin, 46; defense of Catholicism, 49; early life, 52; emergence as ethnic leader, 53
Hibernian Provident Society, 21
Higham, John, 15
Historians, American: and ethnic history, 4–5; and German emigration, 42; and Irish immigration, 18. *See also* Brown; Handlin; Hansen; Higham; McCaffrey
Hoffman, Francis Arnold, 46; early life and immigration, 55; on German American identity, 56–58; German cultural contributions, 56; occupations and offices held, 54–55; retirement

ILLUSTRATION CREDITS

1. The photo of William James MacNeven is from Thomas Addis Emmet, *Memoir of Thomas Addis and Robert Emmet . . .,* 2 vols. (New York: Emmet, 1915), vol. 1, facing p. 332.
2. The photo of Archbishop Hughes is from C. E. McGuire, ed., *Catholic Builders of the Nation,* 5 vols. (Boston: Continental, 1923), vol. 5, facing p. 68.
3. The photo of Das Deutsche Haus is reprinted by permission of the Illinois State Historical Library, Old State Capitol, Springfield, Illinois.
4. The photo of Francis Hoffmann is reprinted by permission of the Illinois State Historical Library, Old State Capitol, Springfield, Illinois.
5. The photo of the Enander memorial is from *Yearbook of the Swedish Historical Society of America* (St. Paul: Veckoblad, 1921-22), 7:29. Translation of the inscription is by Professor Roy Swanson, University of Wisconsin at Milwaukee.
6. The photo of Hans Mattson's church is from Mattson, *Reminiscences: The Story of an Emigrant* (St. Paul: Merrill, 1891), p. 305.
7. The photo of Rabbi Sarasohn is courtesy of Ken Rosett, White Plains, New York.
8. The Harkavy books are in the library of Hebrew Union College, Cincinnati.
9. The cartoon is from the Polish program book by Romuald Piatkowski, *Pamiętnik Wzniesie i Odsłoniecia Pomników . . . Kongresu Narodowego Polskiego* (Chicago: Polish National Alliance, 1911), p. 67. Publishing with permission of © the Washington *Evening Star.* All rights reserved.
10. The photo of Dr. Fronczak is from *Księga Pamiatkowe Zlotego Jubileuszu Osady Polskiej i Parafii: Św. Stanisława . . . Buffalo . . .* (Buffalo: Telegram, 1923), and E. H. Butler Library, State University College at Buffalo.
11. The photo of Cavaliere Fugazi is from *Gli Italiani Negli Stati Uniti* (New York: Italian American Chamber of Commerce, 1906).
12. The photo of the Baldi funeral, from *L'Opinione,* January 4, 1931, is courtesy of Nancy Baldi Berlin, Chadds Ford, Pennsylvania.